W9-DAJ-972

Twenty-First-Century Africa:

Towards a New Vision of Self-Sustainable Development

Edited by
Ann Seidman and Frederick Anang

Task Force Advisory Committee:
Beverly Grier   **Allen Isaacman**
Goran Hyden   **Georges Nzongola-Ntalaja**
Ann Seidman, Chair

Africa World Press (Trenton, New Jersey)
African Studies Association Press (Atlanta, Georgia)

Africa World Press, Inc.
P.O. Box 1892
Trenton, N.J. 08607

ISBN 0-86543-329-1   Cloth
      0-86543-330-5   Paper

Cover design by Carles Juzang

Printed in the United States of America

Acknowledgements

The Task Force expresses sincere appreciation to the John D. and Catherine T. MacArthur Foundation and the African Development Foundation for their contributions which made this first phase of its efforts possible.

The editors would like to express sincere thanks to all the members of the ASA, the Task Force and the Task Groups who have worked so hard over the last year to make this book possible. So many people have contributed through discussions at meetings and workshops that it is impossible to mention them all by name. Hopefully their reward will come in the form of increased participatory research that helps the attainment of self-sustainable development in Africa.

In particular, however, the editors wish to express appreciation to Edna Bay, the Executive Director of the African Studies Association, and her very able and cooperative staff for their invaluable assistance to the Task Force at every stage of its work; to Willie Lamouse-Smith, program chair of the 1990 annual ASA meeting, for facilitating the Task Force Workshop that reviewed substantive papers; to Liz Owens and the staff in the International Development Department at Clark for their on going support; and to Lori Wichhart for taking care of the innumerable details that plaque every manuscript before it goes to press.

The Editors
Clark University
Worcester
1991

Table of Contents

Chapter 1

Introduction

Towards a New Vision of Self-Sustainable Development in Africa

With a land area three times the size of the United States, Africa's vast rich continent possesses all the resources required for modern development. Its many-faceted history and culture reach back through the empires of early antiquity to the first known site of human life. Long before Europeans discovered the Americas, peoples of Africa had built towns and carried on trade with Europe and Asia. Prior to World War II, Africa was a net exporter of food. Today, with a population of over 500 million, Africa ships an infinite variety of mineral and agricultural riches—the raw sinews of modern industry and luxurious consumption—to all corners of the earth. Yet, at the same time, three decades after the peoples of Africa began to throw off the bitter yoke of colonial rule, some 28 African countries, mainly in Sub-Saharan Africa, still rank among the world's forty-two poorest. The World Bank[1] noted that, in the 1980s alone, six more African states had 'slipped' into the lowest income group. Deteriorating economic and social conditions left the average African 20 to 25 percent worse off than in 1979.[2] As the condition for limited financial aid, bilateral and multilateral agencies require African governments to adopt policies that many critics claim push tens of thousands more Africans still deeper into the mire of poverty and dependency.

A 1989 Economic Commission for Africa report, endorsed by almost all African Ministers of Economic Planning, Development and Finance, declared:

"There is mounting evidence that stabilization and structural adjustment programmes are rending the fabric of the African society. Worse still, their severest impact is on the vulnerable groups in the society—children, women and the aged—who constitute two thirds of the population. "[3]

1

Why do African peoples remain so poor?   What kind of an alternative strategy could enable them to shape their own future, to realize the vast potential of their continental resources?

In 1989, the Board of Directors of the African Studies Association of the United States (ASA)—an association of some 2000 scholars, almost all of whom had lived and worked in one capacity or another in Africa—appointed a Task Force to explore ways that US-based researchers might contribute to the attainment of sustainable development in Africa. As the first phase of its efforts, the Task Force sought to cement relations with African scholars and research institutions in order to find ways to work together in the search for answers.[4]

I. Towards a New Vision of Self-Sustainable Democratic Development in Africa:

The Task Force participants undertook their work on the assumption that researchers can and should play an important role in gathering the evidence policy-makers require to test alternative theoretical explanations for Africa's poverty and powerlessness, and assess the probable consequences of the resulting, often conflicting, policy proposals. Researchers should undertake country studies of the causes of the prevalent under- and mis-utilization of human, physical, and financial resources, and the consequences of alternative strategies to change them. Researchers investigating the many different African countries should compare the results of their findings to deepen their theoretical and policy-oriented conclusions. Working together with researchers from other third world countries, they should help policy-makers learn from difficulties encountered elsewhere in order to determine what to avoid in devising new strategies for Africa. In the context of the shrinking global economy, they should exchange information with first world researchers about the potential mutual benefits of accelerated African development. On this foundation, working together with African people and policy-makers, they should contribute to the formulation and implementation of strategies of resource and institutional change essential to attain self-sustainable development.

The Task Force coordinators in seven key areas—economy, state and legal order, environment, education, health, gender and household, and regional integration—brought together task groups to prepare draft review papers outlining the current state of research. These papers defined the core debates, and created an intellectual framework for future collaborative research.   After a year of preparatory work, the Task Force brought together African- and US-based scholars in a series of workshops at the 1990 ASA Annual Meeting in Baltimore to assess and revise the initial drafts.   At a four day follow-up workshop in Washington, DC[5], the researchers from Africa, together with the task group coordinators, worked out detailed proposals for further research and the dissemination of the findings to the academy, the public and policy makers, both in Africa and the United States.   The African workshop participants elected a five person steering committee for a parallel Africa Task Force[6] to coordinate the proposed research with existing on-going research projects in Africa.

In the second phase of their work,[7] the joint Task Force aims to contribute through on-going collaborative research to building the more solid foundation of information required to formulate more successful policies for self-sustainable development in Africa. They seek to gather evidence to answer questions as to the kinds of institutions and re-allocation of resources that, on national and regional levels, will enable Africans to achieve increasingly productive employment and steadily rising living standards; and design programs to provide the needed skills, appropriate preventive health measures and better living and working conditions in an environment capable of ensuring a constantly improved quality of life. In so doing, not only in substance, but also in the form of the research process itself, the joint Task Force seeks to contribute to creating democratic governmental and non-governmental structures to enable all Africans, including women and children, to participate and benefit. In sum, the Task Forces have begun working together to institutionalize a participatory research process to help generate and disseminate the information essential to the realization of a 'new vision of self-sustainable democratic development in Africa.'

In addition to mobilizing US Africanists to participate in this task, the US-based Task Force will make special efforts to disseminate the findings to the US public and policy makers. In the late 1980s, TV screens thrust images of starving African women and children into living rooms across middle America. Millions of Americans donated generously to relief campaigns. Yet few realized that, in recent decades, the United States had begun to play a major role in African affairs. US control over a fifth of the votes in the IMF and World Bank gives its government a predominant influence in shaping those agencies' lending policies. Moreover, although the US government spends barely a fourth of one percent of the national product for aid—a smaller fraction than any other leading industrial power—it still constitutes a leading source of bilateral funds for Africa. Unfortunately, a large share of its aid funds finance sophisticated weapons like shoulder-rockets and anti-personnel mines, instead of literacy campaigns and rural clinics.

More than that: Africa's poverty constitutes an integral feature of an on-going global restructuring process in which a downward-spiralling competition aggravates global inequality and poverty. Growing numbers of American blue collar workers lost their jobs and the fringe benefits they had won over the past half-century, as manufacturing industries shifted from the United States to oppressive low wage areas like apartheid South Africa. America's mounting debt to finance its unprecedented peacetime military build-up—including arms sales to impoverished third world areas like those in Africa—forced deep cuts in welfare spending in the US, aggravating the impact of spreading US poverty. The 1990 Census[8] as well as numerous studies, confirmed the "devastating domestic effects"[9] in dichotomizing US society.[10]

If, on the other hand, appropriate US policies contributed to the African people's efforts to improve their production, employment and income structures, the US might expect to sell about ten times more US-made manufactures to each man, woman and child on that continent[11] — a large and growing market for goods American workers might produce. In return, the US could buy essential mineral and agriculture produce, increasingly processed in the context of reshaping comparative advantages in more mutually-beneficial patterns of trade.[12] The joint Task Force will make special efforts to disseminate the findings generated by the collaborative research process, as to the causes of Africa's crisis, to the US public and policy makers in hopes that the peoples of both the United States and Africa will benefit.

As an important part of the overall dissemination process, the joint Task Force is publishing this book which comprises the full set of revised review papers prepared in Phase I. Each chapter outlines the current state of available evidence relating to the main issues in the relevant field and outlines a program of research to help resolve the core debates to lay the basis for improved development strategies. The last chapter describes the problem-solving framework the joint Task Force participants designed at the Washington workshop to facilitate collaborative participatory research. In total, the book aims to provide background materials to stimulate classroom and study group discussions, debates, and further research both in Africa and in the United States. Readers will note that the authors of different chapters adopted somewhat different analytical approaches. Some focused on structured contradictions that appeared difficult to resolve, while others described tensions they seemed to assume could easily be bridged. Furthermore, some devoted more space than others to examining research methodologies for resolving the debates. Hopefully, however, in toto, the book will encourage African and US researchers, together with those from other areas of the world, to embark on new research efforts to lay the foundation for rational policies to surmount the obstacles that impede successful African development.

II. A Participatory, Problem-Solving Methodology

From the outset, the Task Force sought to adapt and develop a critical problem-solving methodology appropriate to the formulation and implementation of a new strategy for African development.[13] This methodology requires that, at every step, policy makers critically consider the full range of alternative available theoretical explanations to formulate hypotheses that logically seem most consistent with their knowledge of the social problems they confront. The hypothesis chosen serves as an heuristic guide—never a dogma!— to examine the further evidence required to test its validity in particular circumstances. The testing process inevitably leads to revisions that deepen the initial explanation. Once thus validated against the evidence, the explanation logically suggests a range of possible proposals for new policies to overcome the causes it identifies. These, too, require research to determine which, given available resources and probable constraints, will most likely succeed.

Thus, this methodology requires evidence at every step in the process of policy formulation: to define the problem; to analyze its causes; to assess existing constraints and resources to decide which of the range of possible policies will most likely overcome the causes; and to monitor the consequences of the policies implemented. This approach guided the preparation of the draft papers, which each task group prepared during Phase I to summarize the current state of research. As outlined in Chapter 9, below, it forms the framework for the next stages of the research.

The Task Force participants generally agreed that the obstacles thwarting Africa's development efforts do not come in neatly labelled disciplinary packages called "economics," "law" "engineering" or "anthropology." Only multidisciplinary research can adequately identify the causes of these complex difficulties and help discover policies capable of overcoming them. Furthermore, at significant points the materials included in the seven task groups' overall surveys overlap; inevitably, each task group's conclusions for future research suggest implications for the research that the others may conduct.

III. The Findings of Phase I: A Summary

Chapters 2 through 8 in this volume present the revised review papers prepared by the Task Force coordinators and revised as a result of the discussions at the 1990 ASA annual meeting workshops. As much as possible, each task group drew on African research materials not always widely available in Africa, far less in the United States. The bibliography at the end of each chapter cites the sources used. The last chapter outlines the details of the proposed participatory research design for further collaborative research to help provide the information required to resolve the core debates in each field.

This book and the proposed future research aim to help lay a sound foundation for formulating and implementing strategies more likely to realize the proposed new vision of African development. The task far exceeds the available intellectual—not to mention financial—resources of any individual òr even any group of researchers. By no means does participation in any aspect of the Task Force or its task groups imply full agreement with the materials included in this volume. Perusal of the chapters below will indicate, not only the existence of differences in emphases and explanations, but even in terms of how to put the materials together. In publishing these papers and outlining the proposed future research, the Task Force invites the readers of this volume to join in a critical review of these findings and to consider ways in which they, too, may contribute to the further collaborative research essential to resolve some of the debates and contribute more effectively to the attainment of sustainable development in Africa.

IV. Chapter Summaries

The remainder of this chapter briefly outlines the main points elaborated in the rest of this book.

Chapter 2: "Towards a New Economic Strategy for Sustainable African Development"

Three predominant categories of theorists purport to explain and propose alternative economic development strategies for Africa. No hard and fast boundaries demarcate these categories; on some points, inevitably, they overlap. Moreover, the theorists grouped in one category not infrequently disagree with one another. Nevertheless, demarcation of these three categories facilitates exposition of the debates among them. Using different methodologies, each category of theorists tends to focus on different aspects of Africa's development problems. The explanations they advance as to the causes of those problems, and the policies they propose to overcome them, not only differ, but in major respects fundamentally contradict one another.

The first category incorporates *mainstream* theories taught in most African universities, and, in the 1980s, generally adopted by the IMF and the World Bank. Adopting an ideal-type model, these theorists typically assume competitive market forces, unimpeded by government intervention, will lead to the best possible pattern of resource allocation. Therefore, they urge African governments to adopt austerity measures, privatize state-owned industries, and introduce what they characterize as democratic market economies, open to world competition. In particular, they recommend African governments to encourage foreign investment and support expanded exports—wherever possible including labor-intensive manufactures—to serve as an engine for growth. Over time, they maintain, this strategy will contribute to the optimal utilization of Africa's human, physical and financial resources in today's changing global context.

Comprising the second category, basic needs/structuralist theorists focus on human needs and the structural impediments that block optimal third world development. They argue that neither the domestic nor the foreign markets available to Africans even begin to approximate the competitive conditions assumed by mainstream theorists. Distorted income distribution at home combined with overcrowded export markets cause mainstream strategies, imposed through foreign aid, to aggravate distorted development and intensify African poverty. Basic needs/structuralists support democratic reforms, but they insist the state must intervene to assist the African poor to meet their basic needs and to enable informal labor market entrepreneurs and peasants to acquire the resources necessary to compete effectively in national and international markets.

Theorists in the third category, transforming institutionalists, agree with basic needs/structuralists that mainstream ideal-type models in no way correspond to African realities. They go further, however, to emphasize that state structures—only marginally changed from those inherited from colonial rule—have fostered the emergence of new African bureaucratic bourgeois classes. Since new government office holders may profit from collaboration with transnational corporate interests, they will not likely exercise state power to implement measures to meet Africans' basic needs. Privatization, however, primarily serves simply to turn over valuable government-financed productive investments to these new class elements, enabling them to further multiply their wealth and power at the expense of the majority. Therefore, transforming institutionalists generally call for involving the peasants, working people, small businesspersons, and intellectuals in building new democratic state institutions and utilizing them to take over the national commanding heights of their national and regional political economies. Once firmly in control of these, they should implement a step-by-step transition to planned social ownership and development of the means of production to provide increasingly productive employment opportunities and a better quality of life for the broad masses of the people.

The Economy task group's research agenda focuses on gathering new evidence designed to bear on the core debates within and between these three categories of theories. In particular, it proposes to re-examine the nature and extent to which in key domestic and foreign markets—especially for basic industries, export-import trade and finance—real world conditions do or could in any way approximate those assumed by mainstream theorists. At the same time, it calls for in-depth analyses of the intractability of the institutional characteristics of African governments which mainstream theorists allege render unrealistic any possibility that they might implement the kinds of incremental structural and institutional policies called for by basic needs/structuralists, far less the more far-reaching ones recommended by the transforming institutionalists.

Chapter 3: "Regional Cooperation and Integration: Achievements, Problems and Prospects"

A general consensus exists among African scholars and policy-makers on the desirability of African unity for development, but serious disagreements persist on the scope, level and strategy for attaining it. Since winning independence, Africa has witnessed the introduction of roughly 200 sets of institutions in support of regional cooperation. Nevertheless, progress towards integration remains disappointing. The East African Community survived for only ten years (1967-1977). West and central African regional integration schemes, like Union douaniere et economique de l'Afrique Centrale and the Economic Community of West African States (ECOWAS) proved relatively unsuccessful. The Southern African Development Coordination Conference (SADCC) and the Preferential Trade Area for Eastern and Southern Africa seem more promising.

Because Africa remains not only the world's poorest developing region, but also the least integrated and most dependent on foreign trade, many Africans view regional integration as a top priority. The core of the argument centers on the efficiency of economies of scale to be obtained by industrialization to serve regional rather than national markets.

A brief historical review suggests a decline of the Pan-Africanist focus on rapid continental political integration. Instead, a less controversial neo-functionalist approach emphasizes regional institutions as stepping stones towards a progressive process of political and economic unification. More than 160 inter-governmental and some 40 non-governmental organizations have proliferated since independence, however, threatening to waste human and financial resources.

A survey of the aims and activities of a cross-section of nine major integration schemes indicates their possibilities and problems. These include the Union of the Arab Maghreb (UAM); the Communaute economique de l'Afrique de l'Ouest (CEAO); The Economic Community of West African States (ECOWAS); the Union douaniere et economique de l'Afrique centrale (UDEAC); the Economic Community of Central African States (ECCAS); the Franc Zone System; The East African Community (EAC); The Preferential Trade Area for Eastern and Southern Africa (PTA); and The Southern African Development Coordination Conference (SADCC). A summary of this widely varied experience suggests that the major problems lie in: (1) the uneven distribution of benefits and costs of integration for which it remains difficult to compensate; (2) institutional deficiencies, including not only proliferation, but over-centralization and politicization; (3) politico-ideological differences, aggravated by militarization, that potentially lead to destabilization; and (4) external dependence, reflected in the fact that African states conduct almost half their total trade with the European Economic Community, while intra-regional trade remains only about five to six percent of the total.

Market integration experiments have generally not succeeded in Africa. Critics object that the market integration model, taken from industrial Europe, remains irrelevant to Africa, which needs to emphasize the regional production base, giving priority to basic industries. Neo-functionalists opine that low levels of development make Africa unsuited for integration, suggesting the need to concentrate, instead, on infrastructure and training.

To develop a strategy for future regional integration, the chapter concludes with an emphasis on step-by-step rationalization of existing regional organizations to harmonize their policies, improve infrastructure, and achieve lean, efficient institutions. Thus African governments should work towards an enabling environment, including removal of tariffs and other human-made barriers, and mobilizing public opinion and popular support. Given the agreement at least on a minimal degree of integration, several questions arise for research: Can the existing African organizations achieve the necessary coordinated development? Can the French-dominated regional groupings play a supportive role, or will they undermine more self-reliant efforts? What institutional changes are required to enable organizations like UAM, ECOWAS, ECCAS and PTA achieve greater dynamism as building blocks on which to erect the projected African Economic Community?

Chapter 4: "Education and Development: Deconstructing a Myth to Construct Reality"

For thirty years, adopting multiple disciplinary foci and theoretical and ideological perspectives, educational and development experts have debated Africa's educational needs. They have formulated divergent assessments of and prescriptions for educational systems, institutions and programs. Overshadowing this diversity of opinion has been a central consensual orthodoxy that education, particularly formal schooling, is an essential, if not the determining, ingredient in the development process.

Within this established orthodoxy, two central assertions have emerged as accepted doctrine: (1) in Africa as throughout the world, education (specifically 'basic' education) is an inalienable right of all human beings; and (2) a minimally educated citizenry (dependent on an accessible and efficient educational system) constitutes the *sine qua non* for economic and social development. This orthodoxy lent international and academic legitimacy to the two converging strands that buttressed an already-established commitment to educational expansion. On the one hand, nascent post-independence state regimes viewed formal education as essential to the attainment of skills required for economic productivity and expansion, improved state administrative capacity and national unity. On the other hand, a sizable and articulate proportion of an increasingly politicized citizenry perceived formal education as vital for improving their own and their progeny's living standards.

As a consequence of this faith in the ameliorative power of education, many African countries recorded an unparalleled (relative to social welfare and other government commitments) expansion of expenditure on formal education. Yet, even before the severe economic down-turn of the past decade, it became obvious that formal education had neither paid the promised dividends in terms of economic development, system capacity and political stability; nor guaranteed employment or improved life chances for the individual citizen. Moreover, after two and a half decades of quantitative growth, a number of African countries experienced a decline both in the quality of education and in the percentage of school-age children attending primary and secondary schools.

The resulting crisis in education confronts policy-makers and educational researchers with two fundamental issues. Firstly, it is essential to understand why the impressive quantitative expansion of education failed to contribute to a corresponding development of productive forces (and employment), or the institutionalization of democratic participation regimes that, while attaining greater national autonomy, responded to their citizens' legitimate needs. The articulation of this cardinal failure affected the second central issue, that of how African educational policy makers, planners and practitioners, on the one hand, and the international education consortia (academic consultants, researchers and aid agencies— bilateral and multilateral), on the other, conceptualized, diagnosed and pragmatically dealt with Africa's education crisis.

Chapter 4 demonstrates that to date, the conceptual parameters confining the discourse relating to these issues have primarily been established outside of Africa (mainly by academics and analysts employed by major bilateral and multilateral lenders). This conceptual paradigm views the educational crisis in Africa as a result of endogenous problems that arise within the African educational system and structure. Consequently, it assigns responsibility for the inadequate social performance in education to the absence of quality, efficiency and relevance. Exogenous factors, when addressed, concern mainly the issue of finance, particularly the need for alternative, non-state sources of funds. The paradigm seldom raises questions concerning the role of the state and the structure of the economy in imposing conditions of political and economic decay which make it difficult, if not impossible, to realize education's constructive development potential.

The dominant discourse is further legitimized by research formulated, administered and analyzed by the same institutions which subvert, on conditional terms, educational reform and expansion in Africa. As a result, a "financial-intellectual" complex has emerged, comprised of a coalition of international agencies and associated consultants and researchers and, at the national level, African educational policy makers. This coalition determines the perception and consequent articulation of educational initiatives relating to: (1) education's relationships to society; (2) pedagogy and curriculum; and (3) the internal and external efficiency of educational administration.

Chapter 4's focus on the important issue of external control of the educational discourse and the consequent policy- orientation limits the space required for adequate treatment of other current issues and debates relating to educational policy in Africa. The authors therefore included an extended thematic annotated bibliography on these as they relate to empowerment and sustainable development.

Based on this review, the Education task group concluded with an emphasis on the need for a new educational discourse within Africa, informed by a participatory dialogue between policy-makers, practitioners (administrators and teachers at every level) and their constituents (parents, students and local communities), and supported by participatory, problem-focused research. This will constitute an essential first step towards gaining a clear understanding of the causes of Africa's educational crisis, and provide the basis for new educational policies and institutions more likely to contribute effectively to self-sustainable development.

Chapter 5: "Health For the Future, the Future of Health"

Since at least the late 1970s, the poor in Africa have enjoyed less and less control over the spaces they inhabit and the resources they require to satisfy their basic health needs. Growing numbers of urban squatters, as well as rural people, especially women, have seen real income and the provision of health care shrink. They find it increasingly difficult to maintain the nutrition and health of their children. They receive less help when they or their children fall ill. One in ten Africans suffers disability. Maternal mortality is shamefully high. Of the thirty countries with the highest death rates for children under five years of age, twenty-one are in Africa. Yet these children die of diseases preventable by immunization, basic sanitation and simple community-based primary care. On top of all this, Africa's rapid urbanization has fostered serious new health risks. These include HIV infection, food poisoning, exposure to toxic waste, residential fire, rape and other forms of abuse.

Africa's seriously deteriorating health conditions interact with the causes and aggravate the consequences of many of the problems analyzed the other chapters.   First, deepening economic hardship in the rural areas is forcing greater numbers of people to migrate to the cities and many more children are abandoned. The survival strategies of these children and youth can include such high risk activities as prostitution in areas of AIDS endemicity, heavy porterage of goods, and recycling of dangerous materials like glass.   Sick or injured children, youth and women place burdens on the system of health care already under stress and overburdened. Often, they can no longer work productively.

Second, in many African countries reduced government expenditures have decreased the availability of health services. Marginal groups such as the homeless, street children, youth, and low income urban women never had much access to these, and now have less.   Falling real incomes of the working poor and semi-employed people have compounded the impact of deteriorating health facilities.   In some cases, attempts to increase economic growth in and around such African cities have introduced new risks, including dumping of toxic wastes that pollute the water and air, and unsafe working conditions.

Third, the business-as-usual activities of local and national institutions, whether public or private, simply do not take into consideration the environmental and health requirements of most people, especially the poor and such marginalized groups as homeless and street children and youth and low income urban women. Exclusion of the poor, especially women, from decision-making processes at all levels has meant that even measures supposedly directed at improvement of the situation through "development" have often had the opposite effect.

Fourth, since many health problems, especially those in Africa's rapidly growing cities, only emerged as especially serious in the 1980s, legal safeguards and entitlements have failed to keep pace.   Thus urban environmentally-linked health problems of marginalized children, youth and women constitute a major challenge for the state and its legal apparatus.

Finally, the causes of deteriorated health conditions lie deeply intertwined with the causes of those studied by the gender and education task force teams.   Explicating these should help to formulate new policy and action proposals, including improved use of the tools of non-formal education, job training, mobilization and self-organization to empower these marginal groups to cope with the challenges of their rapidly changing urban environments.

The insights into urban health hazards by those at risk are an underutilized body of knowledge.   A participatory research process that identifies the specific ways in which 'development' institutions and projects undermine individual and environmental health will lay the foundation for a range of policy measures to ensure that future decision-making processes take these human needs into account. In addition, a participatory process will reveal the creative responses of children, youth and low income women to health risks in their daily environments. Such coping activities could well be incorporated into the programs of municipal governments and ministries, non-government organizations and donor projects.

The proposed participatory research process will take place in West Africa (Nigeria, Ghana, Sierra Leone, Senegal, Cameroon, and Cote d'Ivoire) and East and Southern Africa (Kenya, Tanzania, Zimbabwe, and Mozambique). It will involve those affected by urban health hazards—especially women and children, as well as agencies working with them—in identifying and testing more detailed, middle-level explanations to lay the groundwork for action plans designed to overcome them. Those who take part will engage in a learning process, enhancing their effective participation in planning programs and institutions to deal with their pressing health problems. The information gathered will be made available to agencies like WHO's regional office, the UN Economic Commission for Africa, the African Development Bank, national government ministries, regional donor agencies and non-governmental organizations.

Chapter 6: "Facing Africa's Ecological Crisis"

Closely interrelated factors have contributed, not only to declining productivity and falling living standards in Africa, but also to a deep-rooted ecological crisis. The chapter first describes the tragic plight of Africa's ecological system, including the inability of most African countries to produce sufficient food for its growing populations; the negative environmental impacts on the rural areas where over three fourths of all Africans still live; and the growth of pollution in mushrooming urban centers as industrialization and the disposal of toxic wastes threaten water and air supplies. It suggests the primary ecological challenge remains that of halting the degradation of the rural areas caused by three complex interrelated clusters of causes, including external factors such as the declining terms of trade for agricultural produce and external debt; internal factors, like inappropriate land tenure systems and weak inefficient government institutions; and a range of pressures that stem from climatic changes, the population explosion, and social factors including class and gender differentiation.

The authors then review the current state of research relating to the impact of the wide variety of responses to the ecological crisis. Numerous national and international institutions have carried out macro-level economic development programs, too often centered on dealing with short-term symptoms rather than long-term causes of the difficulties that hamper Africa's attempts to attain sustainable development. Typically, they have failed to adequately integrate measures for dealing with the pressing problems of environmental degradation that remain deeply rooted in those long-term causal circumstances.

The authors reject the simplistic argument, advanced by some environmentalists, that the solution lies in halting technological innovation. A limited technological base constitutes a major factor inhibiting African development efforts. The continent needs, instead, to improve its capacity to acquire and adapt to its own circumstances technologies that can accelerate the spread of increasingly productive employment opportunities and rising living standards. This underscores the necessity to accompany the growing recognition of the significance of ecological issues with more careful analysis of country- and region-specific features in order to develop strategies for more ecologically sustainable development.

A promising approach, the authors suggest, lies in already-emerging community efforts to incorporate into their plans for increased productivity detailed measures to avoid or overcome the environmental hazards that elsewhere have threatened the long-term viability of development programs. They propose participatory research to explore the possibilities and limits of these local level models. This would contribute to identifying those mostly likely to prove effective, as well as mistakes to avoid. The participatory research teams could then generalize and share the lessons of these community experiences within and beyond national boundaries with other communities, non-governmental organizations and local, national and regional governments. In the context of this on-going evaluatory process, the research teams could seek ways to assist non-government and government institutions to integrate grass-roots proposals for maintaining and improving an ecologically sound environment into regional and national plans to accelerate self-sustainable development.

Chapter 7: "Gender Relations and Development: Political Economy and Culture"

This chapter focuses on the <u>interrelated, significant, persistent inequalities</u> that historically have disadvantaged most African women, inequalities aggravated by Africa's political economic crises and the accompanying structural adjustment programs. Explaining why the Gender Relations task group changed its initial name from Gender and Household, the chapter underscores the complexity of the changing households and communities in which African women struggle to support themselves and their families. The fact that they live in very different kinds of regional, ethnic and class backgrounds differentially affects women's access to resources and opportunities for employment. Nevertheless, with few exceptions, almost all experience the consequences of institutionalized gender inequalities.

From an historical perspective, women have by no means always simply remained victims, but have repeatedly struggled to improve their families' and their own lives. The historical evidence, however, suggests this requires a fundamental transformation of the institutions and structures that have impoverished, not only African women, but most Africans.

To explore the ramifications of this hypothesis, the chapter reviews the major collections and articles, published over the last two decades, that deal with several critical aspects of gender relations. Despite African women's limited access to essential resources, many studies document their extensive contributions to cultivating, processing and marketing agricultural produce, especially food crops. Nevertheless, existing institutions and attitudes, many of them fostered by the changes wrought by colonial rule, thwart these women's efforts to acquire new technologies. Studies indicate that the increased productivity resulting from development projects does not always improve the nutrition levels of participating women and their children. Government and project officials not infrequently take advantage of technological advances to increase their own control over resources and accumulations of capital, intensifying the exploitation of women's labor. As illustrated by the women's experience in Zaire, the structural adjustment programs adopted in response to the agrarian crisis of the 1980s accentuated, rather than alleviated, these trends.

The chapter illustrates the harsh reality that women who seek to escape rural poverty or degradation by migrating to the cities encounter other institutionalized disadvantages. Mostly barred from wage employment, they struggle for bare survival primarily as petty traders, domestic servants, and in commercial sex work where the majority live "short, desperately poor, unhealthy lives." Only a few find jobs in new food processing and textiles industries. In West African coastal cities, some women have prospered in trade. Limited primarily to the informal sector and struggling with the official as well as unofficial obstacles, however, most barely eke out a subsistence livelihood. In contrast, male and sometimes corporate traders, enjoying greater access to essential resources, especially credit, appear far more able to take advantage of structural adjustment initiatives designed to foster new class elements' capacity to challenge those currently holding state power.

The chapter points out that ideological blinders have contributed to scapegoating women, especially poor women, for the increasing prevalence of AIDS, a leading cause of death among adults in Central Africa. It reports research findings that show limiting the spread of AIDS requires "attention to the structures and meanings that produce gender subordination in economy, society and households." Already, some efforts seek to adapt a participatory research methodology to involve women and their communities in identifying the ways these factors interact in order to develop more effective prevention strategies. Using an example from another context, the chapter illustrates how a participatory research methodology engages women in a process of understanding and formulating ways of improving gender relations in the context of strategies directed to overall social change and development.

In conclusion, drawing on the lively discussion among participants in the Gender Relations workshop at the 1990 ASA annual meeting and the Washington follow-up workshop, the chapter explains the aims of the task group's two participatory research proposals: 1) to involve leading women researchers in the design and implementation of all the other task groups' proposals to ensure adequate attention to gender relations; and 2) to engage both women and men together in a learning process to help them understand the interrelationships of the spread of AIDS with the complex factors that cause gender inequality and impoverish the majority of Africans to help lay the essential foundation for future sustainable development.

Chapter 8: "Towards Research on the State, the Law and the Processes of Development"

In Africa, as throughout the world, the state and the legal order, broadly conceived, comprise societies' primary instrument for ensuring that, in every critical area, governments play an appropriate underbearer role in the process of attaining democratic self-sustainable development. For this reason, in Africa as elsewhere, independence movements assumed the form of struggles for state power. The culmination of thirty years of African independence in crises that pervaded all areas of development, however, reflected the failure of Africa's new governments—whatever their stated objectives—to exercise state power in the interest of the majority of Africans.

The authors hold that prevailing theories of the state sought to explain that failure on too high a level of abstraction. As a result, they proved inadequate to guide research that might contribute to improvements in the laws that shaped the institutions that comprised the state and the legal order in Africa. Derived from Europe's struggles against the feudal aristocracy, libertarianism initially assumed that, by enshrining the institutions of western democracy in their constitutions, the new governments of Africa would serve the public interest. Instead, they manifestly represented varied combinations of bureaucrats, ethnic elites and transnational corporate interests. Three other categories of theories of the state purported to explain why. These included: modernization, with pluralism as a principle component; various versions of Marxism, and; what some called the non-governance school. None of these, however, proved very useful in assisting Africa's new governors to build participatory state institutions designed to involve the African people in creative realization of self-sustainable development.

To assist policy-makers in achieving that task, the evidence in Africa, as well as elsewhere, suggests the need to disaggregate the state and the legal order into the (sometimes contradictory) constituent sets of social behaviors that shape development processes. They need to formulate and validate middle-level propositions that explain the social behavior of the central role occupants that, in the context of the existing legal order, perpetuates Africa's poverty and powerlessness. This includes the activities of those role occupants who engage relevant state institutions in counterproductive underbearer activities that contradict development goals.

A critical review of the debates as to what factors influence role occupants' social behavior in deciding to obey existing rules of law in Africa, as well as elsewhere, lays the foundation for a research agenda of appropriate categories for investigation: the rules, themselves; the role occupants' opportunity and capacity to obey or disobey them; communication of the rules to them; their own interests; the process by which they decide what to do; and their ideologies. In each of these categories, the authors propose that researchers draw on relevant theory to formulate middle-level propositions to guide their gathering of evidence; those that prove valid may suggest new laws and institutions more likely to overcome the obstacles that, in every arena, tend to block sustainable development.

Researchers should use this agenda, not merely to examine the behavior of the primary role occupants whose social behavior laws seek to change; but also that of those who determine the activities of the law-implementing institutions that may encourage or discourage them from appropriate development activities. The proposed agenda may also usefully guide investigations of why the law-making process produces some kinds of laws and not others. Given the complex character of law-making and implementing institutions, they must also examine the input, conversion, and feedback processes that shape decision-making within which those central role occupants function.

The chapter concludes with a proposal that researchers concerned with the nature and role of the state, per se, may use the research agenda to conduct two sets of investigations. First, in examining the state and the legal order's underbearer role in all aspects of the development process, they may focus on resolving the core debates relating to the complex issues of class, ethnicity and legality (including the problems of corruption). Secondly, together with policy-makers, they should analyze the obstacles to mass democratic participation in order to propose new policies and institutions to involve the African people at all levels in realizing self-sustainable continental development.

Chapter 9: "New Structures for Participatory Problem-Solving Research"

This chapter outlines the participatory, problem-solving research framework and specific projected case studies that emerged from the process of reviewing the materials covered in the existing chapters. By involving community representatives and selected policy makers together with African national research teams, these will achieve two aims: (1) help to find the information necessary to resolve the core debates raised by the reviews of each of the key problem areas as a sound foundation for designing more effective development strategies; and (2) by involving those affected in the research process, help them to acquire the skills and confidence essential to self-reliant sustainable development.

V. Conclusion

In publishing this volume of papers, the Task Force wishes to underscore the fact that the materials and ideas included here represent an effort to identify key issues and debates, and some ideas about how to conduct participatory research that might assist in charting future development strategies. Hopefully, these will stimulate further discussion and encourage the readers, themselves, to engage in that on-going process.

Endnotes

1. World Bank, *Subsaharan Africa—From Crisis to Sustainable Growth*. Washington, D.C.; International Bank for Reconstruction and Development, 1989. pp. 20-21.

2 Adebayo Adediji, Executive Secretary of the United Nations Economic Commission for Africa, in *African News*, October 3, 1988.

3. Economic Commission for Africa, African Alternative Framework to Structural Adjustment Programmes for Socio-Economic Recovery and Transformation (E/ECA/CM. 15/6/Rev.3) Addis Ababa, 1989, p.24.

4. For a list of the Task Force advisory committee and coordinators, see Appendix I. The Task Force expresses sincere appreciation to the John D. and Catherine T. MacArthur Foundation for the generous grant which made it possible to broaden the scope of the first phase of its work, and particularly to increase the participation of colleagues from Africa.

5. The Task Force wishes to thank the African Development Foundation for co-sponsoring and funding this essential workshop. It greatly facilitated the collective African participation which provided an essential ingredient in formulating the tasks to be undertaken in Phase II in terms of both intellectual content and knowledge of existing African research personnel, institutions and networks.

6. For a list of the members of the Steering Committee, see Appendix I.

7. In light of the Task Force extended proposals for research in Phase II, in May 1991, the ASA Board of Directors decided to change the status of the Task Force from that of an ASA Committee to an independent associated organization. On the one hand, this gave the Task Force participants greater flexibility in developing their proposals in cooperation with their African colleagues; and, on the other, ensured continued cooperation with ASA members and committees in providing support for the research in Africa and disseminating the findings to generate greater understanding in the US as the foundation for more continually improved US policies towards Africa.

8. Robert Pear, "U.S. Reports Poverty Is Down but Inequality Is Up," *New York Times*, Sept. 27, 1990.

9. Anthony Lewis, "Abroad at Home: When Decline Hurts," *New York Times*, Sept. 24, 1990.

10. See also Barry Bluestone and Bennet Harrison, *The Deindustrialization of America,* (New York: Basic Books, 1982.; Peter Dicken, *Global Shift: Industrial Change in a Turbulent Worlds,* (London: Harper and Row, 1986);   Folker Frobel, Jurgen Heinrichs and Otto Kreye, *The New International Division of Labor: Structural Unemployment in Industrialized Countries and Industrialization in Developing Countries,* (Cambridge: Cambridge University Press, 1980); Phil O'Keefe, ed., *Regional Restructuring Under Advanced Capitalism* (London: Croom Helm, 1984); Andrew Glyn and Bob Sutcliffe, *British Capitalism, Workers and the Profit Squeeze,* (London: Penguin, 1972.); David Gordon, Richard Edwards and Michael Reich, *Segmented Work, Divided Workers: The Historical Transformation of Labor in the United States* (Cambridge: Cambridge University Press, 1982); Joseph Grunwald and Kenneth Flamm, *The Global Factor: Foreign Assembly in International Trade,* (Washington, DC: The Brookings Institution, 1985); Richard Peet, ed., *International Capitalism and Industrial Restructuring: A Critical Analysis,* (Boston: George Allen and Unwin, 1987); Robert J.S. Ross and Kent C. Trachte, *Global Capitalism – the New Leviathan* (Albany: State University of New York Press, 1990).

11. The United States sells about ten times more goods, per capita, to industrialized Europe than to impoverished Africa. Ann Seidman, *The Roots of Crisis in Southern Africa.,* (Trenton, NJ: Africa World Press, 1985). Chapter 7.

12. At present, Africa's comparative advantage like that of the rest of the Third Word, rests in its cheap, unskilled labor. Any people-oriented development strategy must improve education, skills and technology as the foundation of increased productive employment opportunities and rising living standards for the entire population.

13. For the theoretical background and an illustration of this methodology, see D. Kalyalya, K. Mhlanga, A. Seidman and J. Semboja, *Aid and Development in South Africa,* (Trenton, NJ: Africa World Press, 1988), especially Chapter 2.

Chapter 2

Towards a New Economic Strategy for Sustainable African Development

Task group co-coordinators: Ann Seidman and John Ohiorhenuan

I. Introduction

The crisis of the 1980s threatened to rend the fabric of African society (ECA; 1989). Its underlying causes, however, lay deeply imbedded in the continent's political economy. This chapter summarizes the debates[1] among scholars and policy-makers as to those causes and possible alternative strategies which might lead to self-sustainable development. It adopts the fundamental premise that development must provide increasingly productive employment opportunities and an improved quality of life for all Africans.

To simplify the debate, this review categorizes the relevant analyses into three sets. At best, these categories represent somewhat arbitrarily chosen points along a continuum of theoretical positions, chosen because they distinguish qualitatively differing perspectives, methodologies and explanatory categories. Since African states achieved independence, each of these sets has held sway in different ones at different times. They have influenced development policies in ways far too varied to permit precise location or periodization in the limited space here available.

The three categories include: (1) 'mainstream,' which incorporates the body of theories taught in most African universities, and, in the 1980s, generally underpinned the policies of the International Monetary Fund (IMF) and the World Bank[2]; (2) 'basic needs/structuralist, which generally argues that main- stream theories fail to adequately consider human needs and structural impediments inherent in Third World economies[3]; and (3) 'transforming institutionalist,' which holds that, to meet basic needs and overcome structural problems, Africans must fundamentally transform their inherited state structures and associated political economic institutions.[4]

Because they all deal with the same reality, the theories in the different categories overlap and interact. Grouping them by category by no means implies that their proponents agree on every point. Moreover, the analyses in each category continually change. Within the limits imposed by space, this chapter indicates some of the changes, overlaps, and differences among those in as well as between each category. It first summarizes the debate over the nature of the economic crisis confronting Africa today; then outlines the alternative explanations and proposals for solutions offered by the three predominant sets of theories; and finally outlines the kinds of research required to help resolve the resulting debates to help lay the foundations for an effective alternative strategy for self-sustainable development.

II. The Debate: The Nature and Scope of Africa's Crisis

Most analysts agree that Africa enjoys the resources required for development (World Bank, 1989a: 22, 33ff; Nyerere, 1988: 7-8; ECA, 1989a; Akor, Komba, Nkokoni, Koffi-Tessio, Misana in IDS, 1989). Nevertheless, the overwhelming majority of Africans remain impoverished and their economies seem increasingly embroiled in debt. Some twenty-eight African countries, mainly in Sub-Saharan Africa, rank among the world's forty-two poorest. At the end of the 1980s, the World Bank noted that, during the 1980s, six more African states had 'slipped' into the low income group (World Bank, 1989a; 2, 20-l). Sub-Saharan African debt had mounted to US$250 billion, roughly equal to the region's total product (the regional GNP), and three and one half times its export earnings. Debt service obligations equalled almost half of the region's foreign exchange earnings, although actual payments averaged little over a fourth of its 1985-88 exports. The continent had become a net exporter of capital to the International Monetary Fund, remitting to it US$l billion in 1986 and 1987 (ECA, 1989a: 52; Ighemat in IDS, 1989).

The three categories of theorists and practitioners focus on different aspects of this crisis. Mainstream analysts emphasize inefficiency of production, lagging exports, trade and payments and government deficits, and stagnating per capita incomes. One World Bank report maintained that, in the 1980s, about half the countries in Africa adopting major policy reform programs exhibited elements of success (World Bank, 1989a: 2, Ch. 3). Nominal devaluations and market liberalization led to rising real agricultural prices in many countries, especially for export commodities. Many countries experienced a realignment of real factor costs. Real interest rates became less negative. Real wages for both skilled and unskilled labor declined; in "Tanzania, real wages are now less than half of their 1980 levels."[5] Large increases in aid spurred economic performance. Assessing the social impact, the report admitted, remained difficult, especially because of patchy data. Growing unemployment and deterioration of social services took "a heavy toll in human terms." Better delivery of public services would, in any case, improve only after a lag. Nonetheless, the report concluded, where countries adopted adjustment programs with strong donor support, per capita expenditures might have begun to rise.

In contrast, both basic needs/structuralists and transforming institutionalists stress African economies' growing inability to meet most Africans' basic needs (Eg, ECA Khartoum Declaration, 1988: 37). Both sets of researchers called for new indicators that would reveal the full dimensions of the social impact of crisis, especially on the most vulnerable groups (ECA, 1989a: 24-5, ECA, 1983; and IDS, 1989)[6].

Endorsed by African Ministers of Economic Planning, Development and Finance, a 1989 Economic Commission for Africa (ECA) report declared:

> "There is mounting evidence that stabilization and structural adjustment programmes are rending the fabric of the African society. Worse still, their severest impact is on the vulnerable groups in the society—children, women and the aged—who constitute two thirds of the population. "(ECA, 1989a: 24; see also ECA, 1983)[7]

The transforming institutionalists[8] underscore the extent to which, as the crisis deepened, the majority of Africans—workers, peasants, unemployed, small businesspeople, intellectuals and professionals—experienced increasing alienation and repression.

III. Alternative Explanations and Strategy Proposals

Each category of theories guides researchers and policy-makers to adopt different explanations of Africa's poverty, leading to diametrically opposed policy proposals.

A. The mainstream model

1. <u>Hindrances to competitive optimality</u>. Building on an ideal-type model,[9] mainstream analysts explain that Africa's poverty results primarily from hindrances, especially government policies, that, in both domestic and international markets, block the optimal operation of competitive forces. Unimpeded, these would otherwise provide

incentives for improved efficiency and higher productivity (World Bank, 1984, 1989a). The theoreticians identify the following sets of government policies as inappropriate:

1. Efforts to stimulate industry that reflect an urban bias, discouraging agricultural productivity and industrial competition, like: (a) protective tariffs that shelter inefficient private and public enterprise; (b) government acquisition of shares of ownership mines, plantations, factories; (c) high corporate and income taxes that scare away potential foreign investors.

2. Government agricultural policies (including marketing boards, subsidies, and price controls) — whether to keep down urban wage costs or to enable governments to cream off the profits— that discourage farmers from expanding production or force them to resort to black or parallel markets (eg., Jones and Roemer, 1989).[10] As a result, African economies lose potential foreign exchange earnings for export crops, and increase imports of foodstuffs.

3. Expansion of government administration, social welfare programs, and unproductive projects that augment government expenditures and spur domestic borrowing. This aggravates inflationary pressures, and opens the door for corrupt practices.

4. Government monetary and fiscal policies that foster inflationary pressures, distorting all national prices and market signals, including: (a) holding down interest rates and directing credit; (b) minimum wages; (c) taxes that discourage foreign investment; (d) overvalued currency exchange rates; and (e) borrowing abroad to cover growing import costs, rather than self-financing projects.

2. Structural adjustment programs. These mainstream explanations lead logically to IMF and World Bank "structural adjustments programs" which link loans, needed by African countries to offset persistent deficits and for limited development expenditures, to the re-introduction of competitive market forces. The typical IMF package includes government measures to: reduce budget deficits by laying off workers and reducing social welfare expenditures; freeze wages; lower taxes on higher income recipients (assumed to be potential investors) while raising those on lower income groups; increase interest rates to reduce domestic borrowing; eliminate foreign exchange controls and import licensing to foster increased competition from imported goods;

privatize public enterprises; and devaluate the national currency to lower real costs and prices to sell more exports.

Asserting African governments must make the final choices and take responsibility for their own actions, IMF teams typically make their proposals and evaluations of government compliance in secret (Marshall, 1990). Once a government agrees to these policies, however, an IMF team checks its performance every quarter, withholding subsequent payments until satisfied with its progress.

In the 1980s, the World Bank introduced Structural Adjustment Programs (SAPs) aimed at longer term restructuring of African economies along parallel lines. It requires African governments to adopt reforms to[11]: (l)   expand their activities less rapidly, even in traditional public sector areas, except where they serve private investors; wherever possible, substitute user fees for universal free access to social services; replace parastatal activity by private entrepreneurs, especially in directly productive spheres; (2) encourage increased agricultural exports to increase peasant earnings and foreign exchange; where possible expand industrial exports; and remove trade restrictions which hinder integration into the world market on the basis of comparative advantage; (3) train more middle- and high-level personnel, encourage more applied research, and publish more financial reports and statistical data to facilitate monitoring of performance and preparation of new policies[12]; and (4) set consistent priorities, policies and programs, and coordinate implementation and review. In this context, the Bank urges donor countries to multiply concessional financial flows, linking them, not to particular projects, but to these kinds of overall structural reforms.

World Bank experts claim that their aggregate economic indicators show partial successes. Given more time, these reforms will lead to improved efficiency and eventually to higher living standards.

Some African researchers agreed. Using Sudanese time series data in an econometric model, for example, Zayid (in IDS, 1989) held that boosting exports and devaluation (because of its inflationary impact), only initially adversely affected consumption and welfare. Over time, however, his model indicated the trend would reverse.

3. <u>Some disputes among mainstream theorists</u>. Not all mainstream theorists, of course, agree on all aspects of the IMF-World Bank policies. Some scholars and policy-makers' observations at two US AID financed seminars in Africa exemplified the tenor of their disputes.[13] Deng noted that, although external factors, including oil price rises, world recession, drought, and structural imbalances, contribute to Africa's crisis, the reforms focus primarily on the African

governments' failures.   Nevertheless, his schematic model's preliminary findings suggest apparent modest rural income growth, both in real terms and in relation to urban incomes.   Several participants challenged his finding that rural dwellers benefit. Others observed that the devaluation/stabilization phase creates severe hardships for consumers, and might not generate the model's assumed supply response.

Some participants objected that the reforms neglected the external environment's effect on trade.   A number expressed fears that competitive devaluation would drive down export prices, reducing benefits of export promotion; others argued that, in absence of export incentives, Africa would continue to lose market shares even for traditional exports.

Claiming a 'new consensus' as to African governments' responsibility for their economies' malaise, some participants urged more attention to the nature of the state, itself.   Others held that consensus implied the need to soften conditionality and expect less from reform. Some donors thought the consensus suggested that tying loans to reforms remained risky.

Both seminars considered issues raised by basic needs theorists. Quarcoo described the Ghana government's Program for Mitigating the Social Costs of Adjustment" (PAMSCAD)—backed by $85 million in foreign pledges—to meet the needs of the poorest through community initiated (self-help) projects.   Zayyad observed that Nigeria's SAP program (1986-88, in many respects like the IMF's), failed to attract new foreign investments or to control inflation and rising prices reduced farmers' benefits.

4. Incorporating the human dimension. In 1989, following extensive consultations with African policy makers and researchers, the World Bank's study sought to incorporate basic needs concerns (World Bank, 1989a: esp. Ch. 3).   It emphasized the danger of the population explosion, and African governments' neglect of the 'missing middle': the informal labor market. The study termed the latter a "seedbed" of potential entrepreneurial talent.   There, small scale entrepreneurs, including women, use labor intensive technologies and local resources to provide significant and growing amounts of employment. Supported by appropriate government policies—including adequate expenditures for social and economic infrastructure—they can eventually make an important contribution to self-sustainable African development.[14] The Bank study suggested non-governmental organizations (NGOs) might play a catalytic role in facilitating participation by all social groups,

from the grassroots to chambers of commerce, in the development process.[15]

Despite its acknowledgement of the importance of the human dimension and increased participation, however, the World Bank still supports the long term restructuring of African economies premised on mainstream assumptions. It still urges African governments to focus primarily on creating an enabling environment for private enterprise to expand and diversify exports, including, wherever possible, manufactured goods. It still recommends increased trade liberalization to enable international competition to spur greater efficiency, encouraging Africans to cement partnerships with foreign investors to gain access to their skills and capital.

Even given optimistic assumptions, however, the 1989 World Bank study forecasts growing gaps between exports and imports and investments and savings. Even if creditors reduced African debt service payments to $9 billion a year, and private capital inflow rose to $6 billion, official donors would have to increase their assistance about four percent annually to reach $22 billion (in 1990 prices) by the year 2000. At this level, foreign aid would finance about half of all public expenditures on human resource development and the maintenance and improvement of infrastructure. To attain this goal, The Bank calls for "a global coalition for Africa."

In other words, while incorporating basic needs' concerns, the World Bank still anchors proposals for restructuring African economies to mainstream premises. It encourages domestic entrepreneurs, together with foreign capital, to engage ever more vigorously in world wide competition. It assumes significant increases in foreign assistance. Only if these conditions are met may African economies over the next two decades hope to achieve the efficient productivity essential to overcome poverty.

B. The basic needs/structuralist alternative:

1. Inherent structural impediments. The basic needs/structuralists critique of mainstream policies reaches beyond a concern with the human dimension of development. Its proponents identify the causes of Africa's crisis in structural impediments, imbedded in third world economies and in their relations with first world. These render unrealistic the assumptions that undergird the mainstream model. Furthermore, because mainstream theorists ignore the interaction of causal factors that a more unified approach reveals, their policies inevitably have unintended negative consequences.

The 1989 Economic Commission for Africa (ECA) report identifies as a primary structural obstacle the distorted generation, distribution and expenditure of national income (ECA, 1989a: 25).   Other basic needs/structuralists focus on other obstacles (ECA, 1989a: 29; Onimode, 1989a, b, and IDS, 1989). First, many point out that devotion of the best land and infrastructure to export crops marginalizes small food farmers, especially women. This hinders expanded cultivation of food crops for growing urban populations and causes counterproductive environmental effects (de Vletter, 1981; Koda and Omari, Ihimodu, Suliman in IDS, 1989; Bujra in ROAPE, 1990, Marshall, 1990)[16].

Second, lack of domestic capital leaves foreign firms in control of key sectors of economy, especially industry, trade and finance (Tella in IDS, 1989; Onimode, 1989b: 2-3; Mubako in Makemure et al, 1986: 10, Seidman, 1976, 1986). Foreign and domestic (including parastatal) firms profit by selling cheap labor-intensive exports (crude agricultural and mineral products, and some manufactures);[17] and importing manufactured consumer goods and machinery, equipment, materials for import substitution industries that produce mainly luxury and semi-luxury items for high income group and a few more broadly consumed items like beer and cigarettes (Mudenda; 1985, Singh; 1985, A. Seidman in Makemure et al; 1986). African efforts to introduce export-oriented manufacturing industry encounter additional problems.[18] Transnationals do not willingly transfer technology to enable independent African countries to attain self-reliant industrial development (Ndlela, 1986; Komba in IDS, 1989; Ohiorhenuan, 1989, 1990); instead, they import relatively capital intensive machinery and equipment over which they retain control. Lack of research to discover the best energy sources leads to unnecessary capital expense, pollution and waste (Omo-Fadaka, Nkokoni in IDS, 1989).

Third, many structuralists maintain that, at the international level, structural impediments inevitably push African economies, seeking to expand exports, into debt. As first world markets narrow due to recessions and greater use of synthetics and recycled products, intensified third world competition to sell exports inevitably causes worsened terms of trade and balance of payments deficits. Falling export earnings and tax revenues force African governments to borrow (Mahdi, Folson in IDS, 1989; Payer, 1989b, Campbell, 1989b, Green, 1989b). Domestic borrowing fuels domestic inflation, reducing the population's real incomes, raising costs of producing exports and contributing to 'overvalued' currencies. Borrowing abroad at high interest rates increasingly embroils African economies in growing international debt (Suliman, Ighemat in IDS, 1989). Heavy foreign debt repayments reduce foreign exchange required to buy machinery, parts and materials for import-substitution industries. As a result, industrial output falls to a fraction of capacity (Gilbert, 1990), aggravating goods shortages and unemployment—further undercutting real living standards (Banugire, 1986; Ighemat in IDS, 1989).

Basic needs/structuralists claim that the IMF and World Bank conditions and SAPs aggravate the negative consequences of these underlying structural features (ECA, 1989a: 18-20; Hussain in IDS[19]):

1. Government dismissals of workers augment already widespread unemployment, with ongoing negative multiplier consequences;
2. Government cutbacks in health, education and welfare further reduce already low living standards;
3. Wages freezes cannot halt inflation, typically caused by other factors; but persistent inflationary pressures increase profits while pushing down working peoples' real incomes—further skewing income distribution (eg, Panford, 1989);
4. Regressive taxes impose increased burdens on lower-income groups, further reducing their living standards;
5. High interest rates do not hinder inflationary pressures (caused by other factors), but increase the cost to government of financing its domestic debt and thwart small (primarily African) businesses from obtaining working capital, thus strengthening larger (typically foreign) firms' oligopolistic positions;
6. Elimination of foreign-exchange controls and import licensing enables high income groups to import more luxury and semi-luxury items, reducing foreign exchange for machinery and equipment needed to build factories to provide jobs and produce necessities for lower income groups; to the extent that imports compete with local industries, they squeeze out marginal local firms, eliminating what little domestic industry already exists and further aggravating unemployment;
7. Curtailing state productive activities hinders efforts to direct local investable surpluses into more self-reliant, balanced and integrated economies to provide jobs and higher living standards;
8. Devaluation causes massive under-valuation of African currencies, enabling creditor countries to obtain third world raw materials for extremely low real prices; and raising the costs of imported necessities (including machinery, equipment and fuel required for development), adding to inflationary pressures

(Moseley, 1989).   By intensifying competition among third world countries in the context of stagnant world markets, it further worsens terms of trade. Thus it tends to aggravate all the difficulties listed above.[20]

2. People-centered structural adjustment plus transformation. These explanations lead basic needs structuralists to propose programs that differ in several respects from those of mainstream theorists (eg, Parfitt & Riley, 1989)[21]. The 1989 Economic Commission for Africa's (ECA) Alternative African Framework - Structural Adjustment Programme summarizes their kinds of recommendations for policy directions and instruments in three interrelated macro-economic areas (ECA, 1989a: Chs. 4-6).   The Commission views these as creating a framework which, supplemented by country-specific research, national authorities may adopt as a pragmatic guide.   The World Bank's 1989 study incorporated several of the ECA's basic needs concerns (see pp. 9 ff, above).   Reflecting differences in their underlying explanations, however, the ECA's proposals differ significantly from those of the World Bank in several aspects. The primary difference lies in the ECA's emphasis on the necessity for African governments, while making essential short term adjustments directed at stabilization, to initiate the appropriate process of structural transformation now.   The IMF-World Bank recommend that governments should first stabilize their economies and open them to international competition, assuming growth will follow.   This different emphasis leads the ECA to recommend three significantly different kinds of interrelated policy directions and instruments (references here cite relevant works by other African researchers adopting the basic needs/structuralist approach):

(1) Strengthen and diversify Africa's production capacity and productivity of investment.

   (a) Major policy directions: The ECA's primary disagreement with the World Bank in this area lies in its proposal for vertical and horizontal diversification to produce essential goods and services to meet the needs of the majority of the population. This necessitates a domestic focus rather than intensified efforts to export   (Ndlela, 1984, 1985; Mihyo, 1984; Kaplinsky, 1985; SADCC, 1985; Abdelkader, 1984; Zimbabwe University, 1981a, b, c; Kalyati, 1984).[22]

   (b) Policy instruments and measures: The disagreement emerges sharply in relation to particular policy measures.   The ECA urges land reform, not limited to issues of land title, to give the poor access to land for productive use (Omo-Fadaka in IDS; re women, Iae in IDS, 1989). Rather than deregulating markets, the ECA also proposes government to direct foreign exchange to the import of agriculture and manufacturing inputs and to increase linkages between sectors; allocate credit within guidelines that favor the food subsector and manufacture of essentials (giving special attention, including credit and child care, to women in informal sector) (Koda and Omari in IDS, 1989; Philpott in MSID, 1989); provide loans at subsidized interest rates to certain groups of economic operators (Ighemat in IDS, 1989); establish selective nominal interest rates, (high for speculative activities, low for productive ones), with positive weighted average real interest rates for savings; and to introduce rational multiple exchange rates to improve resource transfers and mobilize capital (and end capital flight).

(2) Improve pattern and level of factor income allocation to stimulate increased production, expand domestic markets and alleviate poverty:

(a) Major policy directions: The 1989 World Bank study seems to endorse some of the ECA's major policy directions in this area, including a pragmatic balance between public and private sectors, creation of an enabling environment with participation and consensus building and a shift of resources from unproductive expenditures, especially military, to increased social expenditures, with a focus on education. The ECA's proposals, however, involve greater government intervention with market forces (eg, Asombang, Onyekakeyah in IDS, 1989; Seidman et al, 1991), including measures to improve income distribution among different socioeconomic categories of households; and to give the poor and disadvantaged greater access to the means of production, especially land

(b) Policy instruments and measures: The remaining debates center on the ECA proposals to: enlarge the tax base and improve collection machinery (Cf Chaligha, 1990; Seidman, 1986); maintain subventions to parastatals in "nationally strategic basic industries" (eg, Semboja in Mazur, 1990); guarantee minimum prices for food crops managed through reserves; introduce selective production subsidies, multiple exchange rates, differential interest rates with selective credit control; and maintain selective price controls.

(3) Improve the pattern of expenditure of income to satisfy required needs:

(a) <u>Major policy directions</u>: Little debate over the major policy directions appears here between the Bank and the ECA.

(b) <u>Policy instruments and measures</u>: In terms of concrete measures, however, the ECA again proposes more direct government action. This would take the form of selective subsidies and pricing policies to increase production of essential commodities; a selective trade policy, differential export subsidies, and intra-African barter trade; and bilateral and multilateral agreements on primary export commodities.

3. <u>The centrality of regional integration</u>. Although both the Bank and the ECA call for increased cooperation between African governments, the ECA stresses the necessity for regional integration, while the Fund and Bank focus on adjustment in individual African countries in ways that foster competition, rather than cooperation, between them.[23] The World Bank's strategic agenda for the 1990s envisages only market integration among African countries, not integration of production structures. The ECA, in contrast, urges government action to pool resources and avoid duplication of production units which may expand output beyond potential national and regional market capacity. It recommends that African states harmonize taxes, exchange rates, pricing and interest policies; and establish joint intercountry commissions to co-ordinate national programs. It offers to help create a comprehensive system for monitor whole transformation process.

4. <u>Popular participation</u>. Both the World Bank and the ECA recommend strengthening existing administrative structures with greater accountability and dedicated, patriotic management in the public sector. Both support local decentralization, grassroots initiatives and community self-management drawing on individual and private sector participation; and introduction of checks and balances to avoid bureaucratic excesses. The ECA, however, lays more stress on involvement of central state planning machinery in the design and implementation of programs to attain short and long-term development objectives. It also urges measures to ensure that ministers responsible for productive and social sectors, as well as all executive agencies and public enterprises, take responsibility for final programs adopted. To engender popular participation and support by the people (see also Mpangala, Shivji, Turok, Suliman, Baranga in IDS, 1989), the ECA seeks to disseminate information to the general public on its proposals, involving all modes of mass media, the public and organized interest groups. In 1990 at Arusha, Tanzania, an ECA-sponsored conference

formulated the African Charter for Popular Participation in Development (ECA, 1990; Khartoum).

5. Foreign aid.   Like the World Bank, the ECA urges mobilization of foreign aid and external debt relief to help finance its proposed programs. Unlike the Bank, however, the ECA underscores the need for an improved international trade environment to avert a repetition of the 1986 situation when, as export prices plummeted (the 1988 commodity wholesale price index for Africa in 1980 prices fell to 54.2), Africa lost almost US$19 billion—more than double the total foreign aid Sub-Saharan Africa received that year. The ECA also placed greater emphasis on the necessity for African government participation in the process of mobilizing external funds as equal partners.

In sum, the *basic needs/structuralists* maintain that the mainstream explanations and policy proposals ignore structural obstacles that inevitably lead uncontrolled market forces to worsen the plight of the most vulnerable segments of population. Their policy recommendations go beyond proposals to fulfil the poor's basic needs. They propose that African governments take direct action to redirect resources—human, physical, and financial—to more balanced, integrated national and regional people-centered development.

C. The transforming institutionalist critique

The transforming institutionalists agree in part with the explanations and policies advanced by the basic needs/structuralists. They assert, however, that, in the context of the changing international division of labor, African class formation and state institutions combine with transnational corporate behavior to cause Africa's poverty and oppression. They argue that only a fundamental transformation of African institutions and patterns of economic development, internally and in relation to developed countries, can achieve self-sustainable development.[24] Just as theorists grouped in the mainstream and basic needs/structuralist categories differ on details among each other, of course, those grouped here as transforming institutionalists disagree about particular aspects of this basic thesis.

1. Classes, the state and transnational corporations in the changing international division of labor.   Most transforming institutionalists agree that Africa's crisis resulted from the nature of the continent's integration in the capitalist economic system, "a manifestation of the severe phase in the cyclical evolution typical of capitalist development."(Musoke in IDS, 1989).[25] They center their attention on several interrelated explanatory factors entirely neglected by mainstream theorists and only partially considered by basic

needs/structuralists. These include the continued export-dependence of African economies fostered by the emergence of new class forces closely interrelated with post-independence African state institutions; and the role of transnational corporations (Seidman, 1990).

Transforming institutionalists hold that, regardless of differences in African governments' declared ideological perspectives, few have done much to alter the inherited domestic political economic institutions which gear their economies to the export of crude materials and import of manufactures (eg., Ihonvbere, Ihimodo in IDS, 1989). In the context of the changing international division of labor, newly institutionalized domestic class and state formations have emerged which have cemented their economic ties to the metropole (the former colonial powers, the United States, and, increasingly to West Germany and Japan) (Nyerere, 1988; Rugamamu, 1987; Akor, Ihonvbere, Danaher, Mpangala in IDS, 1989).

These class and international influences perpetuate institutions and attitudes that hamper the new governments' efforts to build balanced, integrated national and regional economies (Nyerere, 1988). New government administrators and politicians accept the conventional wisdom that they can only achieve industrialization by attracting foreign capital and technologies (eg., Rugamamu. Komba, Mytelka in IDS, 1989; Ohiorhenuan, 1989, 1990), and expanding crude exports to finance import-substitution (eg, Moseley, 1989). Africa's colonial heritage has left them with neither an adequate technological foundation, sufficient numbers of skilled personnel (technological or administrative), nor institutions appropriate for creating more self-reliant economies (eg, Omo-Fadaka, Komba in IDS, 1989; Mytelka, 1989). Military conflicts, involving the purchase of military equipment from abroad at great cost, aggravate these difficulties.[26]

Inherited governmental institutions grind out policies that strengthened newly emerging African capitalist classes. To legitimize their authority, new governments initially multiplied social expenditures and government personnel to provide education, health and economic infrastructure. Because they failed to create self-sustainable productive sectors and expanding revenues, however, they could not continue to finance them (Banugire in IDS, 1989; Seidman, 1986). Furthermore, educational institutions remain authoritarian, hindering the broader population from gaining the skills and knowledge essential for effective participation in socioeconomic transformation programs (Mpangala in IDS, 1989; Tjike, 1988). Not only, as basic needs/structuralists observe, does expanded export agriculture contribute to the neglect of food supplies for growing urban populations, and the small farmers, especially women, who cultivate them (Bujra, Marshall in ROAPE, 1990); it also aggravates rural stratification,[27] a major obstacle to increased popular participation (eg., Mikell, 1990; Ihimodu, Omo-Fadaka in IDS, 1989).[28] Inherited institutions and government agencies typically support larger "progressive" farms (Ihonvbere, Mpangala and Eyoh in IDS, 1989), including those controlled by new government officials. Even where, as in Tanzania, the government attempts to create more democratic institutions—representative village government, multipurpose cooperatives, etc.—hegemonic control of local governments thwart real participation.   Wealthier peasants tend to control peasant cooperatives (Harris in Seidman et al, 1991; Mayoux, 1988; Kalyalya et al, 1988) while the state may even seek to use them "as instruments... (of) greater control over peasant production."(Mpangala, Mmuya in IDS, 1989; Hyden, 1980).

Quite soon in the post-independence era, existing institutional structures 'captured' new government personnel, incorporating them into a growing 'bureaucratic bourgeoisie.' Thus Africa's new governors use their status and income to acquire control over and profit from productive and distributive sectors already geared to export-import trade. Not infrequently, they take advantage of government secrecy to profit from corrupt practices. Where elections take place, members of this class—lacking cohesive constructive programs to achieve transformation—commonly seek to mobilize support among ethnic groups, thus aggravating ethnic conflicts (Akor, Ihonvbere, Shivji, Turok in IDS, 1989, Chaligha, 1990). Increasingly, new ruling classes exercise state power to repress populations who oppose strategies that impoverish them (Ihonvbere, Hussain, Musoke, Mmuya in IDS, 1989). Governments, installed by military coups pledging to oust corrupt leaders, soon degenerate into the same pattern (Ihonvbere in IDS, 1989).

Many transforming institutionalists view foreign capital, not primarily as a potential cure, but a contributing cause of Africans' continuing poverty and powerlessness. Taking advantage of the post World War II technological revolution in shipping, communications, and productive sectors, transnational corporate finance capital rapidly restructures the world capitalist system within which the new African states remain dependent. They devise new forms of obtaining cheap raw materials, selling surplus manufactures and draining away the investable surpluses generated by low paid workers in competing third world countries, including Africa (Rugamamu, 1987; Omo-Fadaka, Campbell, Ihonvbere in IDS, 1989; Harris, 1989a; Seidman, 1990).[29] No longer eager to risk investments to acquire 'real estate' (i.e., productive or distributive facilities) in independent third world countries, transnationals increasingly encourage African governments to buy some or all the shares of ownership in their local affiliates. The transnationals retain control of technology (Komba in IDS, 1989), markets, and management which they provide through profitable contracts guaranteed by both the African (or other third world) governments and their own. This makes it easier for them to shift their purchases of crude agricultural and mineral products, and even labor-intensive manufactures, to the cheapest of many competing third world exporting economies (Makemure et al, 1986). Taking advantage of third world workers desperate for work at wages a fraction of those in the first world, transnationals have shifted major sectors of labor-intensive industrial production to the Third World. By putting them in direct competition with impoverished people in Africa, particularly in South Africa, this tends to undermine first world workers' ability to organize unions, as well as their wages, working and living conditions (Peet, 1987; Nash and Kelly, 1983; Gaventa, 1990; Danaher in IDS, 1989; Seidman et al, 1990). Thus the transnationals reap growing shares of the profits in new forms, including fees-for-services and transfer pricing through which they drain away 10-15 percent of the value of the typical third world country's foreign trade (Murray, 1981; Stoneman, 1985).

In the 1970s and early 1980s, as worsening terms of trade forced third world governments and enterprises to search desperately for new sources of foreign funds transforming institutionalists claimed a new stage of finance capitalism emerged. Transnational corporate banks eagerly supplied government-guaranteed loans at high, floating rates of interest,[30] a new way to 'invest' their accumulating surplus value profitably. High interest rates and debt servicing constituted a new form of extracting surplus value. The third world's difficulties in servicing those loans in the 1980s threatened the stability of the international banking system which required IMF/World Bank assistance to ensure repayment. This, many transforming institutionalists suggest, provides a key to understanding IMF/World Bank policies (Mwase, Mahdi in IDS, 1989).

Even when African governments recognize that transnationals invest to maximize global profits rather than contribute to African development, they fail to impose adequate controls to redirect their investments within the context of nationally- or regionally-oriented strategies (Makemure et al, 1986; Rugamamu, 1987). Following mainstream advice to attract foreign investment, they   typically compete in providing   transnationals liberal tax subsidies (seldom specifying adequate criteria), which primarily serve to reduce their revenues (Chaligha, 1980; Makemure et al, 1986). Some deliberately seek to enable wealthy Africans to acquire shares in transnational firms' local affiliates.   Many attempt to use parastatal institutions (including marketing boards, development corporations, agricultural finance institutions, etc., frequently initially established by pre-independence colonial governments) to capture a share of the surpluses transnational firms generate—not for national requirements, but their own ends. A few African governments nationalize key sectors (banks, export-import and wholesale trade, basic industries), but lack of personnel and knowledge still leads them to contract with foreign firms to acquire technology, markets, management, and—sometimes—capital (Mushi in IDS, 1989; Mytelka, 1989; Ohiorhenuan, 1989; Semobja in Mazur, 1990).

Whatever form their efforts took, in the 1960s and 1970s—when foreign investment flowed more readily to the Third World—the independent African governments generally lost out in the ensuing competition to attract foreign investment. Transnational manufacturing firms, in particular, multiplied their investments in apartheid South Africa, making it the continent's leading industrial state (Makgetla and Seidman, 1980; Seidman, 1985). The few independent African countries that did attract foreign manufacturing investments, often by making major capital expenditures themselves, discovered they tended to undermine rather than support agriculture (Seidman et al, 1991; Mytelka, 1989). In short, none of the African governments' post-independence policies significantly altered the foreign firms' decision-making powers nor altered their countries' lop-sided external dependence (eg, Ezeife in Adedeji, 1981; Rugamamu, 1987).

Some transforming institutionalists note the danger that African governments' efforts to achieve regional cooperation may prove rhetorical, or conceal new forms of collective economic dependence (Nyerere, 1988; Mpangala, Danaher in IDS, 1989; Amin et al., 1988). Several maintain that, because new African rulers do not find it in their interest to change existing structures and institutions, the Organization of African Unity—which requires consensus among African heads of state—will probably implement neither the Lagos Plan of Action nor the ECA's proposals for an alternative adjustment with transformation (eg., Hussain in IDS, 1989).

In short, transforming institutionalists assert that the new African state and emerging class formations combined with transnational finance capital to perpetuate and extend the internal and external structural features that rendered unrealistic the mainstream ideal-type competitive model, and inevitably culminated in Africa's crisis of the '80s. They claim that the IMF and World Bank function essentially as 'financial cops,' seeking to ensure the stability of transnational corporate finance capital, and, if possible, the continued outflow of investable surplus in the form of debt repayments (Stoneman, 1985, Harris in Onimode, 1989a: 20-23; Folson, Musoke in IDS, 1989, Akafrik, 1989). The destruction of social welfare programs ensures the continued outflow of Africa's investable surplus to transnational corporate banks (Ihonvbere in IDS, 1989). African governments' efforts to further open their countries' resources and markets to global competition facilitates further profitable transnational corporate penetration.

Many transforming institutionalists argue that most foreign aid cannot help African countries to surmount the crisis. The expectation that it will constitutes a deception (Musoke in IDS, 1989). Others maintain that foreign aid can only help to ensure self reliance if accompanied by selective government controls (Omo-Fadaka in IDS, 1989; Makemure et al, 1986).

2. Institutional change and structural transformation. The transforming institutionalists' explanations of Africa's poverty and powerlessness logically lead to proposals that differ fundamentally from those of mainstream theorists, and even, in significant respects, from the alternatives proposed by basic needs/structuralists. First, they emphasize the importance of transforming the institutions that comprise the state to ensure that, as society's primary instrument for restructuring the inherited political economy, governments make decisions reflecting the needs and interests of the majority of Africans. Democratization necessitates creating new state institutions at all levels to ensure representation of the interests of working people, peasants, unemployed, professionals, intellectuals,[31] and small businesspersons (Mazur, 1990; Hadjor, 1987: Ch. VIII). This requires extension of human and civil rights (free press[32], political expression, organization), and autonomous social organization of these groups independently of the state. Only this will enable the exploited classes to organize, to check authoritarian rule and to participate in formulating and implementing development strategies prior to, but by no means excluding the possibility of implementing a transition to socialism (Turok, Musoke, Mmuya, Danaher in IDS, 1989).   Some transforming institutionalists go further to emphasize drawing on African culture and traditions of cooperation and solidarity, instead of undermining them as, they claim, does the bilateral and multilateral aid agencies' emphasis on competition. They criticize dependence on foreign resources and ideologies, and urge African experts to work with

the people to formulate appropriate new strategies (Nyerere, 1988, Kalyalya et al, 1988: Ch. 2)[33].

Transforming institutionalists argue that, in the process of transforming themselves, African governments must also introduce policies and create appropriate institutions in all sectors to implement a planned long-term strategy to transform the national political economy. This necessitates sufficient state control of key economic institutions to capture and redirect nationally-generated investable surpluses to finance balanced, integrated national and regional economies capable of providing increasingly productive employment opportunities for the entire population (Mpangala, Musoke in IDS, 1989; Seidman, 1976, 1986).

In many respects, the transforming institutionalists' proposed reallocation of resources resembles that of the basic needs/structuralists. They place even greater emphasis, however, on shifting from export dependence to creating more balanced national and regional industrial and agricultural economies. They also urge establishment, not only of small scale industries, but also appropriate large ones to:[34] (1) serve as poles of growth for the planned spread of industrial and agricultural development; (2) manufacture essential capital goods to increase self-reliant productivity in every sector; and (3) process domestic resources to provide essential national and regional inputs as well as to maximize foreign exchange earnings in world markets (Ohiorhenuan, 1989; Abdelkader, 1984; Ndlela, 1984, 1985, Seidman, 1976).

Some have undertaken research on the impact of current technological changes for the nature and potential role of such large scale Third World industries and their growing industrial labor force in the context of the changing international division of labor (eg, Kaplinsky, 1985; Mytelka, 1989)[35].

More significantly, transforming institutionalists maintain that the formulation and implementation of an appropriate alternative strategy requires creating new participatory institutions to ensure representation of workers' and peasants' interests in the decision-making processes governing the productive sectors (SADRA, 1982; Akor in IDS, 1989; Ohiorhenuan, 1989). They do not all agree on the lessons of the post-independence African changes in ownership and management arrangements. Some still assert the necessity of collective ownership of all means of production (Akor in IDS, 1989). Others recommend selective control over priority sectors, the so-called 'commanding heights': basic industries, finance and foreign and internal wholesale trade (Makemure et al, 1989; Makgetla, Semboja in Mazur, 1990; Seidman, 1976).

But disagreements among transforming institutionalists do not end there. Given existing constraints in terms of trained personnel, finance, and transnational corporate control over global markets and sources of technology, many are beginning to ask what detailed forms of state and collective control will work more effectively (Semboja in Mazur, 1990)?[36]

Africa's past experience, they say, proves that mere state ownership of shares in existing basic enterprises—mines, transport, energy, iron and steel, chemicals and petrochemicals, machine tools and engineering—contributes little national and regional development, far less to ensure construction of essential new industries (Mytelka, 1989; Ohiorhenuan, 1989; Semboja in Mazur, 1990; Seidman, 1976).

In agriculture, some transforming institutionalists point out that small peasant farmers may produce crop yields exceeding those of large farms. Given the problems of producer cooperatives, they suggest creation of new institutions to facilitate peasant farming (Omo-Fadaka in IDS, 1989; Weiner in Seidman et al, 1990). Nevertheless, they recognize the dangers of stratification (Mikell, 1990; Isaacman, 1990) as more advanced technologies require larger farm units to achieve scale economies (eg., Mayoux, 1988; Harris in Mazur, 1990; Kalyalya et al., 1988 re women: Okpala in IDS, 1989).

Most transforming institutionalists recognize that African states past efforts to control banks and financial institutions to capture and re-direct nationally-generated investable surpluses have not proved very successful.[37] Many admit that repeated African governments efforts to exert control over foreign and internal wholesale trading institutions to redirect trade to support self-reliant balanced integrated national and regional development have failed to overcome shortages, blackmarkets and corruption.

In the area of regional and international trade and payments, transforming institutionalists direct more attention than either mainstream or structuralist theorists to the inadequacy of existing institutions (eg, Gordon, 1990). In the early 1980s, a conference in Zimbabwe canvassed alternative legislative means to improve SADCC cooperation to control transnationals (Makemure et al, 1986). Ostegaard exposed the way regional trade and financial institutions thwarted development of a SADCC-oriented tractor industry (Ostegaard, 1987). Akor (in IDS, 1989) called for increased ECOWAS cooperation to exert control over transnationals in West Africa. Nyerere stresses:

"We have to get ourselves organized, both nationally and at regional and all-African levels, to strengthen the reality of our commitment and action for intra-African cooperation.... We need to learn from the experience of past efforts at regional and subregional organizations, and we need to look again at how we support them by our own actions internally and by the stands we take in other international organizations or meetings." (Nyerere, 1988: 16)

A 1986 workshop of economists from eight SADCC country universities proposed that SADCC involve researchers from member countries to explore the appropriate institutional changes required to facilitate improved regional trade and payments agreements (Botswana proposal).

Transforming institutionalists point out that existing institutions tend to block formation of the united front of African and other South governments needed to negotiate with Northern governments and transnational firms for a new international economic order. As Nyerere observed:

"All these attempts at Third World united action suffer from similar weaknesses to those which affect intra-African efforts": (1) political commitment "withers when any participant has to make a small sacrifice"; (2) there exists no "effective machinery for implementing and taking full advantage of any agreements...or... concession won by their united action"; the Group of 77, for example, has no secretariat, while the OECD countries' secretariat includes "hundreds of highly qualified professionals"; and (3) Third World governments and peoples need more knowledge of each other, more trade, and greater cooperation (Nyerere, 1988: 17-19).

Finally, growing numbers of transforming institutionalists recommend that first world trade unions, church groups, intellectuals, professionals, and small businesses support African (and all Third World) liberation and development. They suggest that real development in Africa along the lines they advocate could lay the foundation for mutually beneficial peace and trade capable of providing jobs and raising living standards for both third and first world peoples (Africa Peace Tour, 1987, 1988, and 1989; Danaher in IDS, 1989; Gaventa, 1990; Seidman, 1990).

IV. Recommendations for Further Research in Phase II

A. Research implications of the debate

By the end of the 1980s, something of a consensus seemed to be emerging as to the scope of Africa's poverty and powerlessness. The major remaining debates centered on the causes and measures for overcoming them. The rest of this chapter outlines a research agenda to help resolve those debates as the essential foundation for designing an improved pattern of resource allocation and the institutional changes necessary to achieve it.

B. Resource allocation

1. <u>Area of agreement</u>. In all three categories, most theorists agree that, in the context of growing specialization and exchange, over time industrialization should provide increased productive employment opportunities in all sectors, including agriculture, as the essential foundation for raising the living standards of all Africans.[38] The debates focus on the direction and timing of practical policies and instruments to achieve the desired development of industrial and agricultural resources on a national, regional, and international level.

2. <u>Debates over resource allocation and Africa's role in the world economy</u>. Holding that the solution must be left to the "invisible hand" of (assumed) competitive national and international markets, mainstream theorists urge African policy makers to encourage the expansion of exports in which their countries have a comparative advantage, including, where possible, labor-intensive manufactures. With multiplier effects, exports will create an engine of growth that will eventually spread sustainable development throughout Africa's national and regional economies.

Basic needs/structuralists and transforming institutionalists object that limited world markets cannot absorb the expanding African (and other Third World) exports; instead, competition inevitably forces down export prices and reduce real returns to the people and resources that produce them. Meanwhile, skewed national and regional income distribution thwarts the expected spread effects, generating pockets of wealth in the midst of deepened mass poverty. Basic needs/structuralists and transforming institutionalists therefore call for a different pattern of resource allocation directed to balanced, integrated industrial and agricultural production in the context of national and regional economies planned to ensure increased productive employment opportunities and an improved quality of life for all Africans.

These disagreements suggest the outlines of a research agenda to gather evidence to assess these alternative explanations and proposed policies affecting resource allocation. This research should define more precisely the existing patterns of resource use—human, physical and financial; and the possibilities, limits and likely consequences of alternative approaches.

Social and physical scientists, working in multidisciplinary teams, should undertake this research to:

On the national level:

a) provide facts as to available physical and human resources: the extent, nature and consequences of their current utilization for domestic needs versus export or military purposes; and the potential for obtaining the required investments (human, technological and financial) to improve their utilization;

b) to identify the nature and consequences of the existing pattern of income distribution for the domestically-generated investable surpluses and domestic markets; and its probable effect on investment, consumption, and resource use.

On the regional level:

a) examine existing regional production and trade in agricultural and industrial commodities to assess the probable short and longer-term consequences of alternative patterns of expanded regional specialization and exchange, including the establishment of basic industries to process regional mineral and agricultural resources to meet regional demand.

On the international level:

a) assess the limits as well as the potential of national and regional export strategies, analyze the international supply and demand (including developed country production and restrictions on imports) for each major regional export in crude and in increasingly processed forms; and the associated flows of financial resources: investment and investment income, loans and debt servicing, and grants.

African and US Africanists researchers lack the resources required to compete with these efforts. They can most effectively utilize their limited resources to critically asses this valuable wealth of evidence in terms of its utility for answering the kinds of questions raised by the on-going theoretical and practical debates over resource allocation in terms of its implications for devising alternative strategies for attaining self-sustainable development.[39] Their experience and background may also enable them to suggest additional information these agencies should gather, as well as how best to present and disseminate it.[40]

C. Institutional changes:

Gathering evidence to resolve debates concerning the institutional barriers that may hamper attainment of proposed improved patterns of resource allocation may require African and US Africanists to pioneer in making more complex and innovative research efforts.   As the decade of the 1990s opens, most African and US Africanists in all three theoretical categories profess support for increased popular participation in all aspects of the development process.[41]   However, their on-going debates pose many unanswered questions as to the appropriate institutional changes required to realize it.

Mainstream theorists assert that corrupt, self-seeking politicians inevitably exercise state power in their own interest.   Therefore, only reduced government intervention at national, regional and international levels will enable competitive market forces to attain optimal resource allocation patterns.

Basic needs/structuralists object that, because structural impediments hinder competitive market forces, unregulated markets inevitably enrich the few and impoverish the majority.   Hence, they call for government intervention to protect the poor and overcome the structural obstacles to their participation in an increasingly self-sustaining development process.   Most admit, however, that shortages of administrative and technically trained personnel, combined with the relatively low levels of technology, limit the possibility of effective African government intervention to priority areas. Wherever possible, they agree, governments should leave the remaining resource allocation issues to market force, but they leave the boundaries of those priority areas extremely vague.[42]

Transforming institutionalists hold that the historically-shaped market institutions that perpetuate less than optimal resource allocation patterns also foster the emergence of new African ruling classes. In collaboration with transnational finance capital, these typically exercise state power to enrich themselves at the expense of the mass.   Only a fundamental transformation of state, itself, as well as key political economic institutions can, over time, make possible participatory planning.   Given personnel shortages, they specify that this necessary institutional transformation should begin with the economic "commanding heights": basic industries, export-import trade, and financial institutions.   Only in the course of a prolonged transition period[43] can the state and other collective forms of ownership or control gradually replace private market-oriented activities to ensure the appropriate development of resources, not for the profit of the few, but for the use of the many. Few transforming institutionalists have succeeded in answering the critical question as to the specific institutional changes required to enable the state apparatus and the institutions governing the commanding heights to facilitate this transition in Africa.

These debates suggest that in some areas, competition may spur private groups (aided by non-government organizations?) to contribute to self-sustainable development; but basic needs/structuralists argue that in a significant number it cannot. In any event, the state must at least play a role in creating an enabling environment for private actors; and where they cannot do the job, the state may, itself, have to intervene in the development process.

To clarify if, where and how the state should intervene, multidisciplinary research teams should conduct research on the way the state and key institutional factors interact at every level to shape resource allocation patterns. To do this, they should formulate and assess middle level propositions as to how, historically,[44] the introduction of new technologies, at different paces in different sectors, change not only the attitudes and skills of those who work with them, but the institutions and working rules governing the relationships between them. Revised and validated by evidence, these propositions should logically lead to suggestions for specific changes in institutions and working rules to facilitate the reallocation of resources in a more appropriate pattern.

In short, to make concrete proposals for appropriate institutional changes in specific African-country circumstances, multidisciplinary research teams should focus on a research agenda that helps to answer the key questions as to how existing economic institutions operate in the following three economic areas:

1.   The productive sectors:
     At the national and regional levels:
     a) to assess the nature, extent, and consequences of competition operating in different productive sectors, from those for food crops to those for iron and steel: how many enterprises (firms or individuals, given technologically-imposed economies of scale) actually compete in the relevant market? What institutional factors, if any, limit the entry or exit of the factors of production? Do all potential competitors enjoy full and equal access to relevant information? what consequences does the

pattern of income distribution have on the nature and extent of competition?

b) How do different government policies and systems of ownership, management, and control affect decision-making (the input, conversion and feedback processes) in enterprises in each sector in terms of the amounts and kinds of investment? employers' and workers' incentives for increased output? the kinds of technologies employed and their consequences for productive employment opportunities and the resulting quality of life of producers and consumers? the patterns of income distribution, stratification, and class formation?

At the regional and international levels:

a) What impact do existing structures, institutions and decision-making processes have on the pattern of national and regional resource development as they affect the employment opportunities and quality of life of the people, and their capacity for self-sustained development?

b) How do specific national government policies affect theirs and other nations' benefits or costs from participation in regional and world trade?

c) What role have transnational corporations played in changing the international division of labor and its impact on the productive structures of African national and regional economies?

d) What consequences have bilateral and multilateral institutional relationships, programs, and policies had for African countries' agricultural and industrial development?

e) What can African countries learn from the comparative experiences of other Third World countries (Broad et al, 1990)? regions?

2. Trading institutions and strategies: Most theorists agree that technological innovation and increased agricultural and industrial productivity require and contribute to expanded specialization and exchange—that is, trade. The theoretical debates, however, suggest the need for research on the institutions engaged to answer the following kinds of questions:

On the national and regional levels:

a) What evidence exists as to the reasons for governments' failure to develop adequate infrastructure for transporting, processing and storing domestic produce?

b) What decision-making processes govern retail and wholesale trading institutions? Do wealthy domestic traders, at either the retail or the wholesale level, exercise oligopolistic control, or participate as part of emerging classes to hinder national or regional attainment of self-sustainable development?

c) What effect on trade and expanded productivity, employment, consumption and the quality of life, have the following institutions had: price controls? subsidies? formation of consumer and marketing cooperatives? state ownership of wholesale firms? retail firms? What factors have led to the emergence of parallel markets (Meagher in ROAPE, 1990)? shortages?

On the international level:

a) What institutional factors thwart African national and regional efforts to cooperate to expand output and improve the terms of trade for their exports?

b) What impact have transnational corporate trading institutions' world-wide marketing policies had on the changing patterns of third and first world production, employment and the quality of life?

c) What experiences have African countries had in attempting to institutionalize new regional trade and payments agreements to redirect trade to support regional (as well as national) agricultural and industrial development?

d) What underlying difficulties have hampered Third World countries' efforts to bargain collectively with the first world for international commodity agreements? to work together for mutually-beneficial regional industrial development?

3. Financial institutions and strategies: Given the theoretical debates over the institutional changes required to facilitate the accumulation and reinvestment of capital, more research should focus on the realm of banking and financial institutions to answer several clusters of questions:

On the national level:

a) To what extent do African economies generate investable surplus, and what happens to it?

b) How do existing government policies affect the distribution of income and the re-investment of capital through taxes? government expenditures (including investments)? domestic and foreign debt? central bank policies?

c) How do other domestic financial institutions—banks, insurance and pension funds, credit cooperatives, etc.—affect the accumulation and allocation of capital to various productive sectors? What decision-making processes (including influences of domestic private interests, the state, and transnational corporate financial institutions) determine their behavior in this respect?

On an international level:

a) What effect do transnational corporate bank policies, (including Eurocurrency markets, rescheduling exercises, lending policies, etc.) have on African national and regional efforts to finance self-sustainable development?

b) What institutional factors influence the decision-making processes of multilateral financial institutions like the IMF, the World Bank, the African Development Bank, etc.? What effect do those institutional factors have on African national and regional financial institutions and policies?

c) What can African countries learn from the experiences of other Third World countries in trying cooperate to redirect the flow of national and regional funds?

Endnotes

1. In so doing, it cites a wide range of authors, from the World Bank and Economic Commission for Africa to individual African and US Africanist researchers. It makes no attempt to weigh their relative significance, but includes them to indicate the breadth of materials available on these issues.

2. This category generally rests on a foundation of neoclassical economics.

3. This category falls within the pragmatic tradition of Raul Prebisch, elaborated in the post-World War II era by International Labour Organization (ILO) and some United Nations experts.

4. This category's lineage includes diverse strands ranging from historical materialism and modes of production to dependency theory.

5. Ibid. pp. 35-6.

6. Re Ghana's alleged 'success', see Folson in IDS; Loxley, 1990; re women, Koda and Omari, 1989; Elson, 1989b; Bujra, 1990; re children, Muntemba in IDS; and, re general impact, including the above plus elderly and minorities, see Bathily, Jonah, Bonat and Abdullahi, Bangura in IDS; Marshall, 1990; Meagher, 1990; re health, Wisner, 1989; Musoke in IDS.

7. See Iae re women in Botswana; Koda and Omari, 1989, re women in Tanzania, re women teachers in Nigeria/IDS.

8. Within the transforming institutionalist perspective, Samir Amin, together with the Third World Forum and the United Nations University, organized a network of African researchers to conduct studies under the title, "Strategies for the Future of Africa."   The network involves some 200 researchers, mostly social scientists, working in 33 African countries, (10 West, 4 Central, 3 East and Southern, 6 North).   Coordinators selected participants to work on themes chosen by a Secretariat composed of African scholars.   Most of the working groups met twice, at the beginning and the end of their research.   The network published their findings in various fora, including the *Third World Quarterly* and in book form. (For book titles, see Future, 1989, in bibliography.) In 1989, at the request of SAREC (the research arm of the Swedish aid agency), four experts provided a useful initial summary and evaluation of the network's published and unpublished works. (See Hyden et al,, 1989.)

9. For an early exposition, see Milton Friedman, "The Methodology of Positive Economics." in *Essays on Positive Economics,* (Chicago: University of Chicago Press, 1953).

10. For comparative study of food price stability and welfare of poor in Asia and Near East, see Goldberg, 1989.

11. Compare World Bank, 1981, 1989a.

12. In this connection, the UNDP and World Bank published a provisional volume of tables of African data re key aspects of economic and social development, accompanied by a computer disk designed to facilitate researchers' efforts to make comparative analyses over time and between African countries (see UNDP, 1989.). The study committee that prepared the document sent copies to members of the ASA Task Force's Economy subgroup for comment; other interested ASA members should contact Mark Gallagher, World Bank, 1818 H Street, NW, Washington DC 20433.

13. Sponsored by Michigan University's Research Center for Research on Economic Development.   The Center initiated several studies on relevant issues, including three case studies of privatization in Ivory Coast which, while not providing evidence on post-privatization performance, indicated that consequences depended in part on the mode of privatization (See Wilson, 1989.)

14. The International Labour Organization had sponsored many studies of this informal labor market that substantiated this argument, and many African researchers had undertaken country case studies that led to similar conclusions (cf: IDS; Zimbabwe U, #2,#3; Mabogunje).

15. For importance of participatory research within NGOs, see Gilbert: for a Senegalese case study, see Schmidt; for participatory study of NGO-aided projects, see Kalyalya et al.

16. Neglect of the environment, including forests, water resources, and agricultural land, as well as industrial pollution, aggravated physical constraints on African productive capacity (Nkokoni, 1989; Misana, 1989; Koffi-Tessio, 1989; Baranga, 1989; <case study re subsistence farmers in East Africa>, Mahran, 1989; W.Rugumamu, 1989; Alieu, 1989.

17. Foreign firms invested in manufacturing in Africa primarily in South Africa (Seidman, 1985).

18. re Ghana's experience, see Folson, 1989.

19. For summary of initial criticisms, see Seidman, 1986: 242-244; for earlier debates, see South North Conference, Killick, Payer; for case studies, see Cheru; Banugire in IDS; Onimode, 1989a; for special problems re women, see Brock-Utne, Mahmoud, Koda and Omari, Okpala in IDS; for a Chinese scholar's review of ECA vs. World Bank program, see Tang, 1990.

20. Some basic needs/structuralists agree that devaluation may sometimes be necessary, but that governments should only devalue their national currencies in the context of carefully formulated and implemented plans, taking into account country-specific structural constraints, to build more self-reliant, balanced national and regional economies (eg., Loxley, 1990;).   Others, including the UN Economic Commission for Africa, urges governments
to rule out generalized devaluation, and instead utilize multiple exchange rates to implement their plan goals.

21. A group of non-government organizations (NGOs) set up a working group that concluded that even in its 1989 study, the World Bank's continued emphasis on orthodox adjustment and export promotion failed to address their criticisms and left unanswered many questions (See NGO Working Group, 1989.)

22. For more detailed consideration of required industrial structure, see Steel, 1984; and A. Seidman in Makemure et al., 1986.

23. Because of their importance, the Task Force established a Subgroup specifically to deal with issues relating to regional integration. Chaired by Guy Martin, that Subgroup prepared a review paper, now Chapter 3 of this book.

24. Nyerere, 1988; see also Amin and Third World Forum Group in SAREC, 1989; T. Moyo, Omo-Fadaka, 1989; special problems re women, IDS, 1989; Mazur, 1990.

25. In South Africa, an emerging working class contributed to the development of new historical research (see Radical History Review).

26. These took many forms, including direct attacks (as in South African destabilization in Southern Africa (United Nations, 1989); surrogate 'revolts' (UNITA, with South African and US support in Angola; and MNR, with SA backing, in Mozambique); conflicts over inherited colonial borders (Sudan, Ethiopia, Moroccan attacks on Polisario Front, the Libyan-Chad conflict).

27. For details, see Isaacman, 1990.

28. Note: Green Revolution tended to aggravate inequality (Cheru 1989b; Loxley, Bujra, Marshall in ROAPE, 1990). For an in-depth discussion of rural social protest, see Isaacman, 1990.

29. For review of background theories, see Ross and Trachte, 1990.

30. Mahdi (in IDS) noted the difficulty researchers confronted in obtaining data on the foreign debt since bank confidentiality prohibits efforts to obtain original bank documents; international agencies and financial journals did not publish half the necessary information relating to Eurocurrency loans, and lacked data relating to medium term private debts.

31. Some, however, argue that some intellectuals view it as in their interests to service those in power without regard to the welfare of the mass (see Oli Adimaly, letter to editor, West Africa, 16-22 July, 1990, p. 2096.

32. Some argue, however, that "free press" may simply give those with sufficient capital the opportunity to publish their biases (cf. Panford comments at Task Force workshop, ASA Annual Meeting, Baltimore, 1990).

33. Re implications for women, IFAA collective. For debate on content of the term "democracy", see Shivji in IDS; Mkandawire-Anyang, 1988.

34. The ECA does incorporate large industries in its long-term perspective approach for the years 1980 to 2008.

35. Already, some African research centers focus on technology research, including the Nigerian Institute of Social and Economic Research, and the Institute of Development Studies in Tanzania. Re implications for labor, see, eg., G. Seidman in Mazur.

36. See also review paper re the State and the Legal Order, ch. 8 below.

37. See Seidman, 1986, for outline and annotated bibliography re mainstream vs. Marxist approaches.

38. For this reason, the United Nations designated 1980-190 as the Industrial Development Decade for Africa. The Economic Commission for Africa, the United Nations Industrial Development Organization, and the Organization of African Unity prepared a joint program of action focusing on the transfer of industrial technology and promotion of intra-African industrial cooperation. The Lima Declaration proposed that, by the year 2000, Africa should double its industrial output to two percent of worldwide manufacturing value added.

39. As an example of the potential significance of this role, see the ECA 1989b; Khan.

40. In the late 1980s, a joint United Nations Development Programme and World Bank team undertook to compile and transform African country data in a detailed computerized form that permits researchers to make comparisons. The team generously made the draft computer program available to ASA Task Force economy group members for their comments and suggestions. (See United Nations Development Programme and the World Bank, *African Economic and Financial Data*, [Washington: World Bank, 1989] for hard copy of the more recent provisional statistics. The computerized version includes more historical data.)   This illustrated the potential role of the ASA Task Force network in facilitating African and US Africanist researchers' contribution to the important task of collecting and disseminating this kind of valuable information.

41. Kwamina Panford (1990) argues that popular participation and basic needs may be diametrically opposed, creating a problem of reconciling both in real life (comment at Task Force workshop, ASA 1990 Annual Meeting).

42. Killick (1989) argues this must depend on the national context.

43. President Nyerere of Tanzania reportedly remarked that Tanzania's efforts to implement a transition to socialism had taken far longer than he had anticipated.

44. Regarding the role of historical factors, including examples, and the necessity of studying them to understand past popular participation in Africa, see Coifman, 1990.

Bibliography

Abdelkader, Djefflat. 1984. "Les difficulties de l'integration interindustrielle en Algerie et la dependeance technologique" Paper presented at meeting on African Regional Perspectives (Dakar: United Nations University, mimeo).

Adedeji, A. 1989: *Towards a Dynamic African Economy.* London: Frank Cass.

Adedeji, A., Ed. 1981. *Indigenization of African Economies* (London: Hutchinson University Library for Africa.

Africa Recovery: a periodical published by the UNDP, UNFPA, UNICEF and the World Food Programme (New York; United Nations, DPI, room S-l061).

Akafrik, Arbeitskreis Afrika. 1989. *International Counter-Congress – West-Berlin Declaration.* AKAFRIK: lingener Str. 9, 4400 Munster, West Germany.

Anthony, C.G. 1988. *Mechanization and Maize: Agriculture and the Politics of Technology Transfer in East Africa.* New York: Columbia University Press.

Anyang, Peter. 1988. "Political Instability and the Prospects for Democracy in Africa," *Africa Development,* Vol XIII, no. 1, 1988, pp. 71-86.

Banugire F.R. 1986. "Towards an Appropriate Financial System for Rural Transformation in Uganda," in Griendshilds, ed., *Agriculture, Growth and Instability.* London: Gower.

----- 1987. "The Impact of the Economic Crisis on Fixed Income Earners," in Dodge & Wiebe, eds, *Beyond Crisis - Development Issues in Uganda.* New York: ASA and Kampala: MISR.

----- 1989. "Privatization as an Instrument of Social and Economic Development," paper presented to the Seminar on the Marketing Concept, Makerere, March, 1989.

Baratou, K. 1988. "Notes Towards a Balance Sheet of a Decade's Experience with Orthodox Stabilization and Structural Adjustment," Proceedings of the Conference on Southern Africa - Economic Experience Since Independence, Zimbabwe Economic Society, Harare, 16-18 November, 1988.

Belinda Bozzoli and Peter Delius, 1990. Guest eds. "History from South Africa," *Radical History Review,* Jan, 1990.

Botswana workshop: A proposal for SADCC research relating to financial institutions in SADCC, prepared at a workshop at University of Botswana, Gaborone, 1986.

Broad R., Cavanagh J., and Bello, W. 1990. "Rekindling the Development Debate," Washington, DC: Institute of Policy Studies, mimeographed draft.

Brown, R. and Cummings, R. 1984. *The Lagos Plan vs the Bert Report.* Lawrencevill, VA: Brunswick Publishing Co.

Center for Research on Economic Development, University of Michigan, *Economic Reform in Africa: Lessons from Current Experience.* Report on two conferences held under US AID contract in Nairobi (September 7-8, 1988) and Abidjan (September 13-15, 1988); papers included E.J. Wilson, "The Global Imperatives of Economic Reform in Africa;" L. Deng, "Economic Recovery Program: An Overview of the Adjustment Experience in Africa in the 1980s;" D. Rodrik, "Trade Policy Issues Facing Sub-Saharan Africa;" R.H. Bates, "Economic Reforms in Africa;" L.P. Mureithi, "Some Issues in Economic Policy Reform in Kenya;" P.K. Quarcoo, "Economic Reform in Ghana;" and H. Zayyad, "Public Sector Reforms in Nigeria."

Chaligha, Amon. 1990. "Taxation and the Transition to Socialism in Tanzania." PhD dissertation, Claremont, CA: Claremont University.

Coifman, V. B. 1990. "Towards a Sustainable Strategy for African Economic Development," Paper presented to the ASA Task Force economy workshop, 1990 ASA Annual Meeting, Baltimore.

Cornia, G.A., Jolly, R. and Stewart, F. 1987. *Adjustment with a Human Face: Protecting the Vulnerable and Promoting Growth.* Oxford. Clarendon Press.

de Vletter, F. 1981. "Rural Development and Agricultural Dualism - Case Study of Swaziland. Kwaluseni: Social Science Research Council and University College of Swaziland, mimeo.

ECA, (United Nations Economic Commission for Africa), 1990. *Africa Charter for Popular Participation in Development.* Addis Ababa.

-----. 1989a. *African Alternative Framework to Structural Adjustment Programmes for Socio-Economic Recovery and Transformation.* (E/ECA/CM.15/6/Rev.3)

ECA, 1989b. *Statistics and Policies – ECA Preliminary Observations on the World Bank Report: "Africa's Adjustment and Growth in the 1980s."* 89-10075. New York.

-----. 1988. *Long-term Perspective for Africa, 1980 to 2008.* Addis Ababa.

-----. 1988b. *International Conference on the Human Dimension of Africa's Economic Recovery and Development: Khartoum Declaration.* Addis Ababa. UNECA.

-----. (United Nations Economic Commission for Africa), 1983. *ECA and Africa's Development - 1980-2008 - A preliminary perspective study.* Addis Ababa.

FAO (Food and Agricultural Organization of the United Nations), 1986. *African Agriculture: The Next 25 Years.* Rome.

Federation for Education with Production. 1989. *Report on Harare consultation on education with production in South Africa.* Conference in Harare, Zimbabwe, 12-14 October, 1989.

Future, 1989: "Strategies for the Future of Africa" network, based in Dakar, Senegal; director: Samir Amin. Books published include: M.L. Gakou, *The Crisis in African Agriculture;* F. Yachir, *The World Steel Industry Today; and Mining in Africa Today;* H. A. Amara and B. Founou-Tchuigoua, a collection of studies on African agriculture (forthcoming); P. Anyang' Nyong'o, Popular Struggles for Democracy in Africa; SADCC: prospects for Disengagement in Southern Africa; a collection of 8 case studies in Afro-Arab cooperation in Africa Development (CODESRIA's journal); E. Hansen, ed., *Africa: Perspectives on Peace and Development;* F. Mansour, *Nation, State and Democracy in the Arab World;* S. Amin and F. Yachir, *La Mediterranee dans le Monde;* S. Amin, La Faillite du Developpement and F. Yachir, *Development in the Third World: Old and New Paradigms.*

Gaventa, John. ed., 1990. *Communities in Economic Crisis - Appalachia and the South.* Philadelphia: Temple University Press.

Gilbert, Elon. 1990. "Non-governmental Organizations and Agricultural Research: The Experience of the Gambia." Paper prepared for ASA Annual Meeting, Baltimore.

Goldberg, Ray A. ed. 1989. *Research in Domestic and International Agribusiness Management.* Greenwich, CT, JAI Press, 1989, vol. 9.

Gordon, April. 1990 "Capitalist Reforms in Sub-Saharan Africa: Some Questions and Issues." Paper presented to 1990 ASA Annual Meeting, Baltimore.

Hadjor: Kofi Buenor. 1987. *On transforming Africa - Discourse with Africa's Leaders.* New Jersey, Africa World Press.

Heath, John. ed. *Public Enterprises at the Crossroads.* United Kingdom. Routledge, forthcoming.

Hyden, Goran. 1980. *Beyond Ujamaa in Tanzania. Underdevelopment and Uncaptured Peasantry.* London. Heinemann.

Hyden, Goran, Meillassoux, Claude, Ndulu, Benno and Nzongola-Ntalaja. 1989. *Strategies for the future of Africa - An Evaluation.* Stockholm: Graphic Systems for SAREC DOCUMENTATION -Evaluations.

IDS (Institute of Development Studies), Papers prepared for Conference on Alternative Development Strategies at Institute for Development Studies(IDS) at University of Dar es Salaam, December 12-14, 1989, co-sponsored by IDS and Institute for African Alternatives (IFAA); the call for papers or this conference generated some 70 papers, mainly by African authors, representing a wide range of views on a wide variety of issues, many of which IFAA is publishing.The papers included: M.E. Akor, "Mobilizing the Domestic Resources of ECOWAS' Traumatized Economies for Economic Development;" E.K.Alieu, "Natural Resources in Sustainable Development: Where do we Strike the Balance?" W. Asombang, "The Environment, Optimum Use of Resources and the Dynamics of Sustainable Development in a Mineral-led Economy: The Case of Namibia;" F.R. Banugire, "Missing Links in the Management of the Uganda Economy Towards an Alternative Structural Adjustment Policy Framework;" D. Baranga, "Lowered Agricultural Productivity Caused by Encroachment on Foreign Habitats;" B. Brock-Utne, "The Schooling Prospects of Tanzania Female Students in a Situation of Economic Crisis;" H. Campbell, "The Debt Crisis and the Restructuring of Capital Internationally: Implications for Democracy and Reconstruction in Southern Africa;" D. Chanda, "Zambia: Another Development Option;" A.E. Chinyio and N.F. Owor, "Motivating Research Schemes;" J.B. Endely, "Strategies and Programmes for Women in the Agricultural Sector in Africa;" K. Danaher, "Adjusting to What? Structural Adjustment and the African Struggle for People's Democracy;" D.L. Eyoh, "Equity, Popular Participation and Rural Development: Ideology and Rhetoric in the Nigerian Experience;" K.G.Folson, "Structural Adjustment as Structural Immobilization: Structural Adjustment and Industrialization in Ghana (1983-89);" M. N. Hussain, "The De-Adjustment Mechanisms of IMF Adjustment Programmes: From Sudan's Experience to the African Alternative;" M.J.N.S. Iae, "Women in Development: The Case of Botswana;" IFAA collective, "IFAA Discussion Paper: Alternatives for

African Women;" A. Ighemat, "The Financial Problems of Sub-Saharan Africa and Their Possible solution;" I.I.Ihimodo, "Agricultural Policy in the Development of the Nigerian Economy;" J.O. Ihonvbere, "Structural Adjustment and Prospects for Democracy in Nigeria;" B.O. Koda and C.K. Omari, "Women's Struggles in Coping with Economic Crisis in Household Economy in Tanzania: The case of poor families in Dar es Salaam;" E.M. Koffi-Tessio, "Environment, Water and Agricultural Performance: The African vicious cycle;" A.Y. Komba, "Science, Technology and Sustainable Development for Africa: The crisis, the issues;" A.A. Mahdi, "Third World Debt Problems with Particular Reference to non-oil Developing Countries;" F.B. Mahmoud, "Some Considerations on Women Conditions Under Structural Adjustment Programme in Africa;" H.A. Mahran, "Ecological Destruction in the Sudan: An Empirical Investigation;" S.B. Misana, "Natural Resource conservation for Sustainable Development in Tanzania;" M. Meetarbhan, "Democracy, the Imperatives of Economic Development and Environmental conservation;" Mmuya: "The Post-Colonial State and Democracy in Africa;"T. Moyo, "Africa's Debt Crisis in the '80s: Which Way Out?;" G.P. Mpangal, "The State, Democracy and the Question of Alternative Strategies in the Development of Peasant Agriculture in Africa (with special reference to Tanzania);" I.K.S. Musoke, "The Debt Trap and Structural Adjustment Programmes: Socio-Economic consequences and Political Implications for Countries in Sub-Saharan Africa;" Mwase, N.R.L. "Resolving the African Debt Crisis: Domestic Initiatives - Lessons for Independent Namibia;" S.R. Nkonoki, "The Ecology Crisis and Alternative Development Strategies: Strategies for Environment-balanced Development;" A.J. Nalwanga-Sebina, "The Viability of Resistance Committees for Women in Development in Uganda;" J. Okpala, "Nigerian Women Adjustment with Structural Adjustment Programme;" J.Omo-Fadaka, "The Environment and Sustainable Development;" W. Rugamamu, "Environmental constraints in Achieving sustainable Resource Utilization in the Southern African Subregion;" A. Seidman, "Towards Controlling Multinational Corporations;" I.G. Shivji, "the Pitfalls of the Debate on Democracy;" M. Suliman, "Sustainable Development in Africa;"S. H. Bukurura, "Public Participation in Financing Local Development: the case of Tanzania Development Levy;" S.A. Tella, "Planning for Growth and Development with International Capital: A Case for Africa;" B. Turok, "No Democracy, No Development?" J.E. Zayid, "Exports and Economic Development: Simulations of an Economic Model of the Sudan."

Isaacman, Allen. 1990. "Peasants and Rural Social Protest in Africa," in *African Studies Review*. (Atlanta: African Studies Association) vol. 33, No. 2, September, 1990. pp. 1-120.

Isoun, T.T. 1989. "Discovery and Innovation" in *African Academy of Sciences* Vol. 1, No. 1, March 1989.

Jones, Christine and Roemer, Michael. 1989. eds. "Parallel Markets in Developing Countries." Proceedings of the Workshop sponsored by Harvard Institute for International Development, Nov. 11-12, 1988, *World Development*, Special Issue, Vol. 17 No. 12, Dec. 1989.

Kalyalya, D., Mhlanga, K., Seidman, A. and Semboja, J. eds. 1988. *Aid and Development - Evaluating a Pilot Learning Process in Southern Africa*. Trenton, NJ: Africa World Press.

Kalyati, J. 1984. "The Iron and Steel Industry in Zimbabwe," Paper presented to meeting on African Regional Perspectives. Dakar, United Nations University.

Kaplinsky, R. 1985. "Locational Patterns of Direct Foreign Investment and the New International Division of Labour in Manufacturing." Mimeographed paper presented to Conference on Economic Policies and Planning Under Crisis Conditions in Developing Countries. Harare, Economics Department, University of Zimbabwe.

Khan, Hider Ali. 1990 "Economic Modeling of Structural Adjustment Programs," Paper presented to Structural Adjustments Conference at Phipps Conference Center, University of Denver, Apr. 27, 1990.

Killick, Tony. 1989. *A Reaction Too Far: economic theory and the role of the state in developing countries*. London: Overseas Development Institute.

Killick: Tony Killick, ed. 1982. *Adjustment and Financing in the Developing World*. Washington, DC: International Monetary Fund.

Mabogunje, Akin L. 1990. "Urban Planning and the Post-Colonial State in Africa: A Research Overview," *African Studies Review*. Atlanta: African Studies Association. Vol. 33, No. 2, Sept., 1990, pp. 121-204.

Makemure, K., Ndlela, D., Seidman, A., Seidman, R.B. Eds. 1986. *Transnationals in Southern Africa*. Papers from a conference on Maximizing the Benefits of Transnational Corporations. Harare: Zimbabwe Publishing House. Chapters include: S. Mubako, Zimbabwe Minister of Justice, "Opening Address;" A. and B. Seidman, "Transnational Corporations and Poverty in Southern Africa.", B. wa Mutharika, "A Framework for Developing a Collective Bargaining Position for the SADCC Countries.", S. Zorn, "Negotiations with Transnational Corporations and Alternatives to Negotiation.", D. B. Ndlela,

"Negotiations on the Transfer of Technology and the Implications for SADCC.", C. Stoneman, "Transfer Pricing.", A. Seidman, "The Potential for Taxing Transnational Corporations.", N. Makgetla, A. and R. Seidman, "Toward a SADCC Investment Code: Laws on Foreign Investment in the Third World.", G. Wittich, "Regional Integration: The Experience of the Council for Mutual Economic Assistance.", A. Sajo, "The Socialist Countries' Experiences in Negotiations with Transnational Corporations: A Lawyer's Approach." and Appendix II: "Recommendations of Workshop Committees" on Aid and loans: technology transfer, alternative tax policies, and investment codes."

Makgetla, Neva and Seidman, Ann. 1980. *Outposts of Monopoly Capital.* Westport, CT: Lawrence Hill.

Mayoux, Linda. 1988. ed. *Not All Are Equal: African Women in Cooperatives.* Report of a Conference held at the Institute for African Alternatives, 10-11 September, 1988. London: Institute for African Alternatives.

Mazur, Robert. 1990. ed. *Breaking the Links.* Trenton, NJ. Africa World Press. including: S. Amin, "Peace, National and Regional Security and Development: Some Reflections on the African Experience." T. Szentes, "Socialism in Theory and Practice." N. S. Makgetla, "Using Development Theory to Solve Problems: An Application to South Africa." W.G. Martin and I. Wallerstein, "Southern Africa in the world-Economy, 1870-2000: Strategic Problems in World-Historical Perspective." S. Nkomo, "Confrontation and the Challenge for Independent Development: The Case of Lesotho." Renosi Mokate, "Realigning Botswana's Trade Structure: Constraints and Possibilities for SADCC." J.J. Semboja and Lucian A. Msambichaka, "The Political Economy of State-Owned Enterprises in the Third World: The Case of Tanzania." T. Moyo, "Development Banks in the Era of 'Socialist Transition'." B. Davidson, "The Keys to Peace in African Regional Conflicts: Lessons from Eritrea and Ethiopia." G.W. Seidman, "From Trade Union to Working-Class Mobilization: The Politicization of South Africa's Non-Racial Labor Unions." R.B.Seidman, "What Constitutional Lessons Does Zimbabwe's Experience Teach?"

Mihyo, P.B. 1984. "The Transfer of Technology to Tanzania's Public Enterprises," Mimeograph, Dar es Salaam: Law Faculty.

Mikell, G. 1990. "Global Formulae, Local Responses: Rural Economic Differentiation in Ghana." Paper presented at colloquium to honor St. Clair Drake, San Francisco State University, April 19-21, 1990.

Mkandawire, Thandika, 1988. "Comments on Democracy and Political Instability" and Anyang's "Rejoinder" in *Africa Development*. Vol. XIII, No. 3, 1988.

Moseley, K.P. 1989. "West African Industry and the Debt Crisis: A Research Report." Paper presented to 32nd Annual Meeting of the African Studies Association, Atlanta, 2 Nov. 1989.

MSID (Minnesota Studies in International Development Internships). 1989. University of Minnesota; Papers by interns include: J.A. Philpott, "Rural Urban Migration: Serer Women Migrants," 1986; and Laura Schmidt, "Toucar ack xola- analysis of a Senegalese development case study."

Mudenda, G. 1985. "The Management of Import Substituting Industrialization in Zambia," mimeographed paper presented to Conference on Economic Policies and Planning Under Crisis Conditions in Developing Countries Harare: Economics Department, University of Zimbabwe.

Murray, Robin. 1981. *Multinationals Beyond the Market*. New York, Wiley.

Mytelka, Lynn Krieger. 1989 "The Unfulfilled Promise of African Industrialization," A Social Science Research Council Paper, *African Studies Review*. Vol 32, No. 3, Dec. 1989.

Nash: June Nash and Kelly, M.P.F., Eds. 1983. *Women, Men and International Division of Labor*. Albany State University Press, New York

Ndlela, D.B. 1985. "The Capital Goods Sector ad Implications for Planning Industrialization in Zimbabwe." Mimeographed paper presented to Conference on Economic Policies and Planning Under Crisis Conditions in Developing Countries. Harare: Economics Department, University of Zimbabwe.

-----, 1984. "The Capital Goods Sector in Zimbabwe." Mimeographed paper prepared for project, "National Building or Transnationalization in Africa" in framework of the Regional Perspective project of the United Nations University. Harare: Economics Department, University of Zimbabwe.

Nyerere, Julius 1988. "Africa Exists in the Economic South" in *Development & Socioeconomic Progress*. Published by Afro-Asian Peoples' Solidarity Organization, No. 41, 3/1988.

Ohiorhenuan, John F.E. 1990. Ohiorhenuan, "The Industrialization of Very Late Starters: Historical Experience, Prospects and Strategic Options for Nigeria." A Discussion Paper. Sussex: Institute of Development Studies.

Ohiorhenuan, John F.E., 1989. *Capital and the State in Nigeria*. Westport, CT: Greenwood Press.

Onimode, Bade 1989a. ed. *The IMF, The World Bank and The African Debt – The Economic Impact*. Papers from an Institute for African Alternatives Conference (London:Zed Press, 1989), including papers by: E. Anyaoku, "Keynote Address: Impact of IMF-World Bank Policies on the People of Africa;" L. Harris, "The Bretton Woods system and Africa;" B. Onimode, "IMF and World Bank Programmes in Africa;" B. Okogu, "Structural Adjustment Policies in African Countries: A Theoretical Assessment;" Commonwealth Secretariat, "Reinforcing International Support for African Recovery and Development;" S. Biermann and J. Campbell, "The Chronology of Crisis in Tanzania, 1974-86;" H. Othman and E. Maganya, "Tanzania: The Pitfalls of the Structural Adjustment Programme;" V. Jamal, "Somalia: Economics for an Unconventional Economy;" S. Fanos, "Sudan and the IMF, 1978-83;" C. Fundanga, "The Role of the IMF and World Bank in Zambia;" A. E. Sibanda, "IMF-World Bank Impact on Zimbabwe;" D. Mabirizi, "Impact of IMF-World Bank on Lesotho;" L. Harris, "South Africa's External Debt Crisis;" W. Asombang, "A Future Independent Namibia and the IMF-World Bank: Policy Alternatives;" R.S. Olusegun Wallace, "Structural Adjustment: The Case of West Africa." A. Olukoshi, "Impact of IMF- World Bank Programmes on Nigeria."

Onimode, Bade, 1989b. ed. *The IMF, The World Bank, and the African Debt - The Social and Political Impact*. London: Zed Press. Including papers by: C. Payer, "Causes of the Debt Crisis;" B. Campbell, "Indebtedness in Africa: Consequence, Cause or Symptom of the Crisis?" R.H. Green, "The Broken Pot: The Social Fabric, Economic Disaster and Adjustment in Africa;" D. Elson, "The Impact of Structural Adjustment on Women: concepts and Issues;" F. Cheru, "The Role of the IMF and World Bank in the Agrarian Crisis of Sudan and Tanzania: Sovereignty vs Control;" F.R. Banugire, "Employment, Incomes, Basic Needs and Structural Adjustment Policy in Uganda, 1980-87;" D. Muntemba, "The Impact of IMF-World Bank Programmes on Women and Children in Zambia;" A. Bathily, "Senegal's Structural Adjustment Programme and its Economic and Social Effects: The Political Economy of Regression;" K. Jonah, "The Social Impact of Ghana's Adjustment Programme, 1983-86;"Z. A. Bonat and Y. A. Abdullahi, "The World Bank, IMF and Nigeria's Agricultural and Rural Economy;" Y. Bangura, "Crisis and Adjustment: The Experience of Nigerian Workers."

-----. 1988. *A Political Economy of the African Crisis*. London: Zed Press.

OAU (Organization of African Unity). 1981. *The Lagos Plan of Action for the Economic Development of Africa from 1980 to Year 2000* (LPA). Addis Ababa.

-----. *Lagos Plan of Action for the Implementation of the Monrovian Strategy for the Economic Development of Africa*. Adapted by the 2nd Extraordinary Assembly of OAU Heads of States meeting in Lagos, April 28-29, 1980. Addis Ababa, OAU.

-----. 1986. "The African Priority Programme for Economic Recovery (APPER)." Addis Ababa.

-----. 1982. OAU Council of Ministers' 39th Ordinary Session in Tripoli, Libya. Progress Report of the Secretary General of the OAU and Executive Secretary of UNECA on the implementation of the Lagos Plan of Action and the Final Act of Lagos. Addis Ababa: ECA

Ostergaard, Tom. 1989. *SADCC Beyond Transportation: The Challenge of Industrial Cooperation*. Uppsala: Scandinavian Institute of African Studies.

Panford, Kwamina. 1989. "The Influence of the International Labor Organization (ILO) on African Workers' Union and Collective Bargaining Rights: A Case Study of Ghana." PhD dissertation, Boston: Northeastern University.

Parfitt, T.W. and Riley, S. P. 1989. *The African Debt Crisis*. London: Routledge.

Payer, Charlotte. 1975. *The Debt Trap and the IMF*. New York: Monthly Review Press.

-----, 198 . *The World Bank—A Critical Analysis*. New York: Monthly Review Press.

Peet, Richard. 1987. ed. *International Capitalism and Industrial Restructuring*. Boston: Allen & Unwin.

Pingali, P., Bigot, Y. and Binswanger, H.P. 1987. *Mechanization and the Evolution of Farming Systems in East Africa*. Baltimore: Johns Hopkins for the World Bank.

Raikes, 1989. *Modernizing Hunger: Famine, Food Surplus & Farm Policy*. London: James Currey for Catholic Institute for International Relations.

ROAPE (Review of African Political Economy). 1990. *What Price Economic Reform?* Sheffield, UK: ROAPE, Spring, 1990. Includes J. Loxley, "Structural Adjustment Programmes in Africa: Ghana and Zambia", J. Marshall, "Structural Adjustment & Social Policy in Mozambique", J. Bujra, "Taxing Development: Why Women Must Pay-Gender and the Development Debate in Tanzania," K. Meagher, "The Hidden Economy: Informal and Parallel Trade in Northwestern Uganda," David Seddon, "Politics of Adjustment: Egypt and the IMF," T. Parfitt and S. Bullock, "The Prospects for a New Lome Convention," A. Hoogvelt, "Debt and Indebtedness: The Dynamics of Third World Poverty."

-----, 1988. *Feeding Africa: What Now?* Sheffield, UK: ROAPE, No. 43, 1988; includes L. Cliffe, "Zimbabwe's Agricultural 'Success' & Food Security;" A. Samatar, "The State, Agrarian Change & Crisis in Somalia;" G. Williams, "The World Bank: Economy of Africa's Crisis".

Ross, Robert and Trachte. 1990. *Global Capitalism- the New Leviathan.* Buffalo, NY: SUNY.

Rugamamu, S. 1987. "State Regulation of Foreign Investment in Tanzania." Unpublished PhD Dissertation, Maryland: University of Maryland.

SADCC (Southern African Development Coordination Conference). 1985. "Industry- Progress of the SADCC Regional Plan of Industrial Co-operation," Mimeographed report to Heads of State. Mbabane.

SADRA (Southern African Development Research Association), 1982. Meeting, Roma, Lesotho.

Secretariat of NGO-Bank Committee, ICVA. 1989. *Position Paper of the NGO Working Group on the World Bank.* Geneva, Switzerland.

Seidman, A., Mwanza, K., and Weiner, D. 1990. eds. *Rethinking Agricultural Transformation in Southern Africa.* Trenton, NJ: Africa World Press. Papers from Association of Concerned African Scholars workshop at Brandeis University, May, 1987, including: L. Harris, "Cooperatives in Mozambique."

Seidman, Ann. 1990. *Apartheid, Militarization, and the US South .* Trenton, NJ: Africa World Press.

-----, 1986. *Money, Banking & Public Financing in Africa.* London: Zed Press.

-----, 1985. *The Roots of Crisis in Southern Africa.* Trenton, NJ: Africa World Press.

Seidman, Ann, 1975. *Planning for Development in SubSaharan Africa.* New York: Praeger and Dar es Salaam: Tanzania Publishing House.

Seidman, Robert B. 1976. *State, Law and Development.* New York: Croom-Helm.

Singh, A. 1985: "The Continuing Crisis of the Tanzanian Economy: The Political Economy of Alternative Policy Options." Mimeographed paper presented at Conference on Economic Policies and Planning Under Crisis Conditions." Harare: Economics Department, University of Zimbabwe.

South-North Conference on the International Monetary System and the New International Order, Arusha, Tanzania, 30 June-3 July 1980.

Steel, W.F. 1984. "Industrialization Experience in Sub-Saharan Africa: Objectives, Strategies, Results and issues." Mimeographed paper prepared for High Level Industrial Policy Seminar for Africa (with assistance of J.W. Evans). Berlin.

Stoneman, C. 1985. "Strategy or Ideology? The World Bank/IMF Approach to Development." Paper presented at Conference on Economic Policies and Planning Under Crisis Conditions in Developing Countries. Harare: Economics Department, University of Zimbabwe.

Tang, Yuhua. 1990. "Structural Changes and Strategic Priorities in African Economic Development." Paper presented to ASA Task Force economy workshop at 1990 annual ASA meeting in Baltimore.

Tjike, Victor. 1988. "The Social Responsibility of the African Graduate." Report of a conference of African Students in the UK at University of Oxford, 4 June, 1988 (London: Institute for African Alternatives).

UN (United Nations) Inter-Agency Task Force, Africa Recovery Programme/Economic Commission for Africa. 1989. *South African DESTABILIZATIONS - The Economic Cost of Frontline Resistance to Apartheid.* New York: United Nations.

UN. 1988. *The Khartoum Declaration.* Khartoum, Sudan, 5-8 March, 1988.

UN, 1986. *The UN Programme of Action for African Economic Recovery and Development.* New York and Addis Ababa, UN Economic Commission for Africa.

UN Advisory Group. 1989. "Report on UN Secretary General's Advisory Group on Financial Flows to Africa." New York: United Nations, 24 February, 1989.

UNICEF, (United Nations International Children's Fund). 1989. *The State of the World's Children*. New York: Oxford University Press.

UNDP (United Nations Development Programme) and the World Bank. 1989. *African Economic and Financial Data*. Washington, DC.

UNESCO (United Nations Educational, Scientific and Cultural Organization). Statistical Yearbook, (Paris) Various years.

University of Zimbabwe. 1981. Economics Department research series re industry in Zimbabwe. Harare: Economics Department, University of Zimbabwe, mimeo. #1: "Long Vacation Pilot Research Project on the Ingredients of an Industrial Strategy to Stimulate Rural Development: The formal sector;" #2: "A Survey of Small Scale Enterprises in the Informal Sector;" #3: "Rural Industries in Zimbabwe."

Wilson, E. III. 1989. *The Political Economy of Economic reform in the Cote d'Ivoire: A Micro-level Study of Three Privatization Transactions*. Ann Arbor, MI: Center for Research on Economic Development.

Wisner, B. 1989. *Power and Need in Africa*. Trenton, NJ: Africa World Press.

World Bank. 1989a: *Sub-Saharan Africa - From Crisis to Sustainable Growth*. Washington, DC: IBRD.

-----, 1989b. *World development Report 1989 - Financial Systems and Development, World Development Indicators*. New York: Oxford University Press.

-----, and the UNDP. 1989. *Africa's Adjustment and Growth in the 1980s*. World Bank, Washington, D.C.

World Bank. 1988: *Report on Adjustment Lending*. Washington, DC. 8 Aug, 1988.

-----, 1987. *World Bank Annual Report, 1987*. Washington DC.

-----, 1986. *Poverty and Hunger: Issues and Options for Food Security in Developing Countries*. Washington, D.C.

-----, 1984. *Towards Sustained Development in Sub-Saharan Africa: A Joint Programme of Action*. Washington, DC: International Bank for Reconstruction and Development.

Chapter 3

African Regional Cooperation and Integration: Achievements, Problems and Prospects

By Guy Martin

I. Introduction

Ever since they became independent in the early sixties, African states have consistently pursued policies of regional cooperation and integration as a means of promoting socioeconomic development and of reducing their dependence on the West. While African scholars and policy-makers generally agree on the need and desirability of African unity, they seriously disagree on the level, strategy and ultimate goal of unification, as well as on the scope of cooperation.

While many institutions for regional cooperation and integration were created soon after independence, progress toward integration has been disappointing. Thus, the East African Community survived for only ten years (1967-1977). West and central African regional integration schemes, such as the 'Union douaniere et economique de l'Afrique centrale' (December 1964), and the Economic Community of West African States (May 1975) have been generally unsuccessful. The Southern African Development Coordination Conference (April 1980) and the Preferential Trade Area for Eastern and Southern Africa (December 1981) have been more promising.

This Chapter provides a briefing on this subject. Part I states the case for regional cooperation and integration in Africa; Part II reviews contending approaches and perspectives on regional cooperation and integration; Part III surveys the aims and activities of nine African regional cooperation and integration schemes; Part IV identifies the problems of, and assesses the prospects for regional cooperation and integration in Africa.

II. The Case for Regional Integration in Africa

Of all the developing regions of the world, Africa is, by far, the poorest, least developed and most heterogeneous. Of the fifty African countries, thirty-two have fewer than eight million inhabitants and thirty-four are in the low-income category, with an average GNP per capita of US$355 (UNDP/World Bank, 1989: Table 1.1). According to a recent World Bank report (*Intra-Regional Trade in Sub-Saharan Africa*), overall intra-African trade has barely increased, as a proportion of total trade, in the last twenty years. GATT statistics indicate that intra-African trade has remained around 4 percent of total trade during the 1980s, significantly below the levels of the early 1970s (GATT, 1987: lll). According to the OECD, the total external debt of Sub-Saharan African countries at end-1988 amounted to US$142 billion, representing about 11 percent of the total external debt of developing countries at that time (OECD, 1989: Table A). This means that Africa is not only the poorest developing region, the most foreign-trade dependent economy and the most dependent on the markets of the developed countries; it is also the least regionally integrated and the slowest growing in terms of mutual interdependence.

This appalling economic situation has convinced African scholars and policy-makers that regionalism (or collective self-reliance) is the most appropriate strategy to achieve autonomous, self-reliant and self-sustained development. Thus, the February 1979 OAU Monrovia Symposium on the future development prospects of Africa called for "the creation of an African common market based on progressive co-ordination and integration, which would evolve in the form of concentric circles reflecting the economic areas that currently exist on the continent." Similarly, the 1980 OAU Lagos plan of action (LPA) and Final Act of Lagos (FAL) proposed the eventual establishment of an African Common Market (ACM) as a first step towards the creation of an African Economic Community (AEC) by the year 2000. Africa's Priority Programme for Economic Recovery 1986-1990 (APPER), adopted on 20 July 1985 by the 21st OAU Assembly of Heads of State and Government, acknowledges that "Economic integration through sub-regional, regional and continental cooperation is today a top priority which will enable the economies of the African countries to be viable within a system of international relations characterized by inequality in the balance of power" (OAU, 1985: sect. 101, 44). Similarly, the United Nations Programme of Action for Africa's Economic Recovery and Development (UN-PAAERD) adopted at the UN General Assembly's Special Session on Africa on 1 June 1986 states that "[T]he international community reaffirms its belief in the strategy for collective self-reliance among developing countries and reiterates its conviction that economic and technical co-operation among these countries should constitute a key element in the economic recovery of Africa and to the mutual benefit of developing countries ...." (UN, 1986)

The Lagos Plan of Action's proposed African Economic Community aims "to promote collective, accelerated, self-reliant and self-sustaining development of Member States; co-operation among these States; and their integration in the economic, social, and cultural fields" (OAU, 1981: 6; OAU, 1980: 128). This goal is to be achieved in two stages. During the first stage (decade of the 1980s), the objective is to strengthen the existing regional economic communities and to establish economic groupings in the other regions of Africa, so as to cover the continent as a whole (north, west, central, eastern and southern Africa); to effectively strengthen sectoral integration at the continental level; and to promote coordination and harmonization among the existing and future economic groupings for the gradual establishment of an African common Market. During the second stage (decade of the 1990s), sectoral integration should be further strengthened, and measures towards the progressive establishment of a common market and an African Economic Community should be taken. In this context, the following sub-regional organizations have been successively created: the 16 member states Economic Community of West African States/ECOWAS (Lagos, 28 May 1975); the 16 member states Preferential Trade Area for Eastern and Southern Africa/PTA (Lusaka, 21 December 1981); the 10 member states Economic Community of Central African States/CEEAC (Libreville, 18 October 1983); and the 5 member states Union of the Arab Maghbreb (Marrakech, 17 February 1989). This elaborate network of sub-regional organizations thus extends over the whole African continent.

III. Contending Approaches and Perspectives

Ever since the early days of independence, African scholars and politicians have been deeply divided on the issue of African unity. A first group (the *Panafricanists*) favored political integration as a prerequisite to economic integration. Its members (Cheikh Anta Diop, Modibo Keita, Kwame Nkrumah, Sekou Toure) advocated the immediate and total integration of the African continent, and the setting up of a single continental government with common institutions. Another group (the *Gradualists* or *Functionalists*), anxious to preserve the African states' recently-acquired sovereignty, favored a more gradual approach to African integration. This group (Felix Houphouet-Boigny, Jomo Kenyatta, Leopold Senghor) held that economic integration should precede political integration. Its members favored a loose cooperation in non-controversial (technical and economic) areas and viewed regional institutions as a stepping-stone for the progressive political and economic unification of the continent. With the passing away of the Panafricanists from the African political scene, neo-functionalism has become the dominant approach and serves as the model to most, if not all, current regional integration schemes in Africa. In this regard, it should be noted that *cooperation* and *integration* are two distinct concepts. Briefly stated, cooperation refers to joint action, by two or more states, in the form of common programmes or projects in functionally-specific areas, while integration implies the creation of new, supra-national institutions within which common policies are planned and implemented.

Another major distinction should be established between *market integration* and *production integration*. According to conventional neoclassical theory, market integration constitutes a means of expanding economic opportunities through specialization based on comparative advantage and economies of scale. This theory analyzes the effects of integration essentially in terms of the *trade creation* and *trade diversion*. Trade creation refers to a shift from the consumption of higher-cost domestic products to the lower-cost products of other member states. Trade diversion refers to a shift in the source of imports from lower-cost sources outside the regional bloc to a higher-cost source within it. A union that is on balance trade-creating is regarded as beneficial, whereas a trade-diverting union is regarded as detrimental (Viner, 1950). The core of the argument for integration is that "so long as there are economies of scale to be obtained, or so long as there are possibilities for specialization between countries on the lines of comparative advantage, industrialization to serve the wider regional market will be more efficient than industrialization within the confines of each national market" (Hazlewood, 1975: 11).

Furthermore, neoclassical theory views market integration as a gradual process evolving through five successive stages. These are: (1) the formation of a *free-trade area* (abolition of trade barriers among member countries); (2) a *customs union* (establishment of a common tariff policy toward non-member countries); (3) a *common market* (free movement of factors of production as well as of commodities within the area); (4) a   complete *economic union* (harmonization of national economic policies among the member countries); and (5) total *economic integration* (unification of economic and social policies and setting up of a supra-national authority) (Belassa, 1962: 2).

IV. African Regional Cooperation and Integration Experiments, 1960-1990

Many institutions for regional cooperation and integration were created soon after independence in Africa. There are at present more than 200 such organizations on the continent; more than 160 are inter-governmental and the rest non-governmental. A recent UN-ECA report identified 32 inter-governmental organizations in west Africa alone. This institutional proliferation has resulted in multiple membership, duplication, waste of human and financial resources, and lack of inter-institutional coordination.

The same report has devised a useful typology of African inter-governmental organizations, based on their objectives. According to this criteria, one may distinguish between: (1) *economic communities*, aiming at establishing an economic union via the stages of free-trade area, customs union and common market; (2) *development organizations*, whose purpose is to harmonize policies in various economic sectors, such as agriculture, transport and energy; (3) *technical/service organizations*, which coordinate policies with respect to a particular sector or project; (4) *monetary and financial institutions*, which are specialized technical/ service organizations; and (5) *professional associations*, which actually belong to the category of non-governmental organizations(UN/CEA, 1983:22-24).

Table 3-1 provides a synopsis of the various African organizations existing in each category. What follows is a brief survey of the aims and activities of a cross-section of African economic communities, development organizations, and monetary and financial institutions.

A. The Union of the Arab Maghreb (UAM)

On 17 February 1989 in Marrakech (Morocco), five Heads of State and Government (Algeria, Libya, Mauritania, Morocco and Tunisia) signed the Treaty constituting the Union of the Arab Maghreb ('Union du Maghreb Arabe'/UMA). Thus, after several unsuccessful attempts (including the 1964 Permanent Advisory Committee for the Maghreb/'Comite Permanent Consultatif du Maghreb'/ CPCM), the dream of Maghreb unity was finally realized. Together, these countries have an area of 5,784 million sq. kms., a population of about 60 million, and an average GNP per capita of US$1,874. The distribution of population and resources remains, however, very uneven. Algeria and Morocco between them have 46.4 million inhabitants, i.e. more than

Table 3-1

Major African Regional Organizations

Organization	Founding date	Member states	Aims
CPCM-Maghreb Permanent Consulta- tive Committee	October 1964	[4] Algeria, Lybia, Morocco, Tunisia	Common market
UAM-Union of the Arab Maghreb	February 1989	[5] Algeria, Libya, Mauritania, Morocco, Tunisia	Economic, social & cultural
Entente Council	May 1959	[5] Benin, Burkina, CI, Niger, Togo	Economic & Technical cooperation
OCAM-Organisation commune africaine et mauricienne	February 1965	[9] Benin, Burkina, CAR, CI, Mauritius, Niger, Rwanda, Senegal Togo	Economic & Technical cooperation
CEAO-Communaute economique de l'Afrique de l'Ouest	April 1973	[7] Benin, Burkina, CI, Mali, Mauritania, Niger Senegal	Common market
ECOWAS-Economic Community of West African States	May 1975	[16] Benin, Burkina, CI, CV, Gambia, Ghana, Guinea, Guinea Bissau, Liberia, Mali, Mauritania, Niger, Nigeria, Senegal, Sierra- Leone, Togo	Common market & Economic Community
MRU-Mano River Union	October 1973	[3] Guinea, Liberia Sierra Leone	Customs union
Senegambia Confederation	December 1981	[2] Senegal, Gambia	Political union

Organization	Founding date	Member states	Aims
UDEAC-Union douaniere & economique de l'Afrique centrale	December 1964	[6] Cameroon, CAR, Chad, Congo, Equat. Guinea, Gabon	Common market
ECCAS-Economic Community of Central African States	October 1983	[10] Burundi, Cameroon, CAR, Chad, Congo, Eq. Guinea, Gabon, Rwanda, Sao Tome & P., Zaire	Common market
CEPGL-Communaute economique des Pays des Grands Lacs	September 1976	[3] Burundi, Rwanda, Zaire	Common market
EAC-East African Community	December 1967 to 1977	[3] Kenya, Tanzania, Uganda	Common market
PTA-Preferential Trade Area for Eastern & Southern Africa	December 1981	[16] Burundi, Comoros, Djibouti, Ethiopia, Kenya, Lesotho, Malawi, Mauritius, Mozam-bique, Rwanda, Somalia, Swaziland, Tanzania, Uganda, Zambia, Zimbabwe	Common market & Economic Community
SADCC-Southern African Development Coordination Conference	April 1980	[9] Angola, Botswana, Lesotho, Maawi, Mozambique, Swaziland, Tanzania, Zambia, Zimbabwe	Project-oriented Economic cooperation

Note: CAR=Central African Republic; CI=Côte d'Ivoire; CV=Cape Verde three-quarters of the Union's total population. The combined GNP per capita of Algeria and Libya (US$8,140) is seven times greater than that of the other three member countries combined (US$1,230) (UNDP/World Bank, 1989: 1.1). As a share of total Maghrebian foreign trade, intra-union trade actually declined from 3 percent in 1962 to 1.5 percent in 1985.

The UAM, whose institutionalization is still in progress, aims at a achieving an economic union by stages, through the progressive implementation of an economic, social and cultural programme of action whose details have yet to be worked out. The recent opening of the borders between Libya and Tunisia, and between Algeria and Morocco, has already demonstrated the potential for the growth of trade, as well as the benefits of a free movement of labor within the sub-region. In spite of these favorable circumstances, the risk of failure of this new attempt at regional integration remains high for two reasons: the necessarily limited short-term gains that may be expected from integration; and, the continuing economic difficulties of the Maghreb countries, which may stimulate a resurgence of nationalism.

B. The 'Communaute economique de l'Afrique de l'Ouest' (CEAO)

CEAO is the successor organization to UDEAO ('Union douaniere et economique de l'Afrique occidentale'), a free-trade area set up within the framework of the former French West African Federation. The organization was established through the Abidjan Treaty of 12 April 1973, and its present membership includes seven Francophone west African states, namely Benin, Burkina Faso, Cote d'Ivoire, Mali, Mauritania, Niger and Senegal. All CEAO member states (except Mauritania) are also members of the Franc zone system and of its affiliated institutions (UMOA, BCEAO and BOAD).

CEAO currently constitutes an *organized trade zone*, i.e. a type of free trade area with various tariff structures and customs regulations. It aims to develop into a customs union within twelve years of its creation and, ultimately, into a full-fledged common market. CEAO also seeks to promote cooperation and integration in such areas as agriculture, livestock, fishing, industry, transport and communications, and tourism. The two main instruments of this regional integration structure are the Regional Cooperation Tax ('Taxe de Cooperation Regionale'/TCR), designed as an instrument of trade liberalization in industrial products within CEAO; and the Community Development Fund ('Fonds Communautaire de Developpement/FCD), a scheme designed to compensate the least developed, most geographically disadvantaged member states for losses incurred through the operation of the TCR. A third instrument, the Community Development Solidarity and Guarantee Fund ('Fonds de Solidarite et d'Intervention pour le Developpement de la Communaute'/FOSIDEC), was set up in October 1978 as a loan guarantee and investment fund in favor of the member states or public and private firms operating in those states.

Since it started operating in 1974, CEAO has achieved a measure of success toward integration. Thus, the number of firms whose products have been approved under the regional tax regime has increased from 91 in 1975 to 222 in 1980, representing a 143 percent increase. During the same period, the number of products traded under this regime has risen from 129 to 403, an increase of 125 percent. The value of manufactured goods traded within CEAO increased 241 percent from US$14,000 in 1976 to US$48,000 in (CEA, 1983: 28). Similarly, intra-community trade has increased in value from US$73 million in 1970 to US$396 million in 1981, US$406 million in 1983 and US$300 million in 1986. Intra-community trade as a percentage of total exports has increased from 6.9 percent in 1980 to 11.6 percent in 1983, falling back to 6.5 percent in 1986 (UNCTAD, Handbook). Furthermore, CEAO has established a common nomenclature and harmonized duties and sales taxes. Finally, CEAO initiated in October 1978 a number of common projects in the areas of small-scale irrigation, fisheries and solar energy, and common higher training institutions in the fields of management, fisheries, geology and mining, and textiles.

According to the World Bank, "Among Africa's market integration schemes the CEAO has been most successful" (World Bank, 1989:149). While this may be the case, it is also true that the organization has experienced various problems and difficulties. First of all, there has been little or no progress towards implementing the measures of positive integration required to establish an economic community. The common external tariff, scheduled for January 1985, has yet to come into effect. In addition, most member states continue to operate certain trade restrictions in defiance of the Treaty provisions. Furthermore , the absence of a regional industrial policy results in duplication of industrial development efforts. In fact, the industrial development of the CEAO countries is heavily dependent upon investment by foreign (French, U.S.) multinational corporations. Indeed, intra-community trade (and the regional tax regime) mostly tend to benefit these foreign corporations. Thus, CEAO very much appears as a 'penetrated organization', externally-oriented and dependent (CEA, 1983: 28-30; Robson, 1983: 41-2).

C. The Economic Community of West African States (ECOWAS)

The Treaty establishing ECOWAS was signed on 28 May 1975 in Lagos. The organization now has 16 member states (Cape Verde, Cote d'Ivoire, Benin, Burkina Faso, Gambia, Ghana, Guinea, Guinea Bissau, Liberia, Mali, Mauritania, Niger, Nigeria, Senegal, Sierra Leone and Togo). The sheer size of this vast economic grouping, with a total population of over 185 million and a combined Gross Domestic Product (GDP) of US$122,437 billion is clearly impressive and augurs well for the economic potential and future of the Community. More significantly, ECOWAS constitutes the first regional integration attempt ever to transcend the traditional historical and linguistic cleavage between French, English and Portuguese-speaking African states.

According to Article 2 (2) of the Treaty, ECOWAS aims at establishing an economic union, via the stages of free trade area, a customs union (within 15 years) and a common market. Additional protocols (of November 1976, April 1978, May 1979 and June 1981) cover budgetary contributions, a Fund for Cooperation, Compensation and Development, the re-export of goods, rules of origin, the assessment of revenue effects of trade liberalization, privileges and immunities, the free movement of persons, and non-aggression and defense. For products to qualify for tariff concessions within the Community, a local ownership rule requires eventual 51 per cent local ownership, as well as 35 percent local value added. The Community's activities began slowly. The Treaty officially became operational in March 1977, but its substantive implementation actually started only in May 1979. Progress has been achieved in a number of areas. Measures have been taken to abolish visas and entry permits for short stays. A special fund for improving telecommunications and a voluntary fund for energy resources development have been established. Finally, since its creation, the ECOWAS Secretariat has undertaken no less than 12 studies on various aspects of sub-regional economic cooperation and integration, notably on trade and customs, currency convertibility and monetary integration, fiscal matters, agriculture, industrial development, transport and telecommunications, and immigration.

While institution-building has proceeded apace, no significant progress has yet been made towards positive integration in ECOWAS. Intra-community trade has remained low, and even shown a tendency to steadily decline. Thus, the value of intra-ECOWAS trade has decreased from US$1,056 million in 1980 to US$500 million in 1984 and US$491 million in 1986. During the same time, as a percentage of total exports, intra-community trade decreased from 3.9 percent in 1980 to 2.5 percent in 1984-85, slightly rising to 3.2 percent in 1986 (UNCTAD, Handbook). Indeed, trade liberalization has made little progress: no common external tariff has yet been established, the 1981 deadline for the freezing of tariff rates was not met, and little progress has been made towards implementing the new time-table.

In addition, the less-developed ECOWAS member states fear that the support and compensation arrangements will prove inadequate in the face of the dominant position of Cote d'Ivoire, Nigeria and Senegal. Furthermore, ECOWAS' rule of product origin has become a source of serious disagreements. This rule promotes indigenous manufacturers but restricts exports from Cote d'Ivoire and Senegal (since their industrial plants are considered foreign investment) and discourages foreign investment. More significantly, the pattern of trade has not changed. Cote d'Ivoire and Nigeria still dominate the export of manufactures. On labor mobility, there has been setback rather than progress; in 1981 and 1983, Nigeria expelled more than 1 million Ghanaian migrant workers.

There is no movement of capital within the region because capital markets remain underdeveloped. Lack of progress in the payments system is due to the failure of ECOWAS to establish (in spite of its declared long-term commitment) a single monetary zone, with a common currency and a pooling of foreign exchange reserves. Finally, non-compliance of member states with Community decisions, policies and programmes is a feature of ECOWAS. Such non-compliance includes a failure of member states to fully contribute their agreed payments to the Community budget and their capital contribution to the Fund. For example, by August 1987, nine members had not contributed to the 1985 budget of the Community, thirteen states owed contributions for 1986, and fifteen had not contributed to the 1987 budget. At the end of 1988, the shortage of finance was acute for the secretariat, and crippling for the Fund (ADB, 1989: 81-3).

D. The 'union douaniere et economique de l'Afrique centrale' (UDEAC)

The Treaty creating UDEAC, signed on 8 December 1964 (and effective on 1st January 1966) by five central African countries (Cameroon, Central African Republic/CAR, Chad, Congo and Gabon) in fact constituted a revamping of the Equatorial African Customs Union ('Union Douaniere Equatoriale'/UDE) set up on 23 June 1959 between the four members of the former 'Federation de l'Afrique Equatoriale Francaise'/AEF (the same as above, minus Cameroon). The CAR and Chad withdrew from UDEAC in early 1968, but the CAR rejoined the

Union shortly thereafter, and Chad applied for readmission on 20 December 1983. Equatorial Guinea became the Union's sixth member on 19 December 1983. All UDEAC member states are also members of the Franc zone system and its affiliated institutions (BEAC and BDEAC).

The UDEAC Treaty ultimately aims to create a common market (through the usual steps of a free trade area and a customs union), though no time-limit has been set. In fact, UDEAC has been in a state of encapsulation since 1966. Little or no progress has been made since then towards creating a customs union or in coordinating the development, transport and communication and telecommunication policies and projects of the member states. Barriers remain with respect to the free movement of persons and capital, and convertibility of currency exists not because of specific UDEAC policies, but because of common membership in the Franc zone. The value of intra-community trade has decreased from US$200 million in 1980 to US$100 million in 1984 and US$84 million in 1986. As a percentage of total exports, intra-UDEAC trade decreased from 4.1 percent in 1980 to 2 percent in 1985 and 2.8 percent in 1986 (UNCTAD, Handbook).

Some limited progress has been made in harmonizing statistical information and internal fiscal regimes. However, recent studies have shown that implementation of the UDEAC Treaty provisions and mechanisms has actually resulted in increased market dominance of foreign-owned companies operating within UDEAC, increased economic inefficiency, and the uneven pattern of industrialization, and disarticulation of the regional economy (Jalloh in Jalloh: 206-225; Mytelka in Mazzeo, 1984: 139-146).

E. The Economic Community of Central African States (ECCAS)

In accord with ECA policy and the Lagos Plan of Action recommendations, the December 1982 UDEAC enlarged summit of Heads of State and Government of the region proposed to create a region-wide central African economic union. On 18 October 1983, ten central African states meeting in Libreville (Gabon) adopted the Treaty creating the 'Communaute economique des Etats de l'Afrique centrale'/ CEEAC-ECCAS. Like ECOWAS, ECCAS includes, and attempts to co-exist with other, pre-existing integration schemes like UDEAC and the Economic Community of the Great Lake States/ECGLS. ECCAS, too, transcends traditional colonial cleavages by bringing together former Belgian, French, Portuguese and Spanish colonies.

This ten-nation grouping (Burundi, Cameroon, CAR, Chad, Congo, Equatorial Guinea, Gabon, Rwanda, Sao Tome & Principe, and Zaire) eventually aims at establishing a central African common market and economic community in 12 years (by 1995). This is to be achieved in three, four-year stages: (1) stabilization and harmonization of the existing customs and fiscal regimes, and elaboration of the tariff and non-tariff reduction/ elimination schedule; (2) creation of a free-trade area; and (3) creation of a customs union, with a common external tariff.

Stressing the need for the rapid development of the less-developed, land-locked and otherwise disadvantaged member states, the ECCAS Treaty establishes two funds to contribute to equitable distribution of the benefits and costs of integration: The Cooperation and Development Fund to provide technical and financial assistance to promote development; and the Compensation Fund to provide financial compensation for revenue losses arising from the lowering of tariffs. Recognizing the inadequacy of an exclusive focus on market integration, the ECCAS Treaty seeks to promote cooperation in the major sectors of the economy (agriculture, industry, energy, transport and communication etc.) through 'production integrated mechanisms.'

The very recent establishment of ECCAS precludes any meaningful evaluation of its achievements at this early stage. Yet, the organization has already experienced some financial and institutional difficulties. Thus, financial difficulties led to a five month postponement of the third summit meeting, due to take place in January 1987 in Bangui (CAR). The fourth summit (Kinshasa, February 1988) drew back from the progress already achieved by rescinding earlier decisions to consolidate customs regimes and to establish a clearing house. The stabilization and harmonization of the member states' customs and fiscal regimes, due to be completed by 1984, has yet to be achieved. However, two important decisions adopted at the sixth summit meeting (Kigali, January 1990) augur well for the future of this young Community: the creation of an ECCAS development bank by 1990; and the free movement of persons, goods and capital, to be realized by 1 January 1991.

F. Monetary and Financial Institutions: The Franc Zone System

The Franc Zone was set up as a monetary cooperation arrangement between France and her former west and central African colonies following their independence in the early sixties. Characterized by a very centralized decision-making structure, the zone is organized around four major principles: (1) free convertibility, at par, of the local (CFA Franc)and French (French Franc) currencies; (2) free movement of capital within the zone; (3) pooling of gold and foreign exchange reserves in a common French Treasury account ('Compte d'Operations');

and (4) common rules and regulations for foreign commercial and financial transactions.

Clustered around France, the Franc zone system includes: (1) France; (2) seven west African states member of the West African Monetary Union ('Union monetaire ouest-africaine/UMOA)—including six out of seven CEAO member states —, namely Benin, Burkina, Cote d'Ivoire, Mali, Niger, Senegal and Togo; (3) six central African States member of the 'Banque des Etats de l'Afrique Centrale'/BEAC— including all six UDEAC member states —, namely Cameroon, CAR, Chad, Congo, Equatorial Guinea and Gabon; and (4) the Federal Islamic Republic of the Comoros.

In addition to the two sub-regional central banks, namely the 'Banque centrale des Etats de l'Afrique de l'Ouest'/BCEAO, based in Dakar (Senegal), and 'Banque des Etats de l'Afrique centrale'/BEAC based in Yaounde (Cameroon), the Franc zone system includes two regional development banks: the West African Development Bank ('Banque ouest-africaine de developpement'/BOAD), created in 1973 and based in Lome (Togo); and the Central African Development Bank ('Banque de developpement des Etats de l'Afrique centrale'/BDEAC, created in 1975 and based in Brazzaville (Congo).

In exchange for the guaranteed convertibility of the French Franc, the Franc Zone African member states have accepted limits on budget deficit and domestic credit expansion. More significantly, by accepting strict membership rules and regulations of the union, they have entrusted all their monetary and financial responsibilities to France in what amounts to a voluntary surrender of sovereignty. Indeed, France controls these states' issuance and circulation of currency, their monetary and financial regulations, their banking activities, their credit allocation and, ultimately, their budgetary and economic policies (Martin, 1986: 205-235).

G. The East African Community (EAC)

The East African Community (EAC) was formally established on 1 December 1967 by the coming into force of the Treaty for East African Cooperation signed by the three partner states (Kenya, Tanzania and Uganda) earlier that year. The Community's demise can be dated to the middle of 1977, when the partner states failed to approve the 1977-78 EAC budget. Thus, the Community died before its tenth birthday. Yet, it had been one of the most successful regional integration experiments in the developing world. What had gone wrong?

As Arthur Hazlewood rightly observes, the three countries' economies had been even more closely integrated before independence.

At that time, the integration arrangement comprised a customs union with a common external tariff and free trade between the countries, common customs and income tax administrations, common transport and communications services, a common university, common research services, and a common currency. By the time the Treaty was signed, however, the common currency had been abandoned, and the operation of the customs union was being seriously inhibited by quantitative restrictions (Hazlewood in Onwuka & Sesay, 1985: 173).

The Treaty aimed to put cooperation between the partner states on a firm footing of mutual advantage. It set up a formal structure for administering Community institutions and provided measures to achieve an acceptable distribution of the benefits of integration between the member states. The main features were: the introduction of a 'transfer tax' to give limited protection for industries in the less-developed states against competition from those in the more developed states; the establishment of an East African Development Bank (EADB) which was to allocate its investments disproportionately in favor of Tanzania and Uganda; and, the relocation of the headquarters of some of the common services (including the Community secretariat), so that they were not concentrated in Kenya. Formally, the main structure—including the common external tariff—stood until the final collapse, but the common market became increasingly a dead letter and some of the common services effectively disintegrated. The EADB survived the final collapse but in a largely moribund condition (Hazlewood in Onwuka & Sesay, 1985: 174).

Many scholars have studied the demise of the EAC, providing significant insights of relevance to the relative lack of success of other African regional integration experiments. Among the major problems identified by these authors are: the uneven distribution of benefits; institutional difficulties; politico-ideological factors; and, external dependence (Hazlewood in Onwuka & Sesay, 1985: 172-189; Mazzeo in Potholm & Fredland, 1980: 81-122; Mazzeo, 1984: 150-170; Ravenhill, 1979: 227-246; Ravenhill in Potholm & Fredland, 1980: 37-61). These will be briefly examined in Part IV.

H. The Preferential Trade Area for Eastern and Southern Africa (PTA)

The creation of the PTA grew out of the UN-ECA's long-term strategy to create two large sub-regional groupings, one in eastern Africa, the other in southern Africa; it also came about as a result of the collapse of the EAC in 1977. The PTA project was actually initiated in October 1977 within the Lusaka-based MULPOC (Multinational Programming & Operational Center), one of five sub-regional centers established by the UN-ECA in Africa in March 1977. Negotiations on the PTA Treaty lasted from March 1978 to October 1981. The PTA Treaty was eventually signed at the Lusaka meeting of Heads of State and Government on 21 December 1981. From ten original signatories, the membership of PTA has now grown to 16 (Burundi, Comoros, Djibouti, Ethiopia, Kenya, Lesotho, Malawi, Mauritius, Mozambique, Rwanda, Somalia, Swaziland, Tanzania, Uganda, Zambia and Zimbabwe). The potential members of PTA—who, for various reasons, have not joined but enjoy observer status—are Angola, Botswana, Madagascar, and the Seychelles.

The PTA was initially conceived as a free-trade area as a first step towards the establishment of a customs union, a common market and, eventually, of an economic community. Thus, to the extent that it aims at rapidly moving beyond the stage of a mere free-trade area to become a genuine common market by 1992, the PTA is somewhat of a misnomer. The PTA combines a market integration approach (trade liberalization measures, i.e. reduction of tariff and non-tariff barriers and customs facilitation) with a production integration approach (common projects in the agricultural, industrial and transport and communications sectors).

Trade links among the PTA member countries are still weak. Thus, between 1980 and 1985, intra-PTA trade constituted only about 6.54 percent of these countries' total trade. Naturally, one of the main objectives of the PTA Treaty is to promote intra-PTA trade, notably through the gradual reduction and eventual elimination among member countries of customs duties and non-tariff barriers (NTBs) to trade on a common list of—initially 212—selected commodities which are of both export and import interest to the member states. The list is regularly amended to progressively include all the commodities traded within the subregion by 1992. Zero tariff levels and complete elimination of non-tariff barriers should be achieved by September 1992. According to the PTA's rule of product origin, goods are accepted as originating in a member country only if they have been produced in that country by enterprises which are subject to management by a majority of nationals and to at least 51 percent equity holding by nationals of that country.

The multilateral clearing system for eastern and southern Africa set up under the PTA Treaty aims to enhance cooperation and the settlement of payments for intra-regional trade in goods and services. Under this scheme, member countries are able to use national currencies in the settlement of payments during a transactions period of two calendar months, with only net balances at the end of this period requiring settlement in convertible currencies (through the Federal

Reserve Bank of New York). Intra-regional settlements are expressed and recorded in terms of the PTA unit of account (UAPTA), which is equal to the Special Drawing Right (SDR) of the International Monetary Fund (IMF)(i.e. US$1.14). The PTA Multilateral Clearing Facility (or Clearing House) started operating on 1 February 1984 in Harare (Zimbabwe). The Reserve Bank of Zimbabwe provisionally performs the functions of Executive Secretary of the Clearing House until 1 January 1992, when the Clearing House shall become fully autonomous.

In the sector of transport and communications, programmes for the rehabilitation and upgrading of sub-standard inter-state roads and railways systems, and for the construction of new links, were adopted in 1985. A 'Road Customs Transit Declaration Document', for a PTA harmonized customs control transit system to facilitate uninhibited cross-border transit by PTA vehicles, was introduced in all PTA countries in July 1986. In July 1987, a PTA 'Motor Vehicle Insurance Scheme', the 'Yellow Card', came into effect to eliminate the costly and cumbersome practice of taking out an insurance cover for every cross-border transit operation. Other subregional programmes and projects were initiated in the areas of air transport, inland-water and coastal maritime transportation systems, telecommunications, agriculture, and industry and energy. Finally, the PTA regularly conducts trade promotion activities such as buyer/seller meetings and PTA trade fairs.

Because of the non-compliance of most member states with the initially approved tariff reduction time-table and tariff rates publication requirement, the PTA Council decided to postpone the deadline for the complete elimination of tariffs to the year 2000 (instead of 1992, as initially scheduled). Thus, the member states should reduce their intra-PTA tariffs by 10 percent per year every year between October 1988 and October 1996; the remaining 50 percent should be eliminated in two steps: 20 percent in 1998, and 30 percent in 2000.

Three major points of contention soon surfaced between the economically more advanced member states—mainly Kenya and Zimbabwe—and the least-developed, geographically disadvantaged micro-states of the subregion—Comoros, Mauritius, Djibouti, Rwanda and Burundi—over the issue of the equitable distribution of the benefits and costs of integration: (1) the restrictive definition of the rules of origin in terms of the 51 percent minimum national equity holding rule; (2) the reduction and elimination of customs duties and 'other charges of equivalent effect' by Comoros and Djibouti; and, (3) the formula for contribution to the PTA budget.

Admittedly, the overwhelming industrial and trade dominance of Kenyan and Zimbabwean manufacturers partly explains the persistent dissatisfaction of some of the smaller member states. Indeed, a study just completed assessed the costs and benefits to PTA member states of implementing the Treaty provisions and programs. It recommended measures likely to enhance the equitable distribution of costs and benefits among the member states.

Monetary and financial cooperation within the PTA has, on the whole, been fairly successful. So far, all the member states (except Djibouti) have utilized the multilateral clearing facility for payment of contributions to the PTA institutions and some of their intra-PTA trade. A total of UAPTA 217.7 million have passed through the Clearing House since it began operating on 1 February 1984. Indeed, the volume of trade settled through the Clearing House has progressed slowly, but steadily, from 9 percent of total intra-PTA trade in 1984 to 10 percent in 1985, 15 percent in 1986 and 20 percent in 1987 (Nomvete, 1987: 8-10). Finally, it should be noted that contrary to a situation usually prevailing in most African regional organizations, basically the PTA remains financially sound.

I. The Southern African Development Coordination Conference (SADCC)

SADCC grew out of a political grouping, the Frontline States, whose objective was (and still is) to bring about independence under majority rule in Zimbabwe, Namibia and South Africa. SADCC came into being at the Lusaka summit meeting of April 1980 with a membership of nine states—Angola, Botswana, Lesotho, Malawi, Mozambique, Swaziland, Tanzania, Zambia and Zimbabwe. It explicitly sought to reduce the member states' economic dependence on South Africa through cooperation on specific projects in priority areas such as transport and communications, food security, and energy.

Taking into account the failings of EAC and ECOWAS, SADCC has avoided the market integration approach and has, instead, adopted an incremental, project-oriented, regional cooperation approach. SADCC's relative success as a regional cooperation organization is partly due to its focus on actions rather than on institution-building. Indeed, one way in which SADCC differs from other African integration schemes is in the manner in which responsibility for particular sectoral programs has been allocated to particular member states. Thus, transport and communications is the responsibility of Mozambique, food security that of Zimbabwe, industrial development that of Tanzania, and mining development that of Zambia. SADCC has avoided the establishment of a dominant regional bureaucracy. In that sense, it is a multinational, rather than supranational, organization.

SADCC has given the area of transport and communications the highest priority. Other areas of cooperation which are part of the Conference's regional programme of action include: food security; industrial development; energy conservation; manpower training; forestry, fisheries and wildlife; mining development; and soil conservation and land utilization. Over 80 percent of SADCC programmes and projects are financed through foreign aid. Annual meetings between SADCC and its international development cooperation partners have, therefore, become a specific feature of SADCC's mode of operation. Thus, at the Maputo Pledging Conference (November 1980), ninety-seven projects, for a total estimated cost of US$1,912 million (and a total amount pledged of US$650 million), were adopted as part of the transport and communications programme.

The situation facing the SADCC states suddenly deteriorated in the years following its creation. Thus, between 1981 and 1986, SADCC member states experienced economic recession, increased external financial dependence, severe drought, and intensified South African-backed attacks on the rural population, transport and other facilities. In spite of SADCC's programmes and activities, the subregion became more dependent on trade and transport links with South Africa. However, by 1988, the situation had substantially improved. The 1988 SADCC Conference brought a large increase in the amount of aid pledged. In 1988, the improved security situation led to the reopening and upgrading of the Zimbabwe-Maputo railway line. On 21 March 1990, Namibia became independent and has become SADCC's tenth member state.   However, the process of gradual political change leading to majority rule which is currently unfolding in South Africa severely undermines SADCC's counter-dependence strategy and ultimately threatens the very 'raison d'etre' (or existence) of the organization.

Critics have declared market integration a failure. In fact, few, if any, of the various African cooperation and integration schemes surveyed in this paper have achieved their stated goals and objectives. This section attempts to identify the nature and extent of the problems and difficulties experienced by these schemes with a view to drawing lessons of general validity in terms of the viability and prospects of regional cooperation and integration in Africa. The purpose of this evaluation is to determine the extent to which regionalism (or collective self-reliance) is an appropriate strategy to achieve autonomous, self-reliant and self-sustaining development in Africa.

Table 3-2

Africa's Intra-Regional Trade
(value in $ millions)   (% of total exports)

	1970 value ($mn)	%	1980 value ($mn)	%	1982 value ($mn)	%	1984 value ($mn)	%	1986 value ($mn)	%
UDEAC	33	3.4	200	4.1	150	3.6	100	3.5	84	3.0
CEAO	73	9.1	296	6.9	374	10.7	306	7.4	300	6.5
ECOWAS	61	2.1	1056	3.9	900	4.1	500	2.5	491	3.2
M R U	—	—	2	0.1	3	0.1	4	0.4	4	0.4
CEPGL	2	0.2	5	0.2	7	0.2	10	0.7	8	0.6

Source: UNCTAD, *Handbook of International Trade and Development Statistics, Supplement* 1986, table 1.13; *Handbook* 1988, table 1.13.

V. Problems and prospects of regional cooperation and integration in Africa

A. Lessons from Experience: Problems of Regional Cooperation and Integration

A number of scholars have studied African regional cooperation and integration experiments, gaining many insights of relevance to their relative lack of success. Among the major problems they identified are: (1) the uneven distribution of the benefits and costs of integration; (2) institutional deficiencies; (3) politico-ideological factors; and (4) external dependence. These will be examined in turn.

1. <u>The uneven distribution of the benefits and costs of integration</u>. Assuming that one accepts the premises on which market integration is based, and supposing that full economic union is achieved, the fact remains that member states will necessarily differ in size and capabilities. They will thus demonstrate dissimilar abilities to take advantage of specialization, economies of scale, augmentation of factor input, and opportunities to improve market structures. Economic integration, then, tends to yield unequal benefits. Consequently, deliberate policies designed to distribute more evenly, or acceptably, whatever net benefits might accrue to the partner states must be

devised. Typically, redistributive mechanisms take the form of financial or fiscal compensatory schemes.

The fairly elaborate compensatory mechanisms set up within CEAO (TCR, FCD and FOSIDEC) have resulted in a relatively satisfactory redistribution of benefits in favor of the least-developed CEAO member states. UDEAC's single tax scheme and solidarity fund have been less successful, and real or perceived unequal distribution of benefits has been a major bone of contention within the organization. Similarly, the functioning of the ECOWAS Fund, which started operating in 1980, has, from the beginning, been plagued with financial difficulties and institutional malfunctions which have seriously affected its efficacy. The ECCAS Treaty duly takes into account the problem of unequal distribution of the benefits and costs of integration by stressing the need for the rapid development of the less-developed, land-locked and otherwise disadvantaged members states. The Cooperation and Development Fund (provision of technical and financial assistance to promote development), and the Compensation Fund (for revenue losses arising from tariff reduction) are to primarily focus their activities on such members.

The compensatory mechanisms of the EAC Treaty (transfer tax and EADB) were inadequate to persuade the partner states that continued cooperation was worthwhile. Within the PTA, the smaller member states—Comoros, Djibouti, Mauritius, Rwanda and Burundi—have expressed their serious concern about the tendency for the two subregional economic 'giants', Kenya and Zimbabwe, to dominate the organization. Indeed, in spite of the numerous derogations to the Treaty provisions granted to them, Comoros and Djibouti, in particular, appear very reluctant members of the PTA. They frequently tend not to implement the organization's decisions and threaten to withdraw whenever they feel any particular community decision endangers their legitimate national interests. They seem unlikely to be convinced by the arguments of the study team on the 'Equitable Distribution of Costs and Benefits in the PTA' that actual government revenue losses resulting from the implementation of the PTA tariff reduction programme are negligible, and that appropriate developmental policies could correct any real or perceived unequal distribution of economic benefits within the organization.

The truth is that no compensatory mechanism can ensure an equitable (and acceptable) distribution of the benefits and costs of integration, if only because different member states' perceptions differ—as the cases of the EAC and of the PTA clearly demonstrate. The distribution may lead some members to think that they are 'giving'

too much, while others think they are 'receiving' too little.
Ultimately, the settlement of such an issue calls for a politico-
diplomatic, rather than strictly economic, approach and requires a
political decision—even if economists can help by presenting the facts.

2. Institutional Deficiencies. Institutional proliferation is one of
the African regional organizations' major deficiencies. As indicated
above (section III), there are more than 200 regional cooperation and
integration organizations in Africa; more than 160 are inter-
governmental and the rest non-governmental. A recent UN-ECA report
has identified no less than 32 inter-governmental organizations in West
Africa alone. To a large extent, the activities of these organizations
overlap and are not coordinated, resulting in duplication of functions
and multiple membership. Thus, 7 out of 16 of the West African
countries belong to at least 17 of the 32 West African regional
organizations; Niger alone belongs to no less than 25; Mauritania
belongs to 3 different economic communities: CEAO, CEDEAO and
UAM. Similarly, the CEAO, Mano River Union (MRU) and
Senegambia Confederation member states are also members of
ECOWAS; the UDEAC member states are also members of ECCAS; and,
in southern Africa, the SADCC member states belong to the PTA. Such
multiple membership inevitably leads to problems of incompatible and
potentially conflicting objectives, and raises the issue of divided
loyalties and primary allegiance; it also stretches to the limit the
African countries' already-scarce human, administrative and financial
resources.

Over-centralization and over-politicization of these organizations'
decision-making process constitutes another major institutional problem
of most African regional organizations. To the extent that this process
requires agreement at the highest political level (Heads of State and
Government), it is bound to create difficulties because of overriding
concern with the preservation of sovereignty and the defence of
national interests, to the detriment of supra-national and community
interests. The experience of European integration suggests that
sustained political will is necessary for acceptance of the constraints on
national sovereignty that are involved in the harmonization of
economic policies and the eventual transfer of political and economic
power and authority to supra-national institutions.

Table 3-3

African Regional Organizations: Typical Institutional Set-up

Organ	Members	Frequency of meetings	Functions
Authority	Heads of State and Government	once a year	Supreme policy-making body
Council of Ministers	Ministers responsible for regional cooperation	twice a year	Policy-coordinating body
Executive Secretariat	Executive Secretary; Experts and Administrators	permanent	Administrative body
Tribunal	ad-hoc judges	permanent	Judicial body
Development Bank/Fund	Manager; Experts and Administrators	permanent	Financing economic and social development

3. Politico-ideological factors. The variety of political ideologies and related development strategies found in Africa might account for the slow pace of cooperation and integration in the region. Thus, all the ideological tendencies have been represented in the UAM: Islamic fundamentalism (Libya, Mauritania); Socialism (Algeria); Liberal Monarchy (Morocco); and Liberal Democracy (Tunisia). In ECOWAS, political regimes have ranged from Socialist (Guinea, Guinea-Bissau, Benin, Burkina) to Capitalist (Cote d'Ivoire, Nigeria, Senegal) via Islamic Republic (Mauritania). The same ideological variety is to be found in other African regional organizations such as CEAO, MRU, UDEAC and ECCAS. Similarly, the Kenya-Tanzania ideological conflict is generally cited as one of the main reasons behind the disintegration of the EAC. Within the PTA, political regimes have ranged from orthodox Marxism-Leninism (Ethiopia, Mozambique, Zimbabwe) to unbridled Capitalism (Kenya, Malawi), with moderate Socialism (Uganda, Tanzania) somewhere in-between.

In north Africa, three out of five member states of UAM (Algeria, Libya and Mauritania) are military regimes. In west and central Africa, the proliferation of military coups d'etat (twenty-eight in twenty-three years: 1963-1986) has created a context of endemic political instability. In 1989, out of sixteen ECOWAS member states, twelve are ruled by army officers, and only four (Cape Verde, Cote d'Ivoire, Gambia and Senegal) by civilian leaders. The situation was very similar in UDEAC and ECCAS, where Cameroon and Gabon were the only remaining civilian regimes. This militarization of north, west and central Africa introduces additional instability in these subregions to the extent that military regimes are generally insecure (because of the permanent threat of possible counter-coups), and create a potentially dangerous civilian-military cleavage among the various states in the region.

4. <u>External Dependence</u>. The play of extra-regional power politics is another factor seriously affecting the cohesion of African regional groupings. In particular, France's continuing economic and political dominance over its former colonies is a permanent irritant and a major obstacle to the progress of economic and political integration in west and central Africa (Martin in Aldrich & Connell, 1989: 101-125). Such institutions as CEAO and UDEAC, engineered and supported by France, might have to be scrapped before any progress toward integration within ECOWAS and ECCAS can be realized. Similarly, all CEAO and UDEAC member states (and Comoros within PTA) continue to be economically and financially highly dependent on France because of their common membership in the Franc zone system. The continued existence of this system will, no doubt, prevent any further progress towards monetary integration—a necessary precondition of economic integration—within both ECOWAS and ECCAS.

Equally divisive, from the point of view of the internal cohesion of African regional groupings, is the dual membership of all CEAO, ECOWAS, ECCAS and PTA members. The December 1989 Lome IV Convention links sixty-eight African, Caribbean and Pacific states (ACPs) with the EEC through a ten-year contractual arrangement on trade and aid cooperation. This raises a potential conflict of interest, notably in the area of trade liberalization and trade preferences. This problem is further compounded by the fact that in general, intra-regional trade remains very low—around 5-6 percent of total trade—while trade between Africa and the EEC remains significant—around 30-40 percent of total trade. It could thus be argued that the African states' economic and political links with the EEC through the Lome Convention are incompatible with intra-regional cooperation and integration. This is because the Lome Convention tends to perpetuate and institutionalize neocolonial, North-South links to the detriment of the collective self-reliant South-South strategy of such organizations as ECOWAS, ECCAS and PTA.

Table 3-4

Phased Time-table of Trade Liberalization
in Selected African Regional Organizations

Organization	Entry into force of Treaty	Free Trade Area (1)	Customs Union (2)	Common Market (3)	Economic Community (4)
C E A O	January 1974	1980	1986	**	
M R U	October 1973	1981 (1977)	**		
ECOWAS	June 1975	1989	1992	*	**
U D E A C	January 1966	*	*	**	
E C C A S	October 1983	1992	1996	2000	
P T A	September 1983	2000 (1992)	*	*	**

(1) Complete elimination of tariff and non-tariff barriers;
(2) Common external tariff against third countries;
(3) Free movement of factors of production/commodities;
(4) Harmonization of national economic policies.

*   Intermediary stage of integration (date unspecified);
**   Ultimate goal of integration (date unspecified).

B. The Prospects for Regional Cooperation and Integration in Africa

1. <u>What type of regional cooperation and integration</u>. What type of regional cooperation and integration scheme is best suited to the present African conditions? Should it be market-oriented or production-

oriented? Should it be based on a comprehensive, continental approach or on a gradual, functional approach? Only policy-oriented research can help gather the information to answer these kinds of questions.

African market integration experiments have generally been unsuccessful. Critics argue that the model, taken from the experience of highly industrialized European countries who have a high level of trade among themselves, is not relevant to Africa, where trade among countries and the level of industrialization are low. These critics recommend abandoning market integration and adoption of a new approach that emphasizes broadening the regional production base. This would give priority to regional investment in heavy industries and transport and communication infrastructure. In the absence of market signals, the production approach—implying a state-led development of core industries such as steel, cement, and chemicals—could force the pace of regional integration. Further research could assess the validity of this argument, and, if it seems justified in the case of specific basic industries, the kinds of institutional changes that might contribute to its success.

Other authors are of the opinion that Africa is particularly ill-suited for regional integration: "In Africa, the low levels of development and the limited possibilities for profitable intra-regional exchange simply do not provide the basis for integration at the present time ....(T)he requisites for integration do not presently exist but must be created" (Ravenhill in Onwuka & Sesay, 1985: 210). Such neo-functionalist authors caution against excessive politicization of issues in African regional organizations, and advocate cooperation in non-controversial—social, economic, scientific and technical—areas. They call for concentration on specific programs and projects in the area of postal, transport, communication and telecommunication infrastructure, as well as in the service sector, namely training and research, control of foreign investment, and transfer, adaptation and development of technology (Mazzeo, 1984: 237). Such a 'realistic' and 'pragmatic' approach is designed to prevent African leaders from "chasing inappropriate and largely illusory goals", i.e. from pursuing the "myth of African unity" in search of "the promised land of some kind of pan-African political kingdom or common market" (Ravenhill, 1986: 217; Mazzeo, 1984: 239). Again, research could help identify the policy-measures and institutional changes which might ensure this approach initiated a dynamic towards regional integration.

2. A strategy for future regional cooperation and integration. The essence of the neo-functionalist approach is that an incremental, step-by-step approach based on common economic interests offers the best

prospects for integration. Such an incremental approach should not involve further proliferation of organizations, but bilateral or multilateral agreements between governments that perceive benefits from a mutual liberalization of product and factor markets. Phased programs addressing critical barriers to regional integration are essential. Each phase would include advances in harmonizing policy and maintaining and improving infrastructure. As an urgent first step, regional organizations need to be rationalized. They should be reformed and consolidated into lean and efficient institutions, with a clear mandate and capacity for making decisions. These institutions (UAM, ECOWAS, ECCAS and PTA) could then spearhead the creation of a physical, technical, and legal infrastructure that would support regional exchange in goods, services, labor and capital. Initiation of appropriate institutional measures to attain these goals require in-depth research as to the constraints and resources of existing institutional arrangements.

It is generally agreed that one function African governments must perform if economic integration is to progress is to create what might be called an *enabling environment*. As already indicated, the removal of tariff barriers is not sufficient to create an effective enabling environment in African regional schemes. Other man-made barriers to intra-regional trade must also be reduced and eventually eliminated. These include: quantitative restrictions on imports customs and other administrative regulations; transport, communications and telecommunications bottlenecks; and foreign exchange controls. Beyond actions on policy, infrastructure, and institutions lies a more fundamental need: to mobilize public opinion and popular support to promote the concept that cooperation within Africa is likely to enhance the progress of all African societies. Ultimately, regional integration should benefit the broad masses of the African people. Research should produce the necessary background information to create a more appropriate enabling environment.

While disagreement on the strategy and ultimate goal of African regional unity persists, African scholars and policy-makers generally agree that some minimal degree of regional cooperation and integration must be achieved. In their view, such a strategy of collective self-reliance should contribute to the promotion of the socioeconomic development and to the reduction of the dependency of the African countries on the West. The question is whether the existing African regional organizations are likely to contribute to the achievement of this objective. There is no doubt that the exclusively francophone African organizations (such as CEAO, UDEAC and the Franc zone system) are one of the means by which France maintains her political, economic, military and cultural dominance over her former African colonies. Such neocolonial organizations constitute major obstacles on the way to further regional integration and should be dismantled in order to pave the way for genuine regional and continental African unity.

If this is the case, do such organizations as UAM, ECOWAS, ECCAS and PTA foreshadow the wave of the future? The fact that these institutions have succeeded in transcending the traditional historical and linguistic barriers is already a positive step in the right direction. However, if these organizations are to constitute the building-blocks on which the projected African Common Market and African Economic Community envisaged in the LPA and FAL are to be erected, they will have to demonstrate more dynamism and show greater tangible achievements than has been the case so far. Research should enable policy-makers to determine the possibilities, as well as the obstacles, to making the necessary institutional changes.

Bibliography

African Development Bank (ADB). 1989. "Economic Integration and Development in Africa," pp. 49-125 in *African Development Report 1989*. Abidjan: African Development Bank/ADB.

Asante, S.K.B. 1985. "Development and Regional Integration Since 1980," pp. 79-99 in Adebayo Adedeji & Timothy M. Shaw, eds., *Economic Crisis in Africa: African Perspectives on Development Problems and Potentials*. Boulder, CO: Lynne Rienner Publishers.

_____. 1986. *The Political Economy of Regionalism in Africa: A Decade of ECOWAS*. New York: Praeger Publishers.

Bach, Daniel. 1983. "The Politics of West African Economic Co-operation: CEAO and ECOWAS." *The Journal of Modern African Studies*, vol. 21, no. 4 (December): 605-623.

Bela Balassa. 1962. *The Theory of Economic Integration*. New York: George Allen & Unwin.

CEA. 1983. *Propositions Visant a Renforcer l'Integration Economique en Afrique de l'Ouest*. Addis Ababa: Commission Economique pour l'Afrique/CEA.

Diouf, Makhtar. 1984. *Integration Economique: Perspectes Africaines.* Paris/Dakar: Editions Publisud/Nouvelles Editions Africaines.

GATT. 1987. *International Trade 1986-87.* Geneva: GATT.

Hazlewood, Arthur. 1975. *Economic Integration: The East African Experience.* London: Heinemann.

_____. 1985. "What Should be Done to Promote Economic Integration in Africa in the 1980s and Beyond," pp. 197-212 in P. Ndegwa, L.P. Mureithi & R.H. Green, eds., *Development Options for Africa in the 1980s and Beyond.* Nairobi: Oxford University Press.

Jalloh, Abdul Aziz. 1976. "Regional Integration in Africa: Lessons from the Past and Prospects for the Future." *Africa Development,* vol. I, no. 2 (September): 44-57.

Kiggundu, Suleiman I. 1983. *A Planned Approach to a Common Market in Developing Countries.* Nairobi: Coign Publications.

Martin, Guy. 1986. "The Franc Zone, Underdevelopment and Dependency in Francophone Africa." Third World Quarterly, vol. 8, no. 1 (January) 205-235.

_____. 1987. "Regional Integration in West Africa: The Role of ECOWAS," pp.171-182 in Emmanuel Hansen, ed, *Africa: Perspectes on Peace and Development.* London & Tokyo: Zed Books/UNU.

_____. 1987. *African Regional Integration Since Independence: Lessons from the West and Central African Experiences.* Lusaka: PTA [PTA/PUB/II/8], March

_____. 1989. "Une Nouvelle Experience d'Integration Regionale en   Afrique: la ZEP." *Africa Development,* vol. X, no. 1: 5-18.

_____. 1989. "The PTA: Achievements, Problems and Prospects." *Afrika Spectrum,* vol. 24, no. 2: 157-171.

_____. 1989. "France and Africa", in Robert Aldrich & John Connell, eds., *France in World Politics.* London: Routledge.

Mazzeo, Domenico, ed., 1984. *African Regional Organizations.*   Cambridge, UK: Cambridge University Press.

Ndongko, Wilfred A. (Ed). 1985. *Economic Cooperation and Integration in Africa.* Dakar: CODESRIA Book Series.

Nomvete, Bax D. 1987. A Brief to the Sixth Meeting of the PTA Authority on Problem-Areas that are Delaying the Implementation Activities of the PTA (PTA/AUTH/VI/3, November).

Organization of African Unity (OAU). 1985. *Africa's Priority Programme for Economic Recovery 1986-1990*.

_____. 1981. *Lagos Plan of Action for the Economic Development of Africa, 1980-2000*.

_____. 1980. *Final Act of Lagos*.

Organisation for Economic Co-operation and Development (OECD). 1989. *External Debt Statistics*. Paris.

Olatunde Ojo. 1985. "Regional Co-operation and Integration," pp. 142-183 in O.J.C.B. Ojo, D.K. Orwa & C.M.B. Utete, *African International Relations*. London: Longman.

Olofin, Sam. 1977. "ECOWAS and the Lome Convention: An Experiment in Complementary or Conflicting Customs Union Arrangements?" *Journal of Common Market Studies*, vol. 16, no. 1, (September): 53-72.

Onwuka, Ralph I. & Amadu Sesay, eds., 1985 *The Future of Regionalism in Africa*. London: Macmillan.

Potholm, C.P. and Fredland, R.A. Eds. 1980. *Integration and Disintegration in East Africa*. University Press of America.

Ravenhill, John. 1986. "Collective Self-Reliance or Collective Self-Delusion: Is the Lagos Plan a Viable Alternate?" in John Ravenhill, ed., *Africa in Economic Crisis*. London: Macmillan.

_____. 1979. "Regional Integration and Development in Africa: Lessons from the East African Community," *Journal of Commonwealth & Comparative Politics*, vol. 27, no. 3 (November).

Robson, Peter. 1983. *Integration, Development and Equity: Economic Integration in West Africa*. London: George Allen & Unwin.

Robson, Peter. 1985. "Regional Integration and the Crisis in Sub-Saharan Africa." T*he Journal of Modern African Studies*, vol. 23, no. 4 (December) 603-622.

Thisen, J.K., "Alternate Approaches to Economic Integration in Africa." *Africa Development*, vol. X, no. 1 (1989): 19-60.

United Nations Development Programme (UNDP) and the World Bank. 1989. *African Economic and Financial Data*. Washington, DC: World Bank.

United Nations (UN). 1986. *United Nations Programme of Action for Africa's Economic Recovery and Development*. New York: United Nations.

United Nations Conference on Trade and Development (UNCTAD). Handbook of International Trade and Development Statistics, various supplements.

Viner, Jacob. 1950. *The Customs Union Issue*. New York. Carnegie Endowment for International Peace.

World Bank. 1989. *Sub-Saharan Africa: From Crisis to Sustainable Growth. A Long-Term Perspective Study*. Washington, D.C.: The World Bank.

Chapter 4

Education and Development: Deconstructing a Myth to Construct Reality

By Joel Samoff, John Metzler and Tahir Salie

I. Editor's Note

For thirty years, educational and development experts, adopting multiple disciplinary foci and theoretical and ideological perspectives, have debated Africa's educational needs. They have formulated divergent assessments of and prescriptions for educational systems, institutions and programs. Overshadowing this diversity of opinion a central consensual orthodoxy holds that education, particularly formal schooling, is an essential, if not the determining, ingredient in the development process.

This orthodoxy rests on two central assertions: (1) In Africa as throughout the world, education (specifically 'basic' education) is an inalienable right of all human beings; and (2) a minimally educated citizenry (dependent on an accessible and efficient educational system) constitutes the *sine qua non* for economic and social development. These assertions have lent international and academic legitimacy to the two converging strands that buttressed an already-established commitment to educational expansion. On the one hand, nascent post-independence state regimes viewed formal education as essential to the attainment of skills required for economic productivity and expansion, improved state administrative capacity, and national unity. On the other hand, a sizable and articulate proportion of an increasingly politicized citizenry perceived formal education as vital for improving their own and their progeny's living standards.

As a consequence of this faith in the ameliorative power of education, many African countries recorded an unparalleled (relative to social welfare and other government commitments) expansion of expenditure on formal education. Yet, even before the severe economic down-turn of the past decade, it became obvious that formal education had neither paid the anticipated dividends in terms of economic development, system capacity and political stability; nor guaranteed employment or improved life chances for the individual formally educated citizen.   Moreover, after two and a half decades of quantitative growth, in the past five years a number of African countries experienced a decline both in the quality of education and in the percentage of school-age children attending primary and secondary schools.

The resulting crisis in education confronts policy-makers and educational researchers with two fundamental issues.   Firstly, it is essential to understand why the impressive quantitative expansion of education has not resulted in a correspondent development of productive forces (and employment), or in the institutionalization of democratic participation (in many countries), or in regimes that, while attempting greater national autonomy, respond more completely to their citizens' legitimate needs.   The articulation of this cardinal dilemma affected the second central issue, that of how African educational policy makers, planners and practitioners, on the one hand, and the international education consortia (academic consultants, researchers and aid agencies—bilateral and multilateral), on the other, conceptualized, diagnosed and pragmatically deal with the myriad of issues (many socially constructed) confronting Africa's educational policy makers and practitioners.

Joel Samoff, the initial coordinator of the Education task group, prepared the second section of this chapter.   Presented as the basis for discussion, it appeared to reflect a significant agreement among the US Africanists and African scholars present at the Education workshop at the ASA's 1990 Annual Meeting.   It suggests that, to date, the conceptual parameters confining the discourse relating to these issues have primarily been established and legitimized outside of Africa (mainly by academics and analysts employed by major bilateral and multilateral lenders), who constitute an influential 'financial-intellectual' complex.

To supplement this focus, one of the coordinators who subsequently assumed responsibility for the Education task group, John Metzler, and Tahir Salie, a South African educator, prepared the extended thematic bibliographical review on additional issues and debates concerning educational policy that bear on empowerment and sustainable development in Africa: the education/school-society relationship; education and economic/social development; educational equity and access and the education of women; international influences on education, including the world economy, donor agencies, and 'the financial-intellectual' complex; and searching for alternatives to fund education.

II. The Financial-Intellectual Complex

A. Introduction
With appropriate substance and ceremony, a distinguished group of educators met in Jomtien, Thailand, in March 1990, to declare their support for making education available to everyone on the planet. At this World conference on Education for All, sponsored by UNDP, UNESCO, UNICEF and the World Bank, some 1,500 participants from 155 governments, 20 inter-governmental bodies and 150 non-governmental organizations adopted by acclamation a World Declaration on Education for All and a Framework for Action. Its central tenet confirmed that all people should have access to basic education both as a basic right of citizenship and because development, however conceived, requires an educated populace. The language is unequivocal and dramatic[1]:

> "(E)ducation is a fundamental right for all people, women and men, of all ages throughout our world....an indispensable key to, though not a sufficient condition for, personal and social improvement....(A) sound basic education is fundamental to—self-reliant development.

> Every person—child, youth and adult—shall be able to benefit from educational opportunities designed to meet their basic learning needs.

> National, regional and local educational authorities have a unique obligation to provide basic education for all....

> Noble goals, with which few would disagree, though of course many countries do not have the means to achieve them rapidly."[2]

But why? Why should everyone be educated? And to achieve that goal, why assign the highest priority to basic (primary) education, rather than, say, adult education, or teacher education?   If basic education is a fundamental human right, then other rationales are unnecessary. If, however, universal basic education is an instrumental goal—a necessary if not sufficient foundation for some other important goal(s)—then these 'why' questions must be addressed.

There are many answers to these 'why' questions, but the answer that seems most important as we enter the 1990s, especially to those who disburse funds to support African education, is that research shows that investing in primary education yields the best return. That is, support for this focus on primary education rests on the claim that research has persuasively demonstrated that investing in primary education promises the greatest progress toward development (however defined).

This formulation—"research shows that..."—and its synonyms are ubiquitous. Among the large number of possible examples are (emphasis added):

> "Substantial <u>evidence from research supports</u> the proposition that within broad limits (between 25 and 50 pupils) changes in class size influence pupil achievement modestly or not at all" (World Bank, 1988 :40).
> "The <u>increasing body of evidence</u> on the payoff in various amounts and kinds of teacher training <u>indicates</u> that, for primary school teachers, preservice training that consists of more than general secondary education and a minimum exposure to pedagogical theory is not cost effective."
> There is <u>strong evidence that</u> increasing the provision of instructional materials, especially textbooks, is the most cost-effective way of raising the quality of primary education." (Ibid: 42).

The very ubiquity of the 'research shows...' claim reflects a striking contemporary phenomenon: the creation of a financial-intellectual complex, spawned by the development business.[3] This part of this chapter focuses on the childhood of that financial-intellectual complex (the contemporary situation), and especially the rapid growth of its influence. It particularly aims to highlight the ways in which its style and language structure the education and development discourse, nurture a fascination with flashy but ephemeral understandings, entrench misunderstandings and legitimize shaky propositions. Its aim is not to advance and substantiate causal claims, but rather to explore influences and interactions. Many propositions that a hypothesis-testing approach would require would necessarily prove counter-factual, for example: (referring to a country where the expansion of secondary education was sharply restrained to permit more rapid achievement of universal primary education) 'a higher priority assigned to secondary education is associated with lower unemployment rates.' Therefore, it seems fruitful to explore interconnections and reciprocal influences.[4]

B. The cachet of capital

Nearly everywhere in Africa, schooling expanded rapidly after the end of European rule. Although the mix of pressures for expansion differed among countries, three were generally of particular importance. First, expanded access to education was both a premise and promise of the nationalist movement. Once in power, the new leadership assumed an obligation to build more schools. Indeed, in part, their legitimacy and the legitimacy of the state depended on that construction process. Unlike clinics and hospitals, clean water supplies or even tarred roads, schools could appear quickly throughout the countryside. The new schools were the locally visible evidence that the leadership was benefitting the populace. Citizens' demands for schooling paralleled, and, in places, exceeded the leadership's sense of obligation. Combined, obligation and demand elevated education to a basic right of citizenship.

The intensity of popular demand reflected, not only the promise of the nationalist era, but also the widely shared understanding that schooling was the single most important route to individual and social benefits: secure employment, influence, prestige, affluence, status and authority. Social mobility and political recruitment are of course everywhere far more complex than this suggests. It was clear to everyone, however, that schooling mattered, and that, for improving one's own or the community standard of living, it mattered a great deal. That was, and is, especially true in those societies where the leadership sought to reduce the role of race, religion, region, ethnicity and perhaps gender as criteria for selection and promotion in employment and public service. That perception of the role of schooling in determining individual life chances was reinforced by the image of meritocracy.

The local artisans and guardians of this image comprised much of what writing on Africa characterizes as a 'modernizing middle class.' The new leadership was drawn from a stratum that was 'middle' in that it was intermediary between the Europeans who governed and the less educated mass of the population. It was deemed 'modernizing' in that pursuing its own interests—those of civil servants, managers, teachers, intellectuals—required overcoming the influence and authority of the residue of pre-European and European-constructed authority systems. Rejecting Fanon's warning about the "pitfalls of national consciousness," commentators expect this stratum of the population, like the European bourgeoisie that came to power by displacing the aristocracy and landed nobility, to energize and intensify the process of modernization precisely because it seemed in their interest to do so. Hence, a meritocracy becomes the self-justifying hallmark of modernization, its image becomes a sacred icon for those who claim to be its bearers.

Modernization was assumed to require meritocratic advancement, which thereby became a principal indicator of a society's modernity. In the developmentalism that washed over Africa, reliance on ascriptive criteria was associated with the backwardness that should be overcome.[5]

Schools were needed to develop the pool of educated and skilled personnel that progress required. That is, education was, and is, widely presumed to be a requisite for development:

> "Greater investment in education can, at this time in Africa's history, be expected to yield broad economic benefits. ...the stock of human capital in Africa will determine whether Africans can harness the universal explosion of scientific and technical knowledge for the region's benefit—or whether Africa will fall farther and farther behind the world's industrial nations" (Ibid: 6-7).

> "Increased investment in education can accelerate growth in several ways....Education is intrinsic to development in the widest sense; empowering people, especially the poor, with basic cognitive skills is the surest way to render them self-reliant citizens." (World Bank, 1989: 77).

1. <u>Dependence on external funding</u>. With a sorely limited legacy, the task was enormous. Schooling, pulled by popular demand and pushed by the need for highly educated and skilled personnel, became an inexhaustible sink for capital. Since there were other pressing claims for available funds, and especially as economic crises succeeded the initial developmental optimism, the recourse was to external funding.[6] For many, perhaps most, African countries, external provision of assistance has become the center of gravity for education and development initiatives. Over time, it has come to seem not only obvious, but unexceptional that new initiatives and reform programs require external support, and therefore responsiveness to the agenda and preferences of the funding agency(ies)[7].

Sometimes the relationship between those who seek and those who provide funds is aggressively manipulative. The funding agency may make the provision of support conditional on the adoption of specific policies, priorities, or programs. Support for vocational schools, for example, may be contingent on implementation of a strategy designed to increase female enrollment. Or to secure support for a preferred program, the leadership in an African country may mobilize support to bring pressure on the funding agency. Where, for example, the African leadership desires to acquire microcomputers, it may communicate directly with energetic individual and organizational advocates of instructional use of microcomputers in the prospective funding agency's home country.

At other times, the relationship is less directly influential. The funding agency may finance research intended to support its preferred programmatic orientation. Or the African educators may tailor their requests more or less explicitly to fit the funding agency's agenda. They may begin their planning by exploring the funding agency's current high priority goals and developing a request for assistance congruent with that priority. Occasionally the paths of influence are far more circuitous. A desire to win support for a high priority goal in one project may promote a willingness to accommodate a low priority goal in another.

Even more fundamental patterns of influence may be imbedded in other interactions between providers and recipients of funds. Overseas education and training may involve an intellectual socialization that inclines those who assume positions of authority on their return home to approach problems, specify the relevant factors and delimit solutions in terms of a particular understanding of development, or economics or education. That understanding then subsequently influences the initiatives and reforms proposed. There may be no request to support student-centered learning, not because the funding agency specifically opposes it, but rather because the training and socialization of African educators have never addressed it as a serious alternative.

This need not primarily reflect external ignorance of or insensitivity to African values, philosophies of education, or policy preferences (though distance from Africa and disdain for things African remain widespread) (King, 1986). Rather, what is most powerful and most insidious in this relationship is the internalization within Africa of world views, research approaches and procedures for creating and validating knowledge that effectively perpetuate Africa's dependence and poverty.

However direct or indirect the influence, the presumption that education reform requires external funding places the support relationship at the center of education planning. Whatever the initiative, it must accommodate the nature and content of that relationship.

African countries may, and do, seek support from several external agencies. Occasionally, it is possible to secure funding from one agency for a project that another has been unwilling to finance. By the end of the 1980s, however, a remarkable convergence in the orientations and priorities of diverse national and transnational funding agencies became apparent. A review of education sector studies commissioned by a wide range of national and transnational agencies during the last half of the 1980s showed a striking commonality of orientation, approach and priorities (Samoff, 1990). Increasingly, the World Bank has come to be the lead agency in setting the education and development agenda.

Several factors contributed to the World Bank's interest in and ability to assume this role. By the end of the 1960s, the World Bank's senior leadership increasingly charged both operations and support staff to focus on poverty and the poor to stimulate and enhance development (formally, of course, the World Bank has always been the International Bank for Reconstruction and Development). The World Bank's resources—both those it controls directly and those it can mobilize from other sources—far exceeds those available to other agencies for supporting projects and financing the research that has come to play a critical role in shaping the agenda. The World Bank's significantly expanded professional staff enables it to command expertise far more directly and extensively than can other agencies. That professional staff also extends the range of settings in which the World Bank can assert the initiative and not simply react to the circumstances. In addition to its command of expertise, the World Bank has become pivotal in communication among the education policy-makers of other agencies and from different countries. Its library of documentation and the ability to access it far surpass the comparable capabilities of other agencies and governments. It is not uncommon for one agency to learn about another agency's activities through World Bank intermediation. Nor is it uncommon for one country to learn of similar projects in another country through World Bank documentation, conferences or consultants. That the World Bank and the International Monetary Fund (IMF) most often pursue congruent or parallel agenda permits the World Bank to employ the leverage generated by IMF conditionalities. The conservative governments in the United States and England (and perhaps Japan) have shaped many of the World Bank's major development policies and have been inclined to follow its leadership on other policies. The severity of Africa's economic crises has increased the importance of external funding for nearly all sectors, and made imperative debt rescheduling and payment deferrals,[8] correspondingly reducing African countries' leverage in their negotiations with the World Bank.

2. The role of research. The organization, orientation and rhythm of the funding agencies both condition the sorts of projects they will support, and establish a particular role for research. In general, the disbursers of funds prefer certainties to tentative propositions; large projects with visible impact to more numerous but less visible small projects; and projects with clear short term outcomes to projects whose implementation may be uneven and slow, with consequential outcomes years in the future. Within those agencies, professional advancement is often a function of the rapidity with which projects deemed successful are developed and funded. Even though at the abstract level education reform is understood as a complex process that may take a long time to come to fruition, project managers with little concrete results to show after a few years are unlikely to be promoted quickly. For similar reasons, while project managers may recognize the advantages of small projects, although these require as much preparation and administration as a single large one, they generally incline toward apparent economies of scale. Those project managers who most successfully move money relatively quickly are unlikely to hold the same post when the consequences of the projects they funded become visible.

Quite understandably, project managers want to know what works. Especially in agencies like the World Bank,[9] where the dominant perspective is economic, or perhaps econometric, 'what works' must be specified in explicit and quantitative terms. The assertion that "investment in primary education yields a greater return than spending on higher education" provides a relatively clear guide to action. A conditional and situationally specific statement does not. The statement that "whether or not investment in primary education yields a higher return than spending on higher education depends on the organization and philosophy of the government, the interests of the particular coalition that is currently most influential in the ministry of education, the support of the party and teachers' union, and the world price of coffee" can be used to support a wide range of alternative, and perhaps incompatible, policies. Project managers simply cannot do their job if each decision depends on a detailed and timely analysis of the political economy of the affected district, region, or country.

In the scientism and super-rationality of the external funding process, research becomes the primary strategy for establishing clear guides to action and for legitimizing actions taken (in practice it may be difficult to distinguish one role from the other). In this context, the importance of the 'research shows...' claim becomes important. How are project managers to advance particular proposals as worth pursuing? How are they to defend their decisions to support one project and not another? Consistency with general agency policies and priorities is necessary but not sufficient. Accommodation to the policies and sensitivities of the recipient country constrains the range of potential projects and may require protracted negotiations, but only in exceptional circumstances do the recipient's preferences provide sufficient rationale for funding a proposed project.

The prevailing super-rational and utilitarian ethos requires an affirmation in the form of 'it (this investment) is (cost)-effective,' or 'it will work,' or 'this strategy works best.' While the assessment of a senior manager with extensive relevant experience may still occasionally provide sufficient warrant to proceed, most often the affirmation of effectiveness must rest on appropriate research findings.[10] The greater the role in the approval process played by individuals considered as 'hard' scientists (a self-description common among but not limited to economists), the greater the pressure for explicit and unambiguous research findings expressed in quantitative terms.

This demand for research combines with trends in contemporary social science to make appropriate research relatively expensive to undertake and complex to administer. That in turn leads to an increasingly prominent role for the agencies with the resources and professional staff most able to initiate and support an appropriate research program. In this way, the World Bank is not only a source of funds for education projects, and not only a prominent client for research. It becomes, as well, the principal agency commissioning, undertaking and managing research on education and development in Africa.

C. The conjunction of research and finance

The remainder of section II outlines the most visible and significant manifestations and consequences introduced by this arrangement. To highlight their importance, it addresses each as problematic, noting what an alternative approach might suggest.

1. <u>A delimited discourse</u>. The conjunction of project support and focused research within a single institution functions to structure the education and development discourse. Within the legitimate terminology are embedded particular conceptualizations, orientations, prejudices and policy preferences. That terminology takes as part of the environment—as 'given' and therefore not requiring explicit justification or even critical attention—important issues on which

policy discussion ought to focus.   That terminology also obscures important issues, thereby far too frequently misdirecting the search for understanding.

Several widely-used examples, drawn from a much larger set, illustrate the effect of this discourse-structuring terminology. For each, a brief critique suggests the possible implications of an alternative perspective.   The examples provided, however, serve only to illustrate that alternatives exist, not to make a strong case for any particular one.

• Wastage (referring to those who begin but do not complete an educational program): Since nearly all students who do not complete their schooling are pushed out (rather than drop out), the high attrition rate is a normal feature of the education system, not an unexpected, abnormal or even unavoidable waste. It reflects decisions that effectively determine the number of places available at each higher education level, and the intentional design of selection and promotion procedures. Examination results and perhaps other criteria may specify who, among the students, will proceed; but the threshold for promotion is a function of educational policy, not individual achievement.   Indeed, many students who pass (score high on examinations) may not proceed. In these circumstances, if attrition is considered problematic, it should be addressed as such. Concern with wastage directs attention to individual motivation and the quality of instruction. In contrast, concern with attrition requires attention to the basic assumptions and organization of the educational system, and to the types of students not permitted to proceed. Are females, or students from a particular region, religion or socioeconomic stratum more likely to be excluded?

• Cost recovery (referring to direct payments by students and their parents for their education): This concept obscures who pays for education in Africa, where, in most countries, taxes on traded commodities, especially exports, provide the largest source of government revenue. That is, the mass of the citizenry pays the cost of education through direct and indirect taxes on production, rather than incomes. Imposing school fees is not cost recovery, but rather increases the portion of educational costs paid by students and their families. It has nothing to do with charging for what was previously 'free'—since it never has been free—but rather determining which segments of the population will bear what portion of the costs.

• Informal sector (referring essentially to economic activities not adequately recorded in official records and statistics, including but not limited to petty commerce, street vendors, sidewalk artisans, tree-shaded auto repair and the like): This usage is, in part, a legacy of the construct, dual economy, and perhaps marks its return to legitimacy. Much of the early literature on Africa's independence era characterized African economies as dual, constituted by an inherently uneasy cohabitation of modernity and tradition. The modern sector produced for export, included European administrators, company representatives and educated Africans, and aspired to the values, patterns of interaction and life styles of contemporary Europe. The traditional sector produced for local consumption ('subsistence'), included the mass of Africans, and struggled to maintain the values, social networks and daily customs of a distant past. This presumes the duality of 'modernization,' the distance between 'we' and 'they,' and the incessant individual and collective turmoil fueled by the fundamental incompatibility between the old and the new. It fit quite well with the other baggage Europeans brought to Africa. It had a certain plausibility, confirmed by the readily apparent differences between urban and rural. As critics of this perspective demonstrated the extent and solidity of links between these sectors—especially the flows of labor, small-scale commodities and wages—the construct's popularity waned. Where dual economy focused on separation, incompatibility, and distance, the critics emphasized Africa's integration into a global economy and the incipient homogenization of cultures.

Within the context of the dual economy, the modern sector came to be defined as the economy: registered firms, wage employment, tax-paying citizens. In national statistics, the much more extensive but presumably anachronistic and disappearing parallel economy went largely unrecorded. In this regard, attention to the informal sector[11] brought an important corrective to the study of economics in Africa. The unregistered and unrecorded acquired a new legitimacy. Their durability and rationality were formally recognized.

That very recognition, however, restored duality to the center of economic analysis. This usage in part reflects a process of labelling that characterizes as qualitatively different, and often of lesser significance, those economic activities that economists and other social scientists did not study carefully and still find difficult to study systematically. Within education, it is now fashionable to preach the importance of 'training for the informal sector' to compensate for the modern sector's apparent inability to generate employment at the rate at which young people finish school.

In fact, as is increasingly widely acknowledged, the economy of the 'informal' sector is neither very informal nor invisible. Patterns of employment are reasonably clearly structured and supported by a rich institutional network involving hierarchical chains of authority, functional specialization, reliable sources of credit and even small scale bureaucracy. Nor are these activities either marginal to the national economy or invisible.[12] That economists and others have not been as successful in documenting these activities does not require employing terminology that reinvigorates the notion of duality and suggests their relative unimportance.   Nor does their invisibility to officialdom indicate that the entrepreneurship that unregistered producers and merchants manifest and the business skills they employ are in some fundamental way different from those of their registered counterparts.

• Relevant (usually used to refer to curriculum deemed appropriate for students likely to become rudimentary-technology farmers): In the incessant search for whom to blame for the current state of affairs, the 'irrelevant curriculum' is widely criticized. The basic premise is that school curricula nearly everywhere in Africa emphasizes the arts, humanities and social sciences at the expense of mathematics, science and technology. This, it is argued, has two undesirable consequences. First, far too many of Africa's secondary and tertiary level students concentrate in the humanities and social sciences, prolonging the continuing shortage of scientists and technicians. Second, since the study of English or French, history and the like is concerned with how people lived in societies very distant in space and time, students complete their schooling with disdain for their own society and few, if any, marketable skills. Unemployment, frustration and alienation result.

This presumes that focusing curriculum more on the immediate local setting and including instruction and practical experience in agriculture with a rudimentary technology, would reduce 'educated unemployment' and its accompanying social dislocation. It would even diminish migration to urban areas. Unemployment, however, is neither caused by schools nor is much under their influence. A more agriculturally-oriented curriculum, in the absence of a fundamental transformation of the organization of production and agricultural practices, will do little to reduce unemployment. At the same time, if African schools make it impossible for their students to study plate tectonics, high energy physics and microchip fabrication, how will Africa ever get beyond depending on externally-created knowledge, technology and most important, standards to assess and value that knowledge and technology. Similarly, if young Africans do not understand the global economy, how will they as adults recognize, let alone address, its manifestations within Africa?[13] Hence, neither history nor microchips are in and of themselves irrelevant in contemporary Africa. The serious curriculum problems have less to do with subject focus than assumptions about learning, the role of the teacher, and fostering critical judgement among students.

• <u>Cost-benefit analysis (referring to an orientation centered on reducing the expenditure required to reach a particular goal, like spending per student, per graduate or per school)</u>: While it is reasonable to search for ways to accomplish goals more cheaply, in Africa this approach seems inappropriate. African countries currently allocate far less of their national budget and their gross domestic product on education than do countries in much of the rest of the world.[14] The primary objective, therefore, should not be to spend less on education, but rather to accomplish more per unit of expenditure. That is, the appropriate focus is on maximizing benefits and the effectiveness of services. Although cost-benefit and benefit-effective analyses can be used for similar purposes, their difference in emphasis remains significant. Where the task is to reduce costs, the strategies primarily emphasize cutting expenditures; for example, by double shifts, larger classes and shorter teacher training programs. Where the task is to maximize benefits, the strategies will more likely seek to facilitate learning and enhance the quality of instruction; for example, by continuing teacher education, student-centered science experiments and peer-assisted studying.

• <u>Internal efficiency (essentially, unit cost per student) and external efficiency (essentially, percentage of students who pass, graduate and secure employment)</u>: Especially prominent in external funding agencies' documents, these constructs also focus policy attention in the wrong direction. Just as concern with reducing costs per student will likely prove far less fruitful than increasing the benefit per unit expended, so it seems particularly obfuscating to characterize as 'external inefficiency,' pass and graduation rates which largely reflect official decisions rather than student or school achievement. The willingness to permit student repetition, too, reflects a policy decision (whether for pedagogical or political reasons), not (in)efficiency. The use of common terminology—internal and external efficiency—casts what are fundamentally policy issues as administrative and management problems, presumably amenable to technical solutions.

• <u>The production and/or formation of students</u>:[15] Both the industrial and sculpting metaphors presume the educational process aims to shape and mold students, a presumption that surely requires critical attention. Indeed, many students of education suggest precisely that conception makes schools into barriers, rather than gateways, to learning.

Put somewhat differently, production and formation on the one hand, and learning on the other, reflect very different understandings and models of education. For the former, the primary vision is that someone with expertise, power and authority is to do something to students. For the latter, the students themselves are the principal actors.

2. <u>Fads in education and development</u>. The amalgamation of funding and research also nurtures an intense but ultimately ephemeral fixation on a particular understanding or strategy. These fads in education and development stem from the centralization of communication and the antipathy to the tentative, the uncertain and the conditional within the financial-intellectual complex. Periodic fads flourish in an environment that regards what works as more important than understanding why it works, that emphasizes relatively rapid tangible outcomes at the expense of attention to the quality and consequences of process, and that prefers technical-administrative to social-political explanations and solutions.

A new insight, perspective or approach that captures the attention of the major funding agencies is quickly communicated to their principal consultants and African collaborators, who in turn disseminate it more widely. For a moment, often a very brief one, it acquires extraordinary visibility and influence. It may even be enshrined as a guiding principle for particular projects. Complex problems, however, are rarely amenable to simple solutions, notwithstanding the preference for uncluttered and unencumbered understandings. New evidence is collected, new objections are lodged, new personnel assume responsibility, and disenchantment sets in. The successor to the current fad is already emerging. Acknowledging that their confidence in the previous approach was misplaced seems not to make the advocates of its successor any more reserved or cautious in their enthusiasm. We were wrong before, they say, but 'this time we are sure.'

Hence, there is a continuing search for a prime cause for whatever problem happens to be currently specified as most important. Periodically, it is announced that a prime cause (or its offspring, a prime solution) has been identified. For example, relevant research shows clearly, it is claimed, that the quality of instruction depends heavily on the availability of textbooks and very little on class size. The canons of social science research disappear in the push for clarity and certainty. As the marketing of the new understanding proceeds, few of its distributors are aware of the setting or limitations of the initial research on which it rests or of the content, orientation and disabilities of the interpretation of that research. Subsequent research, however, generally shows that the prime cause is at best partial, and perhaps neither primary nor a cause. The old prime cause is discarded in favor of a new prime cause.

As the fascination with a particular understanding peaks and wanes, it is not uncommon to find complete reversals in recommended policies. The assertion a decade ago that it was desirable to introduce some vocational curriculum in all schools has apparently been succeeded by the equally ardent assertion that vocationalization of that sort is far too expensive and yields far too few benefits for most countries to undertake.

3. <u>Official (but flawed) understandings</u>. A third consequence of the strong connections between providing funds and conducting research is to accord legitimacy and international sanction to approaches and understandings that are at best partial, and at worst simply wrong. Misunderstandings are entrenched. The official overview publications of the World Bank currently have such a commanding presence in the academic arena that few authors address the issues of African development without referring to them. Even authors who reject both the approach and the conclusion of those publications seem to feel obliged to refer to them. Thus, documents commissioned by the World Bank acquire the status of standard references.[16] Even the specification of Africa itself is heavily influenced by the World Bank's view of the world. Carefully noting that, in their usage, Africa = Sub-Saharan Africa, World Bank documents so define the terrain that in much of the development discourse it is *that* Africa that is discussed, and not Africa = member countries of the Organization of African Unity.

"Most of the discussion and all of the statistics about Africa in this study refer to just thirty-nine countries south of the Sahara, and <u>for which the terms Africa and Sub-Saharan Africa are used interchangeably</u>" (World Bank, 1988: viii (emphasis added).

One example of the entrenchment of (mis)understandings is manifested in the current resuscitation of modernization theory, which insists, as it did twenty-five years ago, that the causes of Africa's problems are to be found in Africa: its people, resources, capital, skills, psychological orientation, child-rearing practices and more. Just as poverty is to be explained by the characteristics and (in)abilities of the poor, so the explanation of problems of African education are to be found within and around African schools. The financial-intellectual complex institutionalizes this fundamental misunderstanding in the centers of financial, industrial, and academic authority, entrenching it against the challenge that the primary sources of contemporary problems are to be found in the process by which African countries have been incorporated into the global economy. The financial-intellectual complex's explanatory framework and research agenda largely exclude that analytic perspective, directing attention to things African.

A second example is visible in the discussions of 'educated unemployment.' The widespread adoption of this terminology is itself revealing. What in fact is the problem here? What distinguishes the unemployment of the more educated from that of the less well educated? Surely neither society at large nor the young who cannot find jobs would be better off if they were illiterate as well as unemployed.

That young people who finish school are frustrated in not finding jobs or the jobs they think they should have is primarily a function of job creation (understood broadly), not of schooling. That the apparently rising level of education among the unemployed is perceived as potentially threatening to the political system is primarily a problem for those in power. As suggested above, curriculum revision is unlikely to have much impact. Efforts to reduce unemployment among those who finish school, and to reduce their frustration and alienation, must focus on job creation (including providing tools, start-up capital), not on schooling. In the absence of more jobs—that is, economic growth— neither the subject content nor the political education in schools will do much to reduce their frustration or relieve the elite's concerns.

More generally, the financial-intellectual complex not only consumes and commissions research, but it also specifies the types of research that it will regard as legitimate and capable of generating valid results.   As already suggested, the behavioral sciences mainstream is preferred, especially studies that seek to test hypothesized relationships through the analysis of quantitative data. It is not uncommon for that preference to be employed in the evaluation of research proposals that address topics of particular interest to the development business, even though those proposals may envision little or no direct connection with that business.

It is striking that individual scholars may orient their work very differently in the academic and financial-intellectual complex spheres of operation[17]. In the former, the relevant audience is institutional and disciplinary academic peers and university chairs and deans, while in the latter, the officials of the employing agency constitute the primary relevant audience.   The latter are much more likely to have clear preferences about method, approach, and findings. Much more easily than most universities, research institutes and funding agencies too readily terminate their relationship with a particular scholar.   There is no equivalent within the financial-intellectual complex of the critical review and peer scrutiny of academia. That is especially problematic in the social sciences, since, unlike chemists and physicists intrigued by the claims about low temperature nuclear fusion, skeptical academics cannot attempt to replicate original results of development initiatives in their own laboratories.

4. Legitimizing weak propositions. A fourth consequence of the integration of project funding and development research is to legitimize poorly supported propositions. Project managers are often prepared to accept as valid, findings whose relatively weak foundations would lead most academic researchers to present them tentatively and conditionally. That weaker confidence standard may be satisfactory in an operational setting, where the pressure for prompt decisions exceeds the demand for very high levels of confidence. The conjunction of project management and research within the financial-industrial complex, however, functions to obscure the caveats that were (or should have been) attached to the original research.

This process of legitimizing weak propositions by granting them official sanction and ignoring their tentative character is especially clear in the use of quantitative data.[18] As indicated above, wherever possible, the need for certainty combines with the influence of economists and the premises of contemporary behavioral science to demand quantitative data. Data (or what the data are claimed to show) provide the most compelling support for supporting some policies and rejecting others. Careful scrutiny of the reported data, however, often reveal that the variation from one period to the next is smaller than the margin of error. For example, a one percentage point change in the portion of national expenditures allocated to education may be reported as evidence of a government's increased commitment to education. Yet in practice, the margin of error in both the reported total and education spending is generally much greater than one percent. In those circumstances, it is impossible to be sure that any change has in fact taken place. A careful researcher will say precisely that.[19] Project managers, however, may discount the data problems in order to have a clear finding that supports a particular decision. When that research is filtered through the project process and combined with other research in a general policy document—that is, when the project funding process subsumes the research—a finding of no clear relationship is transformed into a confidently presented and unqualified assertion about the direction of change. The tenuous becomes certain. Having been legitimized and disseminated, the assertion becomes a guide to, and not infrequently a constraint on, subsequent research.

D. The Emperor is naked!

The financial-intellectual complex erects an imposing edifice. The integration of funding and research is seamless. Analyses, explanations and remedies are all supported by an impressive foundation of research conducted by respected scholars and synthesized in systematic, carefully presented and widely disseminated overviews of the state of knowledge in particular domains. The reported findings occupy center stage in academic as well as operational settings.

When pressed, the academics and even, at times, the operational personnel acknowledge the limitations and inconsistencies in the research. When pressed further, they will acknowledge that the research foundation is far less solid than it appears. The defects are not minor. Yet few in either group are prepared to distinguish themselves by characterizing that foundation as hollow and the edifice it supports as a fundamentally weak structure, more like the storefront facades erected on a movie set than like reinforced concrete construction. To switch metaphors, nearly everyone involved sees that the emperor is at least partially disrobed, but no one in the royal court will say that the emperor is naked.

At the largest scale, notwithstanding the privileged place of research, one is left to wonder whether or not more research, more complex research, even better research have led to more successful projects, better policy or accelerated development. Hypothetical and counter-factual claims are of course always difficult to assess. Even so, what are the grounds for optimism? From its record thus far, and from the disabilities it entrenches, it does not seem very likely that the further evolution of the integration of funding and research—the consolidation of the financial-intellectual complex and the institutionalization of its orientation and values—will substantially improve education in Africa.

III. A Thematic Bibliographical Review

The predominant 'supply side' perspective that explains Africa's crisis in education in terms of its quality and effectiveness (a perspective termed by some 'educational determinism') has been challenged by an alternative perspective of school-society relationships. One such approach (some call it 'social-structural determinism') avers that, education—even when efficient—can only play a central reproductive and supportive role in society. Schools, even optimally operated, are not capable of driving social and economic development. Productivity, job creation and economic development/ expansion are primarily determinants of social, economic and political structures and relationships. Effective education can facilitate change, but only in concert with meaningful reform within the social structure in which it takes place. Quality education, therefore, is education which: (1) corresponds closely, in a symmetrical relationship, with the structures and processes of production ('mode of production'); (2) is sensitive to the ideological or political agenda of the educational policy apparatus—that is, the state; and (3) most importantly, is responsive to the aspirations of and inputs from students, parents and practitioners—that is, education that empowers.

Before researchers and/or policy-makers can adequately address the issues of access, quality and relevance from either perspective, they must reach beyond the limitations imposed by both analytic paradigms to investigate the nature and structure of the relationship between social structure—society at large—and educational systems/schools in Africa. This requires a careful analysis of the roles played in the production and reproduction of educational institutions and practice of not just state apparachik (policy makers) and education administrators (policy implementors), but also of teachers, parents and students, whose voices may be silenced in the formulation of policy, but have not been muffled in their expression of support of, or opposition to, the implementation of particular policy initiatives.

As a central thesis, the Education task group concluded that a clearer understanding of this relationship is essential both to adequately frame research to answer questions on the important educational issues of access, quality and relevance; and to undertake participatory research. In this context, the following review of relevant bibliography attempts to systematically and thematically report on the literature (and immanent theories and concepts) that inform the debate of education in Africa and its potential role in facilitating sustainable development. Given spatial limits, the commentary remains brief, and—far from claiming comprehensiveness—the bibliographic entries aim primarily to assist individuals interested in exploring these issues/themes in greater detail.

A. The education/school-society relationship in Africa

Little quality work exists—either in the form of micro-level (local), single-country or comparative multi-country case studies—that investigates the nature of the evolving education-societal relationship in its varied historical and contemporary contexts in Africa. This may be the consequence of the dominant analytic 'supply-side' perspective (see section II of this chapter, above). The inability of educational systems to 'deliver' the ascribed goods, has not, within this paradigm, led to a critique of its underlying assumptions. Rather its advocates emphasize furthering educational reforms to equip schools to perform their mandated tasks.[20]

Interestingly, while this dominant paradigm has been challenged as early as the mid-1960s (e.g. Foster's seminal study of education in Ghana, 1966), much of the subsequent analysis, even from a 'social-structural determinism' perspective, has accentuated the study of society without thoroughly investigating reproductive (dependent) roles the educational system has played in it.

Blakemore, K. and B. Cooksey.   1980. *A Sociology of Education for Africa.* London: George Allen and Unwin.

Bray, M., P. Clarke and D. Stephens. 1986. *Education and Society in Africa.* London: Edward Arnold.

Carnoy, M. and J. Samoff. Eds. 1990. *Education and Social Transformation in the Third World.* Princeton: Princeton University Press.

Chikombah, Cowden E.M. 1988. *Education Issues in Zimbabwe Since Independence*, Institute of International Education No. 82. Stockholm University: Institute of International Education.

Court, David. 1976. "The Education System as a Response to Inequality in Tanzania and Kenya," *The Journal of Modern African Studies*, 14, 4, 661-690.

Court, D. and D. Ghai. 1974. *Education, Society and Development: New Perspectives From Kenya.* Nairobi: Oxford University Press.

_____ and K. Kinyanjui. 1986. "African Education: Problems in a High-Growth Sector," in R. Berg and J. Seymour. Eds. *Strategies for African Development.* Berkeley: University of California Press.

Cowan, G., J. O'Connell and D.G. Scanlon. Eds. 1965. *Education and Nation Building in Africa.* New York: Praeger.

Draisma, T. 1987. *The Struggle Against Underdevelopment in Zambia Since Independence: What Role For Education?* Amsterdam: Free University Press.

Foster, P.J. 1985. *Education in Sub-Saharan Africa: Some Preliminary Issues,* World Bank Education and Training Department. Washington, D.C.: World Bank.

Foster, P.J. 1965. *Education and Social Change in Ghana*. London: Routledge.

Thompson, A.R. 1981. *Education and Development in Africa*. New York: St. Martin's Press.

UNESCO. 1987. *The Role of Village Schools in the Development of Rural Areas: Sierra Leone and Yugoslavia*. Paris: UNESCO.

_____. 1976. *Education in Africa: Evolution, Reforms, Prospects*. Conference of Ministers of Education of African Member States, Lagos, January 27-February 4, 1976. Paris.

World Bank. 1988. *Education in Sub-Saharan Africa: Policies for Adjustment, Revitalization, and Expansion*. Washington, D.C.: World Bank.

1. Education and economic/social development

The assumption that education plays an essential if not unequalled role as an independent variable in stimulating economic and social development has been examined by research that sought to investigate: (1) the relationship between education and economic growth/ development;   (2) the rates of returns (social and individual) on educational investments; (3) the contribution of education (differentiating by level) to productivity;   and (4) the relationship between schooling and modernization.

A. Education and economic growth

Studies by Schultz (1961) and Denison (1962, 1967) demonstrated a strong explanatory correlation between expansion of formal education in the United States and economic growth. Similar studies carried out in the late 1960s and early 1970s in at least three Africa countries—Ghana, Kenya and Nigeria—demonstrate a similar but weaker correlation (Psacharopoulous and Woodhall, 1985, Table 2-1). However, as Haddad et al (1990: 3-4) point out:

> "growth accounting does not provide a criterion for educational investment policy, since it can only show that <u>should economic growth</u>

occur simultaneously with a considerable investment in education, education will account for a significant percentage of that growth."

Absent continued economic growth (as in most African countries), this limited research (in terms of number of cases) offers little support to the argument that educational expansion will facilitate development in Africa.

Bellew, Rosemary. 1986. *African Education and Socioeconomic Indicators: An Annex to "Education Policies in Sub-Saharan Africa."* World Bank Discussion Paper No. EDT 39. World Bank: Washington, D.C.

Court, David. 1987. "Education and Socioeconomic Development in Africa: The Search for the Missing Link." in *Rural Africana*, No. 28-29.

Denison, E. 1967. *Why Growth Rates Differ: Post War Experience in Nine Western Countries.* Washington D.C.: The Brookings Institution.

Haddad, W.D., M. Carnoy, R. Rinaldi and O. Regel, 1990. *Education Gand Development.* World Bank Discussion Papers #95.

Hinchliffe, K. 1986. *The Monetary and Non-Monetary Returns to Education in Africa*, EDT Discussion Paper No. 46. Washington, D.C.: World Bank.

Psacharopoulos, G. and M. Woodhall, 1985. *Education for Development: An Analysis of Investment Choices*, Baltimore: Johns Hopkins University Press.

Schultz, T. 1961. "Investment in Human Capital," *American Economic Review* (51).

2. Rate of return

Analyses carried out over the past thirty years in Africa have indicated consistently high social and private rates of return to education. Research in twelve African countries suggests: (1) personal rates of return tend to be quite a bit higher than social rates of return; and (2) social (but not personal) rates of return are considerably higher for primary education than for either secondary or tertiary education. Related research indicates that the rate of return for specialized vocational education, to the individual (employability) or society (productivity) is not as high as for general education. These findings, along with other research, has bolstered major multilateral and bilateral donor agencies' lending and policy initiatives that: (1) stressed the priority of primary education; (2) de-emphasized vocational education; and (3) increased individual/family responsibility for financing education, particularly in post-primary schooling.

However, critics have identified a number of problems with:

"many of the empirical estimates of rates of return—particularly in the way costs of education are measured, the fact that the samples used for the estimates are usually drawn only from the urban labor force, and that rates of return are uncorrected for ability differences, social class differences, and unemployment differences among those with different amounts of education." (Haddad et al, 1990, p. 6)

Moreover, these analyses do not take into account those outside the 'formal' employment sector, that is, the large percentage of Africans involved in subsistence farming and the urban/rural 'informal sector.'

Bergmann, H. and U. Bude. 1982. "Theses on Basic Education and Village Development in Black Africa," *International Review of Education*, 28, 1, 97-102.

Berstecher, D. and R. Carr-Hill. 1990. *Primary Education and Economic Recession in the Developing World Since 1980*. Paris: UNESCO.

Bude, U. 1985. *Primary Schools, Local Community and Development in Africa*. Baden-Baden, Federal Republic of Germany: Nomos Verlagsgescllschaft.

Clark, S.H. 1983. *How Secondary School Graduates Perform in the Labor Market*. World Bank Staff Working Paper No. 615.

Foster, P.J. 1965. "The Vocational School Fallacy in Development Planning," in C.A. Anderson and M.J. Bowman. Eds. *Education and Economic Development*. Chicago: Aldine.

Kogoe, Akrima. 1985. *Trends and Issues in Vocational Technical Education in Francophone West Africa*.

Psacharopoulos, G. 1987. *Time Trends of the Returns to Education: Cross-National Evidence*, EDT Discussion Paper No. 94. Washington, D.C.: World Bank.

Psacharopoulos, G. 1986. *To Vocationalize or not to Vocationalize? That is the Curriculum Question*, World Bank Discussion Paper No. EDT 31, Education and Training Series. World Bank: Washington, D.C.

_____. 1985. "Returns to Education: A Further International Update and Implications," *Journal of Human Resources*, 20.

Psacharopoulos, G. and W. Loxley. 1985. *Diversified Secondary Education and Development: Evidence from Colombia and Tanzania*. Baltimore, MD: Johns Hopkins University Press.

World Bank. 1990. *Primary Education: A World Bank Policy Paper*. Washington, D.C.: World Bank.

3. Education and Economic Productivity:
According to some educational economists,

"the single best measure of education's or training's economic impact is the additional productivity of workers and farmers with more education and training over those with less. Productivity measures avoid the pitfalls associated with using earnings as proxy for economic contribution, particularly in labor markets that are highly non-competitive, marked by barriers to entry and other distortions." (Haddad et al, 1990, p. 4).

In spite of a severe lack of adequate data on productivity, particularly for rural small-scale and subsistence farmers, evidence reported from an eighteen country survey indicates that a farmer with four years of education had an average productivity of 8.7 percent higher than one with no education (Lockheed, Jamison and Lau, 1980). However, there remains a dearth in empirical studies on measuring the relationship between schooling and productivity in African countries. Moreover, findings based on data collected in the 1960s and 1970s may have limited predictive value for the 1990s.

Berry, A. 1980. "Education, Income, Productivity and Urban Poverty," in King, K. Ed. *Education and Income*. Washington, D.C.: World Bank.

Education and Productive Work in Africa: A Regional Survey. 1982. Dakar, Senegal: NEIDA.

Eisemon, T.O. and A. Nyamete. 1988. "School Literacy and Agricultural Modernization in Kenya." *Comparative Education Review*, 33.

Eisemon, T.O. and A. Nyamete. 1988. "Schooling and Agricultural Productivity in Western Kenya," *Journal of Eastern African Research and Development.* Number 18

Godfrey, M. 1977. "Education, Training and Productivity: A Kenyan Case Study," *Comparative Education Review,* 21.

Hanson, J.W. 1980. "Is the School the Enemy of the Farm? The African Experience." East Lansing: Michigan State University Africa Rural Economy Program.

Jamison, D. and L. Lau. 1982. *Farmer Education and Farm Efficiency* Baltimore: Johns Hopkins Press.

King, K. 1977. The African Artisan: Education and the Informal Sector in Kenya. London: Heinemann.

Knight, J.B. and R. Sabot. 1986. Overview of Educational Expansion, Productivity and Inequality: A Comparative Analysis of the East African Natural Experiment. EDT Discussion Paper No. 48, Washington, D.C.: World Bank.

Lockheed, M., D. Jamison and L.Lau. 1980. "Framer Education and Farmer Efficiency: A Survey," *Economic Development and Change* 29 (1) 1980.

_____. 1987. "Farmer Education and Farm Efficiency: A Reply," *Economic Development and Cultural Change.* 35, 3, 1987. 4. *Education and Modernity*

4. Education and modernity

Modernity theory contends that the pre-conditions for development (modernization) are not only structural and institutional, but reside primarily in individuals—their values, attitudes, dispositions and perceptions ('world views') which in turn influence the development of institutions, social organizations and societies of which they are contributing members. Modernity theory identifies personality traits which, it contends, are essential to modernization. Members of 'pre-modern' ('traditional,' pre-industrial) societies, the argument is made, lack the personality traits that facilitate development. These attitudinal and behavioral traits include among others: openness to new experiences, assertion of independence from traditional authority and 'superstitions'; a belief in the efficacy of modern science and a rejection of primordial fatalism, time orientation and a willingness to take risks.

Social psychologist Alex Inkles, the leading proponent of this perspective, asserts that in societies in transition from 'traditional' to 'modern,' formal education is the most effective instrument for the transmittal of the attitudinal and behavioral traits essential to modernity. He drew his 'evidence' for this assertion on an eight country comparative study, only one of which, Nigeria, was in Africa.

The ethnocentric philosophical and theoretical assumptions of this perspective have been thoroughly discredited. Studies in Ghana (Weis, 1978; 1979) and Nigeria (Amer and Youtz, 1971) indicate that schooling does not 'produce' modernity traits (as defined by Inkeles), but rather reinforces traits that are already present when students enter school.

Amer, M. and R. Youtz, 1971. "Formal Education and Individual Modernity in an African Society." *American Journal of Sociology.* 76 (4).

Inkeles, A. 1969. "Making Men Modern: On Causes and Consequences of Individual Change in Six Developing Countries," *American Journal of Sociology* 75 (2).

Inkeles, A. and D. Smith. 1974. *Becoming Modern* Cambridge MA: Harvard University Press.

Weis, L. 1978. "The Impact of Secondary Education on Attitudinal Modernization: A Ghanaian Case Study." Ph.D. Dissertation, University of Wisconsin-Madison.

_____. 1979 "Schooling, Attitudes and Modernization: The Case of Ghana," Occasional Papers Series, Comparative Education Center, State University of New York.

B. Educational equity, access, and the education of women

In Africa, as in most areas of the world, young women get less education than young men. Other important groups experience inequity in terms of access and ability to complete a primary or secondary educational cycle. These include handicapped and special need students;[21] rural children/students; children of working class or unemployed parents. Nevertheless, gender discrimination remains more pervasive. Moreover, the recent, but belated, recognition of the cardinal role played by women in production and guaranteeing subsistence, as well as in the nurturing and socialization of the young, has resulted in a consensus of opinion that greater efforts must be exerted to educate young females in Africa.

The persuasive moral-equity and economic arguments for educating young women is further supported by research evidence that the education of future mothers strongly correlates to a reduction in infant mortality and malnutrition, even when employment, income and other economic factors are controlled. In addition, research in Africa, as in other regions, indicates a positive relationship between mothers' education and reducing family fertility.

An additional issue often ignored by social scientists in their discussion and research of women and education relates to sex-role bias and socialization within the class-room. The little research in Africa which has been reported on this issue clearly demonstrates a bias in curricula offerings for female students and teacher attitudes towards and attention to female students in African classrooms; factors which often result in under-achievement and higher drop-out rates among female students.

Assie-Lumumba, N.T. 1983. *Social Inequality and Access to Schooling in the Third World: An African Case*, Monograph 83-4. Houston, Texas: Institute for Higher Education, Law and Governance.

Aubel, Judi. 1986. "'My God, She Has So Many Tasks': Listening to Peasant Women," *Convergence: An International Journal of Adult Education*, 19, (2) 18-28.

Benavot, Aaron. 1989. "Education, Gender, and Economic Development: A Cross-National Study," *Sociology of Education*. 62, 1, 14-32.

Biraimah, Karen L. 1987. *Educational Opportunities and Life Chances: Gender Differentiation Within a Nigerian Elementary School*, Women in International Development Working Paper No. 150. Michigan State University.

_____. 1987. "Class, Gender, and Life Chances: A Nigerian University Case Study," *Comparative Education Review*, 31, 3, 570-82.

_____. 1982. "Different Knowledge for Different Folks: Knowledge Distribution in A Togolese Secondary School." In *Comparative Education*. Edited by P. Altbach et al., New York: Praeger.

Bowman, J. and A. Anderson. 1982. "The Participation of Women in Education in the Third World." In Kelly, G. and C. Elliott Eds. *Women's Education in the Third World: Comparative Perspectives.* Albany: State University of New York Press.

Caldwell, J.C. and P. Caldwell. 1985. "Education and Literacy as Factors in Health." In S. Halstead et al, Eds., *Good Health at Low Cost.* New York: Rockefeller Foundation.

Cochrane, S. 1986. *The Effects of Education on Fertility and Mortality.* EDT Discussion Paper No. 26, Washington, D.C.: World Bank.

Cochrane, S. and S. Farid. 1986. *Fertility in Sub-Saharan Africa: Levels and Their Explanation.* PHN Technical Note No. 85-13. Washington, D.C.: World Bank.

Cochrane, S., D. O'Hara and J. Leslie. 1980. *The Effects of Education on Health.* Staff Working Paper No. 405. Washington, D.C.: World Bank.

Cooksey, B. 1982. "Education and Sexual Inequality in Cameroon." *Journal of Modern African Studies,* 20.

Dall, F. 1989. "A Problem of Gender Access and Primary Education: Mali Case Study." *Harvard Institute of International Development Research Review,* 2, 4, 7.

Davies, Lynn. 1987. "Research Dilemmas Concerning Gender and the Management of Education in Third World Countries." *Comparative Education,* 23, 1, 85-94.

Dorsey, Betty Jo. 1989. *Socialization, Gender, Academic Achievement and Aspirations of Secondary School Pupils in Zimbabwe,* Working Paper No. 3. University of Zimbabwe: Human Resources Research Center.

Duncan, Wendy A. 1988. *School Dropout in Botswana: Gender Differences at Secondary Level.* Institute of International Education No. 81. University of Stockholm: Institute of International Education.

_____. 1985. *Schooling for Girls in Botswana: Education or Domestication?* National Institute of Development Research and Documentation Working Paper No. 49. University of Botswana, Gaborone: NIR.

Dupont, Beatrice. 1981. *Unequal Education: A Study of Sex Differences in Secondary-School Curricula.* Paris: UNESCO.

Finn, J. et al. 1979. "Sex Differences in Educational Attainment: A Cross-National Perspective." *Harvard Educational Review*, 49, 4, 477-503.

Jabre, Bushra. 1988. *Women's Education in Africa: A Survey of Field Projects in Five Countries*. Digest 26. Paris: UNESCO - UNICEF Co-operative Programme.

Kelly, G. 1990. "Education and Equality: Comparative Perspectives on the Expansion of Education and Women in the Post-War Period." *International Journal of Educational Development*. 10 (2/3).

-----. 1987. "Setting State Policy on Women's Education in the Third World: Perspectives from Comparative Research." *Comparative Education*. 23, 1, 95-102.

King, Elizabeth M. *Educating Girls and Women: Investing in Development*. 1990. Washington, D.C.: World Bank.

Martin, C.J. 1984. "Education and Inequality: The Case of Maragoli, Kenya." *International Journal of Educational Development*, 4, 2, 129-36.

McSweeney, B. and M. Freedman. 1980. "Lack of Time as an Obstacle to Women's Education: The Case of Upper Volta." *Comparative Education Review*. 24, 2, 124-39.

Ngau, M. 1988. "Women"s Participation in Education and National Development: The Dilemma of Institutional Bias in Kenya." *URAHAMU* 16 (2)

Nkinyangi, J. 1982. "Access to Primary Education in Kenya: The Contradictions of Public Policy." *Comparative Education Review*. 26, 2, 199-217.

Smock, A.C. 1982. "Sex Differences in Educational Opportunities and Labor Force Participation in Six Countries." [including Egypt, Ghana and Kenya] in P. Altbach et al, eds. *Comparative Education* New York: Praeger.

Stromquist, N.P. 1986. *Empowering Women Through Knowledge: Policies and Practices in International Cooperation in Basic Education*. Palo Alto, CA: School of Education, Stanford University.

Sudarkasa, Niara. 1982. "Sex Roles, Education, and Development in Africa." *Anthropology and Education Quarterly*. 13, 3, 279-88.

Weis, L. 1980. "Women and Education in Ghana: Some problems of Assessing Change." *International Journal of Women's Studies* 3.

C. International influences on education: The world economy, donor agencies and 'the financial-intellectual complex'

Section II of this chapter deals with issue of the growing dependency, economically and 'intellectually,' on the bilateral and multilateral donor agencies, especially the World Bank. The depth of this dependency can be garnered from 1983 data which indicates that on average 17 percent of recurrent educational budgets and 31 percent of capital education budgets in Sub-Saharan African countries came from <u>bilateral aid</u>. That excludes grants and loans from the World bank and African Development Bank. This trend has deepened in late 1980s. The World Bank, for example, is scheduled to increase their support of education from US$625 million between 1985-1989 to US$1.5 billion during 1990-1994.

This financial dependency is coupled with a continued 'intellectual' reliance on knowledge—as manifested in textbooks, professional journal and manuscripts, graduate and specialized training—produced in and disseminated from industrialized countries of the North. As the decade of the 1990s opened, World Bank analysis and consequent lending policy accentuated primary education. The Bank's major educational sector review (World Bank, 1988) recommended a reduction in the growth of university education. These measures would reinforce and deepen academic dependency, by reducing African countries' ability to produce knowledge, to carry out meaningful research and develop scientific and technical competency essential to development (and to the lessening of economic and 'knowledge' dependency).

Bray, Mark. 1984. "International Influences on African Educational Development." *International Journal of Educational Development*. 4, 2, 129-36.

Eshiwani, George S. 1989. "The World Bank Document Revisited," *Comparative Review*. 33, 1, 116-25.

Fuller, B. 1989. "Eroding Economy and Declining School Quality: The Case of Malawi." *IDS Bulletin* 20 (1) January.

Hawes, H. and T. Coombe (eds.). 1986. *Education Priorities and Aid Responses in Sub-Saharan Africa*. London: Institute of Education, University of London.

Hinchliffe, K. 1989. "Economic Austerity, Structural Adjustment and Education: The Case of Nigeria." *IDS Bulletin* Special Issue, "Adjusting Education to Economic Crisis." 20 (1) January.

King, Kenneth. 1988. *Aid and Educational Research in Developing Countries: The Role of the Donor Agencies in the Analysis of Education.* Edinburgh: Center of African Studies, Edinburgh University.

Lockheed, Marlaine E. and Adriaan M. Verspoor. 1990. *Improving Primary Education in Developing Countries: A Review of Policy Options.* Washington, DC. The World Bank.

Maquire, Patricia. 1984. *An Alternative Analysis.* Amherst, MA: University of Massachusetts, Center for International Education.

Orivel, F. and F. Sergent. 1988. "Foreign Aid to Education in Sub-Saharan Africa: How Useful Is It?," *Prospects.* 18, 4, pp. 459-69.

Samoff, Joel. "The Durability of Modernization," *Revista Internacional de Estudios Africanos.* (Forthcoming).

Samoff, Joel. 1990. "Defining What Is and What Is Not an Issue: An Analysis of Assistance Agency Africa Education Sector Studies". Anaheim, CA: Annual conference of the Comparative and International Education Society.

Samoff, Joel. 1982. "Class, Class Conflict, and the State in Africa." *Political Science Quarterly* 97,1: pp. 105-127.

Sifuna, Daniel N. 1983. "Kenya: Twenty Years of Multilateral Aid." *Prospects.* 13, 4, pp. 481-92.

"Summary of World Bank Report," *Comparative Education Review.* 1989. 33, 1, 93-104.

United Nations Development Programme (UNDP), *Human Development Report 1990.* New York: Oxford University Press.

"The World Bank Report: Special Issue" *Zimbabwe Journal of Educational Research.* 1 (1) 1989 [includes interview of the World Bank Report with the Minister of Primary and Secondary Education and the Minister of Higher Education].

World Bank. 1989. *From Crisis to Sustainable Growth.* Washington, DC. The World Bank.

World Bank. 1988. *Education in Sub-Saharan Africa: Policies for Adjustment, Revitalization, and Expansion: A World Bank Policy Study.* Washington. DC. The World Bank.

World Bank. 1988. *Education in Sub-Saharan Africa: Policies for Adjustment, Revitalization and Expansion.* Washington, DC. The World Bank.

World Bank. 1986. *Financing Adjustment with Growth in Sub-Saharan Africa, 1986-1990.* Washington, DC. The World Bank.

World Bank. 1981. *Accelerated Development in Sub-Saharan Africa.* Washington, World Bank.

World Bank and United Nations Development Programme. *Africa's Adjustment and Growth in the 1980s.* Washington, DC. The World Bank.

World Bank, UNDP, UNESCO & UNICEF. 1990. *World Declaration on Education for All and Framework for Action to Meet Basic Learning Needs.* Jomtien, Thailand: Inter-Agency commission for the World Conference on Education for All.

D. The crisis in funding education: searching for alternatives

The near universal agreement that education, while not sufficient, is essential to development, has resulted in a continued commitment to education on the part of African governments, parents and students as well as from the international community. However, the economic crisis confronting Africa, coupled with externally imposed structural adjustment policies and the rapid increase in population of school age children (over 3 percent in most African countries), has led to a serious crisis in funding education. This financial crisis has resulted in a significant reduction in per capita funding and an increase in direct and indirect costs borne by African students and their families. Between 1970 and 1983, the average per capita expenditure on primary school pupils in sub-Saharan African countries declined from US$67 to US$48 in constant dollars; for secondary school pupils the per capita decline was from US$362 to US$223 (World Bank, 1988: Tables A-17, A-19).

These harsh data lend understanding to the recent figures which show that after nearly three decades of quantitative expansion in percentage of school age cohort attending school, since 1985 there has been a significant decline in the percentage of students attending primary school in a number of African countries. According to World Bank data, in 1983 the percentage of primary aged children in school in

Africa peaked at 75 percent; by 1986 this figure had declined to 68 percent (63 percent for females) (World Bank, 1990).

In response to this crisis, donor agencies, particularly the World Bank, have been actively encouraging 'cost-recovery' programs, particularly for secondary and higher education. In African countries, per capita government expenditure averages sixty times higher for university students than for primary school students. Critics of this position point out that 'cost recovery' programs exasperate rather than ameliorate the equity issue, since under such schemes students from lower income groups are effectively shut out of the university. Moreover, it is argued that "cost recovery" programs reduce the percentage of students attending universities. The long term consequence of this policy would be to reduce the size of the skilled labor force, reinforcing continued dependence on expatriate personnel and on outside analysis and solutions for Africa's problems.

Privatization of education has also been suggested as a potential solution to the financial crisis in African education. Evidence from African countries demonstrates that African parents and students are often willing to make great sacrifices to attend private schools in situations where public education is not an option. However there is also evidence that private schools provide inferior quality education for a fee, while students from higher-income families attend higher quality state or state-aided schools, thus facilitating social class reproduction (Samoff, 1987; Armitage and Sabot 1985).

Armitage, J. and R. Sabot. 1985. "Efficiency and Equity Implication of Subsidies of Secondary Education in Kenya." In D. Newberry and N. Stern, eds. *Modern Tax Theories for Developing Countries*. New York: Oxford University Press.

Eicher, J.C. 1984. *Educational Costing and Financing in Developing Countries*. World Bank Staff Working Paper No. 655. Washington, DC. The World Bank.

James, E. 1987. *The Political Economy of Private Education in Developing Countries*. World Bank, EDT Discussion Paper No. 71. Washington, DC. The World Bank.

Jimenez, E. 1987. *Pricing Policy in the Social Sectors: Cost Recovery For Education and Health in Developing Countries*. Baltimore: Johns Hopkins University Press.

Mingat, A. and G. Psacharopoulos. 1985. *Educational Costs and Financing in Africa: Some facts and Possible Lines of Action.* World Bank, EDT Discussion Paper No. 13. Washington, DC. The World Bank.

Psacharopoulos, G. 1987. "Public Versus Private Schools in Developing Countries: Evidence from Colombia and Tanzania." *International Journal of Economic Development.*

Samoff, J. 1987. "School Expansion in Tanzania: Private Initiatives and Public Policy." *Comparative Education Review* 31 (3)

Tan, J.P., et al. 1984. *User Charges for Education: The Ability and Willingness to Pay in Malawi.* World Bank Staff Working Paper No. 661. Washington, DC. The World Bank.

Wolff, L. 1984. *Controlling the Costs of Education in Eastern Africa : A Review of Data, Issues and Policies.* World Bank Staff Working Paper No. 702. Washington, DC. The World Bank.

Woodhall, M. 1983. *Student Loans as a Means of Financing Higher Education: Lessons from International Experience.* World Bank Staff Working Paper No. 599. Washington, DC. The World Bank.

World Bank. 1991. "Education, Nutrition and Health." *Africa Update.* The World Bank External Affairs Unit: Africa Region, 1990/1991: pp. 3. Washington, DC. The World Bank.

World Bank. 1986. *Financing Education in Developing Countries: An Exploration of Policy Options.* Washington, D.C. The World Bank.

E. Qualitative issues: Educational reform and the school effectiveness debate

In the three decades of post-colonial rule African educational ministries have attempted to 'Africanize' the curricula (particularly in history, social studies and literature) to be more appropriate for African children. Attempts have been made in some African countries to reform the overall curricula and radically restructure the educational system. But, many of these attempts (for example the 1978 educational reforms in Zambia) were never implemented, due to strong opposition by powerful interest groups (including teachers) as well as from students and parents.   A common interpretation of the ineffectiveness of the attempts at system reform argues that reformers mistakenly assumed that schools could be used as instruments to restructure society.   In reality, this argument contends, educational reforms, which are perceived to interfere with the functionality of education—i.e. to provide improved life chances (or maintain existing living standards) of its clients, who live and struggle for existence in the 'real world'—will be strongly opposed.

In the past decade the emphasis for reform in African schools has shifted its concentration to issues of classroom quality—improved teaching and learning—and administrative efficiencies. Given the accepted notion that as a natural consequence of a drastic reduction in resources coupled with increased student population, that the general quality of learning has declined for most African students, it would be facile to argue that concern for educational quality is misplaced.   As research has shown, increased quality in the academic preparation of teachers, the availability of learning resources such as textbooks (which are a luxury for the vast majority of African students), etc., pay positive educational dividends.   However, recent research, has also challenged some of the assumptions of the school efficiency paradigm. For example, research in Burundi clearly demonstrates that grade repetition is not always economically or educationally inefficient, as has been commonly held (Schwille, et al. 1991).

However, as section II of this chapter suggests, it is equally superficial to attempt to explain the crisis in African education—or more correctly the educational expression of economic and political crises—solely in terms of the discourse of educational quality and efficiency.   Solving Africa's educational problems, including the cardinal issues of access, retention and learning, can only be addressed with a thorough analysis of the relationship between educational systems and the societies in which they are located.   A society's economic, political and social policies are often concurrent with and inform educational policy and reform. At the same time, they address the wider social, political and economic structures and relationships, which along with the personal aspirations and perceptions of African parents, students and teachers, shape the crises and possibilities of success for African education.

Alkin, Marvin C. 1988. "National Quality Indicators: A World View." *Studies in Educational Evaluation*. 14, 1, pp. 11-24.

Barnes, Victor. 1982. *A Review of Literature on Efficiencies in Primary Education for Sub-Saharan Africa*. U.S. Agency for International Development. Washington, DC.

Berman, E.H. 1989. "A Comparative Analysis of Educational Reform." Paper presented at the annual meeting of the comparative and International Education Society, Boston, March 1989.

Carnoy, M. 1986. "Educational Reform and Planning in the Current Economic Crisis." *Prospects* 16 (2).

Chikombah, C. et al. Eds. 1988. *Education in the New Zimbabwe.* Proceedings of a conference held at Michigan State University in collaboration with the Faculty of Education, University of Zimbabwe, 1986. East Lansing, Michigan: International Networks in Education and Development.

Cohn, E. and R.A. Rossmiller. 1987. *Research in Effective Schools: Implications for Less-Developed Countries.* World Bank Discussion Paper No. EDT 52, Education and Training Series. Washington, D.C. The World Bank.

Court, D. and K. Kinyanjui. 1986. "African Education: Problems in a High-Growth Sector." In R.J. Berg and J.S. Whitaker. Eds. *Strategies for African Development.* Berkeley: University of California Press.

Craig, J. 1987. È EDT Discussion Paper No. 79. Washington, D.C. World Bank.

_____. 1987. *Comparative African Experiences in Implementing Educational Policies.* World Bank Discussion Paper No. 83, Africa Technical Department Series. Washington, D.C. The World Bank.

Fuller, B. 1987. "What School Factors Raise Achievement in the Third World?" *Review of Educational Research.* 57, 3.

Gardner, R. 1985. *"Improving Quality in Primary Education in Developing Countries - Who Makes it Happen?"* Report of a Workshop held in the Department of Education in Developing Countries. London: Department of International and Comparative Education, Institute of Education, University of London.

Ginsburg, G., et al. 1990. "National and World-System Explanations of Educational Reform." *Comparative Education Review* 34 (4).

Heyneman, S.P. and D. Jamison. 1980. "Student Learning in Uganda: Textbook Availability and Other Factors." *Comparative Education Review* 24 (2).

Heyneman, S.P. and W. Loxley. 1983. "The Effect of Primary-School Quality on Achievement Across Twenty-Nine High- and Low-Income Countries," *American Journal of Sociology,* 88, 6, 1162-94.

Lockheed, M.E. and A. Komenan. 1989. "Teaching Quality and Student Achievement in Africa: The Case of Nigeria and Swaziland." *Teaching and Teacher Education*. 5, 2, 93-113.

Lockheed, M. and B. Fuller. 1987. *How Textbooks Affect Achievement*. World Bank EDT Discussion Paper No. 53. Washington, DC. The World Bank.

Lockheed, M. and E. Hanushek. 1987. *Improving the Efficiency of Education in Developing Countries: Review of the Evidence*. World Bank EDT Discussion Paper No. 77. Washington, DC. The World Bank.

Mwamwenda, T. and B. Mwamwenda. 1987. "School Facilities and Student Academic Achievement." *Comparative Education*. 23, 2, pp. 225-36.

Mundangepfupfu, M. 1988. *School Quality and Efficiency in Malawi*. Report of the pilot of the primary school quality survey. Lilongwe: Ministry of Education and Culture.

Pscharopoulos, G. 1985. "Curriculum Diversification in Colombia and Tanzania: An Evaluation." *Comparative Education Review* 29 (2).

Quansah, K.B. 1985. "Current Testing in Africa: Selection or Measure of Real Performance?" *Prospects: Quarterly Review of Education*, 31, 281-88. Report on the Basic English Language Skills Project (BELS). Aug 1985.

Riddell, A.R. 1989. "An Alternative Approach to the Study of School Effectiveness in Third World Countries." *Comparative Education Review* 33 (4) 1989.

Schwille, J., T. Eisemon, R. Hwang, D. Kwon and R. Prouty. 1991. *Is Grade Repetition Always Wasteful? New Data and Unanswered Questions* [from Burundi]. BRIDGES Research Report # 7 January, 1991. Cambridge, Harvard University

Simmons, J. Ed. 1983. *Better Schools: International Lessons for Reform*. New York: Praeger.

Somerset, H.C.A. 1985. *The Quality of Elementary Education in Africa: Some Key Issues*. The World Bank Education and Training Department. Washington, DC. The World Bank.

_____. 1987. *Case Study of Educational Reform: The Kenya Experience, 1983*. World Bank EDT Discussion Paper No. 64. Washington, DC. The World Bank.

Verspoor, A. 1989. *Pathways to Change: Improving the Quality of Education in Developing Countries,* World Bank Discussion Paper No. 53. Washington, DC. The World Bank.

_____. 1986. *Textbooks as Instruments for the Improvement of the Quality of Education."* World Bank EDT Discussion Paper No. 50. Washington, DC. The World Bank.

_____. 1986. *Internal Efficiency and the African School.* World Bank EDT Discussion Paper No. 47. Washington, DC. The World Bank.

_____. 1985. *Implementing Educational Change: The World Bank Experience.* World Bank EDT Discussion Paper No. 44. Washington, DC. The World Bank.

Verspoor, A. and J.Leno. 1986. *Improving Teaching: A Key to Successful Educational Change.* World Bank EDT Discussion Paper. Washington, DC. The World Bank.

Windham, D. M. 1986. *Internal Efficiency and the African School.* World Bank EDT Discussion Paper No. 47. Washington, DC. The World Bank.

F. Curriculum and Pedagogy

Closely associated with the discussions of quality and relevance of education in Africa have been debates on the appropriateness (to the agenda of local/individual empowerment and socioeconomic development) of established curricula and institutionalized forms of the practice of teaching—pedagogy.

Numerous first time observers of an African primary (or secondary) classroom have been astounded by the dominance of the teacher-centered and directed 'chalk-and-talk' style of teaching in which the majority of classroom time is spent in 'call-and-response' rote drills and memorization in the primary classroom and dictation of notes in the secondary class-room. This pedagogy closely corresponds to what Paulo Freire has called the 'banking concept of education,' in which students are treated as empty bank vaults into which externally determined and legitimized knowledge is 'deposited' by the teacher. (Freire: 1970, 59-64) Freire, among other progressive scholars perceive the teacher-centered pedagogy, so prevalent in Africa, as an obstacle to the liberation and empowerment of children and, consequently, to the development of economically viable and politically democratic communities and nations. Other more main-stream scholars and observers share the concern that teacher-center pedagogy stifles African children's creativity, and their ability to become problem solvers and self-directed productive (economically and politically) citizens (Fuller and Heyneman, 1989).[22]

Jansen (1989, 1991) in his review of curriculum reform efforts in Africa, clearly articulates the debates of curriculum relevance, quality and the reasons why curricular reforms have seldom been institutionalized. Johnson identifies five major curriculum themes in post-colonial Africa: the vocational versus academic curriculum; indigenous (included Islamic) versus colonially inherited western forms of curriculum and pedagogy; internal versus external examinations ('standards' and international recognition); language policy; and curriculum control and decision making (who makes curriculum policy—educators or state officials?).

Jansen (1991) further identifies four commonly given reasons for the failure of curriculum reform—or for 'curriculum continuity,' even within African states committed to "scientific socialism': (1) technicist explanation which asserts system inefficiencies and incapacities to adequately administer curricular reform; (2) dependency theory which postulates that colonial, western-based curriculum continues to be dominant because the African states are powerless to challenge this hegemony (of knowledge and curriculum) which reproduces conditions of underdevelopment (including knowledge production); (3) cultural relevance perspective which argues that attempts at curriculum change fail because they do not take into account the socio-cultural contexts of African nations and communities; (4) Legitimation theory, which posits that the African state is forced to promote contradictory and unworkable curriculum reforms in order to compensate for eroding legitimacy—inability to meet social and economic aspirations of the people.

Jansen correctly contends that none of these perspectives adequately explains curriculum continuity in Africa and consequently he calls for serious research which addresses the reasons for curriculum continuity as a necessary antecedent to essential curriculum reform policies.

Adams, M.N. and M. Coulibaly. 1985. "African Traditional Pedagogy in Modern Perspective," *Prospects: Quarterly Review of Education* 15, (2) 275-280.

Ball, S. 1983. "Imperialism, Social Control and the Colonial Curriculum in Africa," *Journal of Curriculum Studies*, 15, 3, 237-263.

Bao, K. Salia 1987. *An Introduction to Curriculum Studies in Africa*. London: Macmillan.

Benavot, A. and D. Kamens. 1989. *The Curricular Content of Primary Education in Developing Countries*, Policy, Planning and Research Working Papers, Education and Employment, WPS No. 237. Washington, D.C.: Population and Human Resources.

Chapman, D. and Winham, D. 1985. "Academic Program 'Failures' and the Vocational School 'Fallacy': Policy Issues in Secondary Education in Somalia," *International Journal of Educational Development*, 5, 4, 269-81.

Freire, P. 1970. *Pedagogy of the Oppressed*. New York: Continuum Publishing Corporation.

———. 1978. *Pedagogy in Progress: Letters to Guinea-Bissau*. New York: Continuum Publishing Corporation.

Fuller, B. and C.W. Snyder 1991. "Vocal Teachers, Silent Pupils? Life in Botswana Classrooms." *Comparative Education Review* 35 (2) 274-294.

———. and S.Heyneman 1989. "Third World School Quality: Current Collapse, Future Potential." *Educational Researcher*. March.

Haket, L. and Hoppers, W. 1986. *Research Programme on Education and Production in Theory and Action (EPTA): Education with Production in East- and Southern Africa. A Bibliography*. Foundation for Education With Production (FEP), Gaborone.

Hamilton, E. and Asiedu, K. 1987. "Vocational-Technical Education in Tropical Africa," *Journal of Negro Education*, 56, 3, 338-355.

Hawes, H. 1985. "Curriculum History: Third World Countries," in Husen, T. and T.N. Postlethwaite (eds.), *The International Encyclopedia of Education, Research and Studies*, Vol. 2C. New York: Pergamon Press.

Hawes, H. 1979. *Curriculum and Reality in African Primary Schools*. London: Longman.

Heyneman, S. 1986. "The Nature of a "Practical Curriculum." *Education With Production* (Botswana) 4 (2).

Jansen, J. 1991. "The State and Curriculum in the Transition to Socialism: The Zimbabwean Experience." *Comparative Education Review* 35 (1) 76-91.

————. 1989. "Curriculum Reconstruction in Post-Colonial Africa: A Review of the Literature." *International Journal of Educational Development*. 9 (3) 219-231.

————. 1988. "Curriculum Change and Contextual Realities in South African Education: Cui Bono?" *Journal of Curriculum Studies*, 20, 6, 521-27.

Kaluba, H. 1986. "Education with Production in Zambia: Lessons from the Experiences of the First Decade," *Education with Production*, 5, 1, 29-39.

Kay, S. 1975. "Curriculum Innovations and Traditional Culture: A Case Study of Kenya," *Comparative Education*, 11, 183-191.

King, K. 1986. *Evaluating the Context of Diversified Secondary Education in Tanzania*, Vocationalizing Education Conference. London: University of London Institute of Education.

Lassa, Peter. 1983. "The Quality of Learning in Nigerian Primary Education: A Note on Curriculum and Community Needs - An Example from Mathematics," *International Review of Education*, 29, 245-46.

Lewin, K. 1985. "Quality in Question: A New Agenda for Curriculum Reform in Developing Countries," *Comparative Education*, 21, 2.

————. 1984. "Selection and Curriculum Reform," *Education Versus Qualifications?* London: Allen and Unwin.

Lillis, K.M. 1983. "Processes of Curriculum Innovation in Kenya," *Comparative Education*, 19, 89-107.

Lillis, K and D. Hogan. 1983. "Dilemmas of Diversification," *Comparative Education*, 19, 1, 89-107.

Maravanyika, O.E. 1986. "Towards a Curriculum Analysis Model for National Development," *Zambezi: The Education Supplement*, 5.

McDowell, D.W. 1980. "The Impact of the National Policy on Education on Indigenous Education in Nigeria," *International Review of Education*, 26, 1, 49-64.

Ogundare, S. 1988. "Curriculum Development: A Description of the Development of the National Curriculum for Primary Social Studies in Nigeria," *Educational Studies*, 14, 1, 43-50.

Prophet, R. and P. Rowell. 1988. "Botswana Curriculum-In-Action: Classroom Observation in Botswana Junior Secondary Schools (1987-1989)" Washington D.C.: USAID Project Report, 1990.

Psacharopoulos, G. and W. Loxley. 1985. *Diversifies Secondary Education and Development: Evidence from Colombia and Tanzania.* Baltimore and London: Johns Hopkins University Press.

Saunders, M and G. Vulliany. 1983. "The Implementation of Curricular Reforms: Tanzania and Papua New Guinea." *Comparative Education Review* 27 (3)

Saunders, M. 1982. "Productive Activity in the Curriculum: Changing the Literate Bias of Secondary Schools in Tanzania," *British Journal of Sociology of Education*, 3, 39-55.

Stuart, J.S. 1988. "Classroom Action Research: Rationale Methods and Practical Applications," *Boleswa Educational Research Journal, Vol. 6.* Botswana: University of Botswana.

Stuart, J., et al. 1986. *Case Studies in Development Studies Teaching in Lesotho Classrooms.* Maseru: National University of Lesotho, Center for African Studies.

_____. 1985. *Research Report No. 9: Classroom Action—Research Case-Studies in Development Studies Teaching in Lesotho Classrooms.* Lesotho: Institute of Southern African Studies, National University of Lesotho.

Synder, C.W. and P.T. Ramatsui. 1990. *Curriculum in the Classroom: The Context of Change in Botswana.* Gabarone: Macmillan-Botswana.

Wilson, D.N. 1987. "Two Decades of Planned Educational Experience in Developing Nations: An Examination of Successes, Failures and Change," *Canadian and International Education*, 16, 2.

Wright, C. 1988. "Internationalizing Educational Research Paradigms: A West African Perspective," *Compare*, 18, 1, 39-51.

Endnotes

1. World Declaration on Education for All, p. 2-3.

2. Although the World Bank was a principal sponsor of this World conference, its projections for Africa have been far less optimistic. Eg., see World Bank, *Education in Sub-Saharan Africa*, p. 19.

3. As a burgeoning business, providing development advice has emerged as the setting for considering both educational goals and projects, which warrants detailed critical analysis in its own right; but that reaches beyond the scope of this essay. It is important to note, however, that: 1) the community of development consultants-for-hire is constituted transnationally; 2) although many, perhaps most, consultants are formally employed by universities or research institutes, they derive significant, perhaps their most significant income from their advisory services; 3) in some, perhaps many Third World countries, the agencies that hire consultants have thereby become principal employers of a large segment of the highly educated personnel in particular disciplines, especially economics; and 4) development consultants' advice, though presented in very different ways to very different agencies and governments, functions to disseminate globally a particular world view and a particular understanding of development. For a critique of one branch of this business (it seems preferable to reserve "industry" for settings where what is produced is more tangible), see Maguire, "Women in Development."

4. It is impossible to discuss what is at issue here without entering the debate itself. To assert that understandings and explanations can be constituted from the exploration of interactions and reciprocal influences is to challenge the prevailing pattern of social sciences, which posits that explanations are constructed through systematic efforts to confirm or reject claims about causal relationships. On this, see Samoff, "Class, Class Conflict, and the State in Africa."

5. Though it is beyond the scope of this essay to develop this point fully, it is important to recognize here: 1) the deep psychological and social roots of the ideology of modernization; 2) the we/they (modern/primitive) duality embedded in that ideology; 3) its incorporation in the languages of both daily discourse and academic research; 4) its institutionalization in schools and schooling; and, for all of those reasons, 5) its pervasiveness and durability. Several of these ideas are elaborated in "The Durability of Modernization."

6. The issue here is not with the motivations of external agencies, national or international. Although there is no lack of carpetbaggers and opportunities, most individuals involved in providing support to African education are genuinely committed to improving the standard of living and quality of life in Africa. At the same time, investors in African education acquire a structural capability to influence both the content and the orientation, not only of schooling in the present, but also fundamental values, world views, and ways of knowing far into the future.

7. External sources of funds for African education are of several sorts and organized both nationally and transnationally. Although it clearly matters to the recipient country whether the funds come as loans or grants, for purposes of this discussion they are here grouped together in the terms funding and assistance.

8. See Chapter 2, above.

9. The World Bank is not, of course, a monolithic organization. Divergence of perspective and priorities among its personnel be much broader and sharper than the policy and programmatic differences between funding agency and recipient country. Nevertheless, official World Bank policies remain influential if not determining in every situation. Within the World Bank, understandings of development and development strategies, of the nature of obstacles to desired changes and tactics for addressing them and of the appropriate role of the World Bank, itself, are sufficiently widely shared to make it reasonable and necessary to treat its ideas, roles and practices in a relatively undifferentiated manner. That sharp critiques of World Bank policies have emerged from its own personnel, and that particular project managers pursue agendas that diverge in some respects from that of the World Bank as a whole, must not obscure the general orientation, trajectory and consequences of World Bank funding.

10. Only some research can play that role. The specification of the sorts of research that can credibly support (or reject) the affirmation of effectiveness is another dimension of the financial-intellectual complex, as discussed above.

11. Also known by other terms, including parallel, invisible, hidden, subterranean, underground, and second economy.

12. For further discussion of the informal sector's relation to the larger economy, see Chapter 2, above.

13. Recognizing this dilemma, some education policy makers favor parallel pathways through the school system, with a few children exposed to these subjects, and the majority oriented toward what they consider more practical

topics. Peasants and workers, however, see this arrangement as both creating and reproducing an elite and denying to their children any chance of proceeding beyond basic education. From their perspective, <u>relevant curriculum</u> and <u>ruralized curriculum</u> are strategies of the powerful to remain powerful. In much of the rest of the world, certainly in the most affluent countries, the tendency has been to delay definitive decisions on career paths.

14. For 1985, if spending on education in industrial countries = 100, in Sub-Saharan Africa, it was 21 (UNDP, *Human Development Report*, 1990, Table 7, pp. 140-141). In 1986, Sub-Saharan African countries spent an average of 3.6% of their Gross National Product on education, compared to 5.2%, or nearly half again as much, in industrial countries (Table 14, pp. 154-155).

15. English speakers' use of "production" and French speakers' preference for "formation" may offer some insight into the history, philosophy, and contemporary context of education in the Anglophone and Francophone worlds—a topic requiring another essay.

16. That the Bank commissions and publishes studies of African development and that these become widely cited is not, in itself, problematic. It is important, however, to recognize the power, influence and academic and development consequences of this historically unique combination of funding of development projects and research. It is appropriate, indeed imperative, to address the World Bank as an institution whose basic policies are largely determined by the interests of a few affluent countries, whose lending program is justified by the extensive research it commissions, and whose own analyses and development agenda have come to constrain and shape the entire development discourse.

17. A review of education sector studies found that academic authors and education funding agency consultants—often the same people working in two settings—rarely referred to the work of the other. The primary source materials generated by the development business are frequently unavailable and even unknown in academic settings. (See Joel Samoff, "Defining What Is and What Is Not an Issue.")

18. That most funding agency documents do not indicate clearly the sources that support their claims about research findings compounds the problem: Even careful and critical readers find it difficult or impossible to locate and assess the reliability and validity of relevant research.

19. Both the problems with reported data and their causes are well known. Even authors sensitive to these problems, however, frequently note them at the beginning of their reports, and then dismiss their own caveats as they proceed

on the ground that, whatever their limitation, "these are the best data available."

20. This overly generalized rendering provides only an "ideal type" of the "supply-side" perspective (not a definitive statement) which has informed the thinking, particularly by international donors and consultants, on education's role in development.

21. Little information exists on education in African countries for handicapped and special needs children, but what is available suggests little special education meets these needs.   The significance of this over-sight is compounded by that fact that, as Chapter 5 on Health in this volume shows, endemic poverty, malnutrition, lack of adequate pre- and post-natal care, etc.—and warfare (e.g Angola and Mozambique) "create" large numbers of handicapped and special needs children/adults.

22. Caution should be exercised when analyzing this seemingly ubiquitous pedagogic phenomenon in the African classroom.   The teacher-centered teaching practice is not necessarily reflective of a lack of educational resources or a function of colonial control, rather common classroom practice and protocol are seemingly deeply rooted in traditional African cultures.   Many expatriate teachers, consultants and researchers (the author included) have been informed in a forceful and unambiguous manner that questioned practices are part of African culture and essential to discipline, cultural authenticity and societal homeostasis.   Clearly, this is an issue which desperately needs rigorous and culturally sensitive classroom research before reforms and new policy initiatives are undertaken.

Chapter 5

Health of the Future/the Future of Health

By Ben Wisner

I. Introduction

African leaders attending the World Summit for Children at the United Nations in September 1990 reminded us of the facts of life in Africa.[1] President Chissano of Mozambique cited his country's infant mortality rate of 159 per thousand live births, one of the highest in the world. Uganda's President Museveni noted that, of the 30 countries with highest death rates for children under five years of age, 21 are African. These children die of diseases preventable by immunization, basic sanitation and simple community-based primary care—dehydration due to diarrhoea, measles, whooping cough, tetanus, and pneumonia. Malaria kills many more and has increased in the 1980s. Blindness, war-related and post-polio disability are widespread. Women suffer increasingly high rates of death in childbirth. Meningitis stalks Africa's dry, dusty zones, while guinea worm cripples tens of thousands in its moister areas. Chronic undernutrition and lack of long term food security makes all of this worse.

These facts are well known by now. An Africa torn by wars, ravaged by drought, haunted by the fear of AIDS has become the conventional image. Nor would one dispute such "facts." Yet there is much more to the reality of health in Africa that is not revealed in such a straightforward recitation.

The 1980s has been a 'lost decade' for Africa economically (UNECA, 1990: 3). Senegal's president Diouf called for bilateral cancellation of all foreign debt, noting that "...a solution can't be found to these [childrens'] problems without a solution to the debt crisis." No discussion of health in Africa can neglect the variety of ways debt has been translated into higher food prices, poorer medical services, and worsening health.[2] In Ghana, for instance, infant mortality had fallen from 132 per thousand live births in 1960 to 107 per thousand live births in 1970 and to 86 per thousand live births in the late 1970s only to climb back up to the 107-120 range in the 1980s. Access to safe domestic water decreased in both urban and rural Ghana. As a percentage of requirement, average caloric availability declined from 97 percent in 1970 to 88 percent in the late 1970s to an alarming 68 percent in the 1980s (Green, 1989: 38). During this critical period (1979-1983) thousands of industrial workers lost their jobs, the cocoa income declined, the price of food rose, and Ghana's budget was cut by nearly 16 percent (Pinstrup-Anderson et al., 1987: 76).

War must also be addressed as a health issue. The conflict in Mozambique has cost more than 500,000 child lives since 1980 (UNICEF, 1989b; Cliff & Noormahomed, 1988), and orphaned 250,000 children. (Smith, 1990: 42). Possibly as many as 70 percent of the African population has suffered severe and prolonged conflicts since the mid-1950s.[3]

The first decade of independence in many African countries saw considerable improvement in health (World Bank, 1981). War, debt, consolidation of non-democratic class interests and forms of state control over economic life played significant roles in reversing these early gains. Rural industrialization, oppression of women, and urbanization have also contributed. The effect of intermittent droughts during two decades has been exacerbated through over-exploitation of land resources by desperate people responding to economic stagnation. Since basic needs are indivisible, it is not surprising that health cannot improve in an environment where shelter, water, food, clothing, education, or even personal security is in doubt.[4]

Since such 'facts' are not self-explanatory or transparent, the choice of a perspective on Africa's health crisis is an important matter. This chapter seeks to adopt the perspective of ordinary Africans themselves rather than 'top down' views that impose causal analysis and problem priorities on the people. African social science has made impressive contributions in this direction by conveying local definitions of health and revealing the decision-making processes of therapy managing groups.[5] African women and children constitute a 'social periphery', (Mburu, 1986) but some researchers have tried to enlist their opinions (Kisseka, 1981; Loewensen, 1986; Raikes, 1989; Ennew & Milne, 1989). Farmers and industrial workers in Africa have more frequently been asked to help to define problems (Richards, 1985; Wisner, 1988: 254-277; Packard, 1989a: 490-1).

II. Conventional approaches to health in Africa

The World Bank, UNICEF, and WHO agree that the major African health challenges for the next century are: chronic malnutrition; diarrhoeal disease and associated domestic water supply and sanitation; malaria and other vector born and communicable diseases; HIV infection; and health care financing.

A. Hunger and food security

Green (1989: 36-37) lists seven groups of people who are highly vulnerable to food insecurity:

(1) victims of sustained drought and/ or ecological degradation whose previous sources of income (herds, seed stock, land improvements) have been wiped out;

(2) land-hungry migrants—often poor, women-headed households—who move into marginal land (in terms of soil, weather, ecological fragility);

(3) isolated or peripheral rural people at the ends of marketing, administrative and supply lines;

(4) small producers who are self-provisioning, but also sell food for cash income;

(5) victims of war;

(6) members of the urban informal sector who cannot match high urban prices with low income and live in crowded, poorly serviced slum or exurban areas;

(7) urban wage earners whose purchasing power has fallen dramatically in the last decade.

The World Bank (1989: 72) notes that one quarter of the population of sub-Saharan Africa eats on average, across good and bad crop years, less than eighty percent of their energy requirements. In addition to emphasizing *the core area of food insecurity* in the drought-prone Sahel and southern Africa, the World Bank goes on to point out other conditions that undermine food security. For instance Kenya is a case "in which income distribution is particularly skewed and a part of the population is very poor, even though the agricultural base and national income levels are strong" (Ibid: 73). The Bank also mentions war—in Angola, Ethiopia, Mozambique—as a cause of food insecurity, as well as countries with poor infrastructure—Uganda, Zaire—and those with large urban populations—Zambia, Sudan.

1. Prevalence of Malnutrition. In the period 1973-1983 Africa is thought to have had an annual average of 22 million cases of malnutrition in children aged 0-4 (Chandler, 1985: 11). This would amount to about one quarter of all cases worldwide and more than twice the number for the whole of Latin America. UNICEF (1985a) estimates that between 1975 and 1981, 60 percent of Ethiopian children suffered mild to moderate malnutrition. For Sudan, the figure was 50 percent; for Tanzania, 43 percent; for Kenya, 30 percent. Severe malnutrition affected 40 percent of under fives in Burkina Faso, 28 percent of those in Cote d'Ivoire and 16 percent in Nigeria (Timberlake, 1988: 37).

Rates don't do justice to the absolute magnitude of the challenge of malnutrition. The greatest numbers are found in few countries (Haaga et al., 1984). Thirteen African countries have a total of more than 12 million underweight children—three-quarters of all the underweight children on the continent. These countries include: Nigeria, Ethiopia, Sudan, Zaire, Kenya, Tanzania and Uganda.

2. Three Examples. Examination of malnutrition in three countries illustrates its relations with skewed patterns of development.

Nigeria. By far the greatest number of malnourished children (3.5 million) are found in Nigeria, Africa's most populous country, where the distortions caused by oil wealth have severely undermined agriculture and aggravated socioeconomic stratification (Watts, 1986; Nafziger, 1988: 123-4). Access to health services is highly inequitable because of a pronounced urban/rural disparity and the predominance of a private health sector which many cannot afford (Stock, 1985a).

One study published in 1981 found that the average rural household in northern Nigeria consumed 11 percent calories more than the required level suggested by the FAO. Households in the first decile, however, suffered a caloric deficit of 25 percent. The poorest 30-40 percent of households were seriously impoverished and needed to borrow grain from high income households during the pre-harvest 'hungry season' (Nafziger, 1988: 123-4).

Kenya. Studies in Kenya reveal 28 percent of children aged 1-4 to be below their expected height-for-age, *stunting*, and a similar proportion below the expected weight-for-age, *wasting* (UNICEF, 1988). Kenya has a very highly skewed income distribution and great pressure on available land. Eighty percent of the country is classified arid and semi-arid. The remaining 20 percent constitutes the well watered and highly fertile volcanic soil once monopolized by the colonial white settlers. Since independence a small elite of African farmers, linked to the government and the dominant political party, have largely replaced the whites. The landless and land poor have migrated to the cities and into the margin of the arid and semi-arid zone where they face the risk of drought (Wisner, 1988: 167-198).

Contrasts by class and geographical region are evident in nutritional data. In 1982, rates of stunting of children in the Kenya provinces of Coast and Nyanza were 36.2 percent and 29.9 percent, more than one third higher than in the provinces of Central and Rift Valley (respectively 20.4 percent and 19.8 percent) (Mwangi & Mwabu, 1986: 776).

Zimbabwe. In Zimbabwe 18 nutrition surveys conducted between 1980-1982 showed that between 21-23 percent of the under five population remained below 75 percent of their expected weight-for-age. Another large scale study of nearly 2,000 Zimbabwean children in 1982 found low weight-for-age in 22 percent of the age group 0-3 years (UNICEF, 1985b: 40). The southern part of the country is more prone to drought and less well provided with health care facilities. In part, this reflects the colonial geographical division of the country along racial lines, depending on agricultural potential, with patterns of urbanization, roads and social infrastructure falling in line. In part, it results from post-colonial tensions between the northern Shona and southern Matabele leadership which slowed investment in the South during the critical period 1983-1988.

One study surveyed health conditions in three adjacent areas that share a common rainfall, soil, etc., but have been differently administered: 1) a small scale commercial farming area (SSCFA) before independence called 'a native purchase area', where Africans were allowed to buy land on the edges of white commercial farming areas); 2) a communal area (CA), formerly termed a 'Tribal Trust Land' reserved for Africans; and 3) a resettlement area (RA), where since independence Africans have settled on land purchased by the government from white farmers (Campbell et al, 1989). While sharing a similar physical endowment, these neighboring zones contrast starkly in such indicators as kilometers of available roads, numbers of shops and markets and access to clinics and water schemes.

Child health and nutrition statistics reflect differences shown in Table 5-1.

B. Childhood diarrhoea, sanitation and communicable diseases

The deadly synergism between infection and malnutrition takes a great toll of African children (Scrimshaw et al., 1968; Scrimshaw, 1987). Preventable childhood diseases, like measles, whooping cough, diphtheria and diarrhoea, caused by a variety of water and fly born pathogens, and tuberculosis tend to exacerbate malnutrition, often interfering with the ability of the child to absorb nutrients.   In turn, malnourishment makes these diseases' impact on the child more severe (Van Ginneken & Muller, 1984; Duggan et al., 1986).

Table 5-1

Child Welfare:
Differences between CA and SSCFA in Zimbabwe

	Poorly served CA	Well-served SSCFA
Undernutrition	very high	high
80% weight-for-age	24%	14%
90% height-for-age	28%	17%
85% weight-for-height	11%	6%
Frequency of diarrhoea	very high	high
% reporting episode in last month for under 5s	43%	35
Food intake	low	higher
no oil or beans in past 24 hours consumed by under 5s	81%	77%
fruit, vegetables consumed 1-2 times by under 5s	71%	82%
no protein consumed in past 24 hours by under 5s	82%	53%
peanuts consumed weekly	10%	20%
oil, margarine consumed daily	34%	50%

Source: Campbell et al., 1989, pp. 61-72.

1. Immunization. UNICEF's standard immunization package protects against measles, whooping cough, diphtheria, tuberculosis, tetanus (especially important to protect pregnant women and their babies), and polio (UNICEF, 1985c). The success of mass immunization campaigns in Africa has been mixed. In small, densely populated countries like Rwanda, Burundi, Guinea-Bissau and Lesotho coverage has been good. Some larger countries with difficult logistical conditions have achieved high levels of coverage through popular

mobilization and maximum use of some of the best developed rural primary health care services on the continent: for instance, Zimbabwe, Tanzania, Burkina Faso, Congo, Cote d'Ivoire, Senegal and Kenya. Higher rates of coverage have been obtained against tuberculosis and measles. Polio and DPT immunization requires several attendances.

Unevenness of coverage may reflect the history of public health priorities before the recent campaigns. For instance, Zambia, Zimbabwe and Botswana all have a long history of tuberculosis brought home by migrant workers returning from the mines in South Africa. For years health authorities have been concerned with TB, as reflected by high rates of immunization.

Some argue that the campaign approaches undertaken by UNICEF and other UN agencies in the 1980s, like universal immunization and the so-called water and sanitation decade (discussed below), constitute desperate attempts to mop up with outside money some of the excess mortality caused by structural adjustment measures required by the World Bank and the IMF (Wisner, 1988: 130-147). Such campaigns function in parallel with the national health care system, and UNICEF has noted that "for poorer countries ... especially those hard-hit by the economic crisis, assistance [with immunization] will have to continue well beyond 1990, and it may have to cover some recurrent expenses normally assumed by governments" (UNICEF, 1987: 28).

2. Diarrhea. International and bilateral donors place a lot of emphasis on control of diarrhoea, or more precisely, on low cost, simple means of replacement of water and electrolytes in children suffering diarrhoea.   The use of such oral rehydration therapy (ORT) has constituted a major success in child health (UNICEF, 1989a: 8). Unfortunately the use of ORT in Africa is still rare.

3. Sanitation and water supply. The best way of dealing with diarrhoea, of course, is to avoid it (Feachem et al, 1983). The U.N. Water supply and Sanitation Decade (1981-1990) had that goal. By the year 1990 all people in the world were to have "reasonable access to safe water" (Agarwal et al., 1981). Average African domestic water consumption is a mere 10 liters per capita per day compared to something like 300-600 liters in industrialized countries (White et al, 1972; Lindskog & Lundquist, 1989: 9-10). In Europe 95 out of 100 people have access to piped water. In Africa 90 percent do not (Timberlake, 1988: 38).

What has the UN Water Decade, financed bilaterally and through the UNDP, managed to accomplish in Africa? Because of the very high rate of urbanization in Africa, a decade's heavy investment has produced only a 5 percent net increase in urban dwellers' access to piped water. Improvements in urban sanitation are similar. Rural access to a protected water source and improved sanitation (usually in the form of a pit latrine) have not grown as rapidly (Wisner, 1988: 87-111; UNDP/WHO, 1990).

Although there has been a net 8 percent increase in rural access to sanitation facilities during the decade, the absolute number of rural dwellers in need has grown by 30 million (equivalent to the population of Sudan, Zaire or South Africa), leaving 303 million people still without access to improved sanitation (Agarwal et al., 1981). Similarly, rural access to protected water supplies increased by a small margin (3 percent), but the number in need increased by 49 million (nearly equivalent to the population of Ethiopia), leaving 229 million people still in need of service (UNDP/WHO, 1990: 17).

Not surprisingly, the incidence of water born, water vectored and water related diseases continued to increase during the 1980s. Africa was seriously affected during the great cholera pandemics of earlier decades (Stock, 1976), but in the 1970s and 1980s the disease became endemic. There have been a number of recent outbreaks, including one in 1984 involving Burkina Faso, Mali, Niger, Nigeria, Cameroon, Ghana, Kenya and Tanzania in which, out of 6,500 reported cases, 600 people died. In 1985 some 2,000 people died of cholera in refugee camps in Sudan (Timberlake, 1988: 39). In 1991, Zimbabwe was seriously affected.

C. Malaria and other diseases

1. <u>Malaria</u>. Despite efforts to control malaria, it has been increasing in many parts of the world, especially in Africa. Eighty percent of all reported cases of malaria occur in Africa, where more than 90 percent of the population lives in malarious areas and where the prevalence of the disease in the general population is 50 percent. Among young African children prevalence approaches 100 percent (Clyde, 1987: 219; Breman & Campbell, 1988: 611; WHO, 1986; World Resources Institute, 1990: 56) An estimated 100,000 African children under one year of age and 575,000 between one and four years die each year from malaria (Breman & Campbell, 1988: 617). Placental malaria—a condition associated with low birth-weight babies—may occur in 20-34 percent of African women living in malarious zones (McGregor, 1984).

Malaria parasites have become increasingly resistant to the most common drugs. In 1990 Kenya suffered nearly 500 deaths in an epidemic of chloroquine-resistant falciparum malaria in highland centers like Eldoret and in western Kenya. During the 1980s, economic hardship had caused many people to migrate from the highlands (where they do not gain partial immunity from frequent childhood exposure to malaria) into the lowlands where malaria is holo-endemic. In secondary towns like Nakuru and Eldoret in Kenya, overburdened by the very high rate of urban growth, the government's structural adjustment measures have deferred maintenance of urban drainage and sewerage systems. This has led to an increase in mosquito breeding sites.

2. Other Diseases. Among the casualties of economic decline in the 1980s are massive national and multi-national projects to control such diseases as river blindness, sleeping sickness and bilharzia (World Bank, 1989: 65). Wars have also contributed to the abandonment of zones where tse-tse fly habitat can regrow, leading to an eventual resurgence of sleeping sickness. Likewise desert locust control has been complicated by war, adding another threat to regional food security.

3. Tuberculosis. is endemic in most of Africa despite vaccination campaigns. This is partly due to the presence of an older, unvaccinated population and partly due to the problems with the vaccine. TB is a particular problem in southern Africa and South Africa (Packard, 1989b). Of great concern is evidence that HIV-infected persons are more at risk of developing clinical TB and eventually spreading it. Simpler diagnostic tests are needed as well as a longer lasting vaccine and shorter-acting drugs for treating active cases (Commission on Health Research for Development, 1990: 22).

D. HIV Infection

As of June 1988, out of a world wide total of 100,410 cases, roughly 11,500 cases of clinical AIDS—11.5 percent—were reported in African countries (Panos Institute, 1989: 156-7). Considerable controversy about the reliability of tests for seropositivity (presence of antibodies against HIV in the blood) includes the suspicion that frequent exposure to malaria can produce antibodies that read as false HIV positives (Chirimuuta & Chirimuuta, 1989). Nevertheless, more and more evidence suggests the virus has infected a large number of Africans— including children, women and men—although they may not show symptoms of the disease. Estimates range as high as 3.5 million infected Africans out of a world wide total of 6.5 million people infected (McKenzie, 1990: 6).

The countries with the highest numbers of reported AIDS cases per million of population (in June 1988) were Congo (595), Burundi (231), Uganda (149), Rwanda (133), Zambia (106), Central African Republic (94), Malawi (79), Tanzania (68) and Kenya (67). The largest absolute numbers of reported cases (June, 1988) were found in Uganda (2,369),

Tanzania (1,608), Kenya (1,497), Congo (1,250), Burundi (1,156), Rwanda (901), Zambia (754), Malawi (583) and Zaire (335) (Panos Institute, 1989: 156-157).

It is likely that life in rural areas is already being disrupted by AIDS mortality. The number of orphaned children is growing rapidly in Uganda and probably elsewhere (Blaikie, 1990). UNICEF estimates that by the year 2000 there could be as many as 10 million orphans in Africa due to AIDS. Even now the burden of treating AIDS patients weighs heavily on limited health facilities and personnel already strained by financial crisis and budget cuts (Anon, 1988: 48).

E. Health care financing

The era of structural adjustment has lead to a severe decrease in public financing of health care in Africa. All over the continent, governments have reduced their total budgets. In addition, some have cut the share of shrinking public revenue allocated to health (Pinstrup-Anderson et al., 1987: 73-83). Considering the low per capita expenditure on health in the first place (something like US$2 per person per year on average), the impact of cuts has had an even more devastating impact.

The remaining funds tend to be spent on urban-based clinical services for a small elite. Despite the rhetoric in favor of primary health care, expenditures on rural and preventive services continue to lag.

1. Cost sharing. In the face of crisis, the World Bank is encouraging a fee-for-service approach. They emphasize that safeguards have to be built into any such cost-sharing approach. Services with high public health significance such as antenatal care and immunization should be exempted; those who cannot pay should have recourse to clear, simple procedures for forgiveness of fees; the fees collected need to be spent on the improvement of services provided (Ellis, 1987; Kanji, 1989). It is argued, for example, the majority of Kenya's rural poor would benefit from selective application of user fees if some of the US$442 million budgeted by the government for urban hospitals (67 percent of the health budget) were freed to improve rural coverage and quality of care. Not only could the poor be excused fees in an organized manner or fees be waived for people referred up the government hospital hierarchy, but whole geographical regions could be exempted on the basis of poor health indicators (e.g. U5M rates) in a procedure referred to as 'health zoning' (Mwabu & Mwangi, 1986: 767; Wood, 1990).[6]

However, the implementation of cost-sharing schemes has not attained these proposed goals of protection of equity and basic needs. In

Ghana, for instance, the fee-for-service system reportedly denied service to the poorest citizens (Waddington & Enyimayew, 1989). In Zimbabwe when the municipal councils raised the fees charged for obstetric services, fewer women used them (Loewensen et al., 1990). In Kenya doubts were expressed early on about the impact of cost-sharing without substantial safeguards (Mwabu & Mwangi, 1986: 766).

   2. Drug procurement policy. A related debate concerns pharmaceuticals. Does one throw open the doors to drug company representatives selling expensive brand names, or does one control drug imports and establish a national capacity to produce a certain number of essential drugs, importing the rest in generic form from international sources who tender the lowest bids (Wang'ombe & Mwabu, 1987; Bennett, 1989)? Mozambique, Zimbabwe and some other countries have opted for the latter course, while Nigeria favors the former. Kenya utilizes a compromise system.

   3. Privatization. Another approach to health care financing recommended by the World Bank is privatization. In many countries including Zimbabwe, Kenya, and Nigeria the private sectors are growing rapidly. These private practitioners are even more urban-biased than government medical services. In addition, doubts have been expressed about the quality of service available in circumstances where the urban poor have few alternatives. In Uganda, government health workers put in short hours at government facilities in order to make ends meet by working outside in the private sector. Banugire (1987: 102) estimates that effective labor time spent in public health clinics has declined from six or seven hours a day to only one. Meanwhile in Uganda the ratio of population to doctor has increased from 11,100: 1 in 1965 to 24,500: 1 in 1981. Private clinics have opened up in rural trading centers as well as Uganda's major cities and towns. Subsequently, rising prices tend to exclude more and more people. Even those who can afford these private services find a low level of professionalism (Banugire, 1987: 102).

III. Alternative approaches

A. Health Priorities

   1. Food security, justice and sustainability. It can sometimes occur that the pursuit of national food security can actually undermine family food security. For instance, in the early 1980s, Kenya implemented a so-called *production first* agricultural policy inspired by World Bank thinking. This policy emphasized the provision of inputs and credit to large, well-established farmers in physically

favored zones, supposedly to generate foreign income from crop exports while building up a food reserve. It had the effect, however, of further marginalizing several million land-poor farmers (Wisner, 1988: 158-179).

Thus, it is not as easy or straight forward to 'famine-proof' an African country as some agencies may believe. In order to understand why hunger persists in Africa the conventional analysis must be stretched at both ends. At the macro level, effective regional strategies must deal with the threat of continuing war and growing indebtedness (Onimode, 1989; Prah, 1988; Mafeje, 1987; Hansen, 1987). At the micro level, issues of equity and democracy have a high priority: gender equity within families (Carney, 1988; Jones, 1986; Aluko & Alfa, 1985; Tadesse, 1982; Dey, 1981), gender equity in society (Pietil & Vickers, 1990; ILO, 1984; Hay & Stichter, 1984; Cutrufelli, 1983), ethnic minority equity (Parkipuny, 1979; Snow, 1984), rural/urban equity and economic justice in class relationships (Lipton, 1977; Mabogunje, 1980; Ellis, 1984; Hadjor, 1987; Ngonzola et al, 1987).

In southern Africa this expanded approach to food security has proposed special assistance to critical geographical zones and populations identified on the basis of: (1) war damage and refugeeism; (2) instability of export prices (e.g. copper, oil, sugar); (3) drought and environmental degradation; and (4) deterioration of farmers' production capacity (e.g. death of oxen) and national infrastructure (e.g. inability to provide timely inputs and collect marketed surplus) (Morgan, 1988).

2. <u>Women's health and women's power</u>. Feminist authors assert that foreign men have for many years defined the health priorities of women. Thus *maternal and child health* (MCH) and *family planning* (FP) have a content that falls short of what women themselves want. In western Kenya women complained that no one in the maternal and child health clinic was interested in their concerns about domestic violence, rape and infertility (Raikes, 1989). Other African women have spoken out on female circumcision (Abdalla, 1982).

Some health risks receive little attention. For instance, few studies explore the respiratory injury African women suffer while cooking indoors over wood fires. Women work longer hours than men but do not eat as well (Agarwal, 1986; Trenchard, 1987; Wisner, 1988: 234-254). Yet they are responsible for most food production, provision of water and domestic fuel, care of the sick, nurturing the young, cooking and cleaning.

Such a daily cycle wears a woman down. What is at issue is whether and how women have the power to define what health is and to name the problems they face. Such an issue is not unique to health care, but raises the more general question of women's power in society (Turshen, 1989: 91).

3. <u>Maternal mortality</u>. Rates of maternal mortality are very high in Africa, reaching above 1,000 per 100,000 as compared to rates as low as 5 per 100,000 in Europe. The African average is near 700 per 100,000. Although figures for Kenya and Zimbabwe are 170 and 150 respectively, Nigeria reports 1,500 per 100,000 (UNICEF, 1989a: 106).

These high rates result from a variety of factors: very early parity (Kisseka, 1990); lack of access to antenatal services (Crowther, 1985); poor referral service for high risk pregnancies (Otolorin et al., 1988); high rates of caesarian-section delivery in hospital (De Muylder, 1986); untreated sepsis following delivery or abortion (Brown, 1978); and poor maternal nutrition (UNICEF, 1989a: 42).

In 1987, an international conference in Nairobi on safe motherhood attempted to launch concerted efforts to cut the rate of maternal deaths by half before the end of the century. Even attainment of this goal would still leave many African women to face severe risks as they give birth well into the next century.

4. <u>Women and structural adjustment</u>. Today, when a women delivers in a hospital in northern Nigeria, her family has to find money to buy all the drugs, dressings and things she may need. Due to the shortage of virtually all material in the hospitals, these must be purchased from private pharmacies (Kisseka, 1990). Economic crisis and budgetary stringency thus very directly affect the quality of maternal care.

Women and children are among the first to feel the effects of structural adjustment, but their voices have rarely been heard. In a rare attempt to let rural women speak for themselves, Marjorie Mbilinyi and Mary Kabelele organized 'speak bitterness' sessions with women at Uyole Farmers' Training Center near Mbeya in Tanzania's southern highlands (Mbilinyi, 1990). Women complained about the gender division of labor; the 'double burden' they bear. They also emphasized how, recently, they had been expected to work even harder on export crops while health services and transportation deteriorated and basic goods (soap, clothing) became scarce. Dorothy Muntemba conducted more structured interviews among urban women in Lusaka, Zambia (Muntemba, 1989). She found that since October 1985, when Zambia began to auction foreign exchange, prices of foodstuffs and other essential items had increased so much that families had reduced or even eliminated various items from meals, especially protein foods.

Women are usually the ones who have had to find ways of making ends meet in the face of the impact of structural adjustment. Women are also generally expected to assume responsibility for home care of the sick and management of the search for therapy. When they feel they are failing to safeguard the health of the family, feelings of shame and guilt are added to the stress of making ends meet (Folta & Deck, 1987). In rural Africa, the poorest and most vulnerable of these women head households on their own.

5. The rights of the child. The full range of rights of the child includes 'child health' (ANPPCAN, 1989).[7] UNICEF and children's rights advocates are to be praised for bringing into full light the magnitude of the health insults suffered by children: child labor, child military service, child prostitution and child homelessness. An estimated 10 million children in Africa live without families, mostly in towns as 'street children' (UNICEF, 1984: 39). Urban health services have little contact with these children who remain 'institutionally invisible'.

6. Hazards and people's control of space. Additional external forces penetrate the life spaces of ordinary Africans to create health hazards. Foreign firms attempt to export toxic waste to Africa (O'Keefe, 1988). Urban squatters in Africa commonly inhabit areas subject to sanitary and often toxic flood hazards. They also live in the shadow of sudden police attacks when municipal authorities decide to move them on. Fire and day-to-day crime add to health risks they confront (Satterthwaite & Hardoy, 1989).

Africa is not the stereotypically rural continent some may think. In fifteen countries, more than 30 percent of the populations live in urban centers. More than one fourth live in urban areas in eighteen additional countries, including three of Africa's most populous: Nigeria, South Africa and Zaire (United Nations, 1985; World Bank, 1988: 284-5). By the year 2020, when Africa is much more urbanized and industrialized, who will control the health and safety of life spaces?

7. Occupational Health and Workers Control. A closely related issue is who controls the health and safely of the workplace. This is becoming a point of struggle between workers and managers. One must not make the mistake of thinking of Africa as non-industrial. It may lack large scale manufacturing, but its plantations, mines, railways, ports and construction industry all present hazards to workers and their families (Loewensen, 1986; Packard, 1989a). Pesticide exposure in Africa is as bad or worse than anywhere in the world. As a consequence of the economic crisis, aging machinery remains poorly maintained, making it even more dangerous.

8. Disability. An estimated 5-10 percent of the African population suffers some degree of disability due to: disease; home, work or traffic accidents; faulty practices surrounding birth; malnutrition; and civil strife or warfare (Ransom, 1990, p. 4). One out of five of the world's 30 million blind persons live in Africa (Anon, 1989: 6). The two leading causes of blindness in these six million Africans are preventable at low cost (UNICEF, 1985c; Eastman, 1987). Blindness due to vitamin A deficiency can be prevented by dietary supplementation (Sommer, 1982: 109-122). Trachoma, a fly born infection that eventually scars the cornea, is preventable by provision of improved water and sanitation. While more costly, programs to control river blindness remain less expensive than rehabilitation of whole families blighted by the progressive loss of sight and economic activity as the life cycle of the disease and the family play themselves out (Evans, 1989; Evans & Murray, 1987; Prost, 1986).

Another major cause of disability in Africa is polio. Prevention is not costly, but at the moment the vaccine requires three separate doses. In Africa the 37 percent drop out rate (1987) after the first dose remains higher than the world average of 25 percent (UNICEF, 1989a: 56).

Other common causes of disability include uncorrected birth defects, poorly set broken bones, and severe burns. The African rate of vehicle accidents per passenger/kilometer is the highest in the world. Industrial accidents also produce spinal cord injuries and other disabilities. Finally, war-related amputations and paralysis (due to poison gas, for instance) are very common in Angola, Mozambique, and the Horn of Africa. In Angola alone at least 20,000 people have lost limbs, mostly from land mines buried by anti-government forces in farmers' fields and in village footpaths (Brennan, 1987: 22; Smith, 1990: 44).

All of the above are also preventable, including some birth defects, if antenatal and obstetric care were more widely available. Nevertheless, the question remains; how to rehabilitate the existing millions of disabled persons?

B. The Challenge

So far this review suggests that, unless altered, the future may condemn millions of Africans to chronic malnutrition, disease and disability, compounded by increasingly perilous conditions of work and dangerous and unhealthy urban living conditions. Famine and very high maternal and child mortality may not be easy to overcome.

Table 5-2 graphically illustrates the future challenge in the seven countries inhabited by nearly 60 percent of the continent's 1987 population.

Table 5-2

21st Century Health Challenge

(number of "+" indicates relative severity of problem)

Country	Food Security	Sanita- tion	Immu- nization	Position of Women	Disease	AIDS
Nigeria	+	++++	++++	++++	++++	+
Zaire	++	+++	+++	+++	++++	+++
South Africa	++	++	?	++	++	++
Sudan	+++	+++	++	++++	+++	+
Ethiopia	+++	+++	+++	+++	+++	+
Kenya	++	++	+	+++	++	++++
Tanzania	+	+	+	++	++	++++

Notes:
a) Food Security combines drought and environmental degradation with income distribution.
b) Sanitation is based on percentage rural and urban population covered and degree of urbanization.
c) Immunization is a reflection of success with vaccines requiring multiple doses.
d) Position of Women is a combination of statistics for maternal mortality (where available) and degree of participation of women in the market economy and politics.
e) Disease summarizes the prevalence of major vector born, parasitic and communicable diseases including guinea worm, river blindness, drug resistant malaria, and tuberculosis.
f) AIDS is a function of numbers of reported AIDS cases per million of population.

Source: These are qualitative assessments based on the material in the foregoing text and a more lengthy review presented at the annual meeting of the African Studies Association in 1990.

C. What Works Now?

Despite the crisis of the last 15 years—the reality of wars, drought, collapse of infrastructure, loss of jobs and income—African efforts in four health-related areas have been extraordinary: community based health care, food production, care of refugees, and environmental management. Here may be the basis for changing a dismal future. The key to improving the future of health is rejection of policies that equate health with health care (Navarro, 1986: 225-227) and separate issues of financial and ecological sustainability from issues of social justice (Hellinger et al., 1988).

1. <u>Community Health Care</u>. Families and communities care for their sick and injured. They always have. Traditional birth attendants, bone setters, herbalists and spiritual doctors remain very active in their contribution to the health of the community. Most Africans mix western and traditional therapies in a variety of ways. There have also been successful pilot schemes in primary health care with participation by community members.[8] These programs produced lessons on how to generate local priorities through village health committees and community assessment. They provided the educational and social support network for projects to combat malaria (Spencer et al., 1987) promote the use of ORT and child feeding, and monitor growth and the rural water supply. Questions remain about the role and training of and compensation for village health workers, but the potential for community mobilization has been demonstrated (Warner, 1977; Vaughan, 1980; Rifkin & Walt, 1988).

Over a five year period one of the most successful projects in 168 villages in Iringa, Tanzania, reduced severe malnutrition by 60 percent and young child deaths by 30 percent. The program centered around community-supported day care centers and has now been expanded to include all 620 villages in Iringa region (UNICEF, 1989a: 66).

2. <u>Food Production</u>. Despite the general impression of famine vulnerability, major successes, like the small farmers' increased contribution to Zimbabwe's marketed maize surplus, have been achieved. Other hopeful signs include: the success of women's cooperatives in Burkina Faso, widespread use of new drought resistant varieties of sorghum, maize and pigeon peas in dryland eastern Kenya, women's gardening groups in Senegal and peri-urban Mozambique, small animal production by women's groups in a number of cities, and some partial success in village cooperatives following Ethiopian land reform. These cases point to the ability of African farmers and women

to cooperate, to adapt knowledge and skills and to produce despite difficult circumstances.[9]

3. Caring for refugees. At the peak of drought and war-related population movements during 1984-86, as many as 5 million refugees crossed African national borders (CIMADE et al., 1986: 3). Many more were displaced within the borders of their own countries. UNHCR and other international and national bodies provided a great deal of support for these people. Yet the cooperation of host populations living near the refugee camps was also essential. Considering the pressures on host populations, their generosity is little short of amazing (Kibreab, 1985; Christensen, 1985).

4. Environmental management. Although aggregate statistics on access to water and sanitation show little progress, individual communities have mobilized successfully to improve environmental hygiene. Their successes do not contradict findings in Malawi, Tanzania, Nigeria and Lesotho that water facilities alone, in the absence of socioeconomic change, bring few health benefits.[10] Nevertheless, their partial success demonstrates a potential for group action to control and to improve the environment.

During the crisis years 1975-1990, women's groups: planted millions of trees; they dug thousands of kilometers of bands to stop erosion and to harvest the run off of rain; they made hundreds of thousands of wells and reservoirs; and protected tens of thousands of springs (Harrison, 1987; Dankelman & Davidson, 1988; Conroy & Litvinoff, 1988; Leach & Mearns, 1988). Is this energy and commitment to one's place and children not a factor to take into account in thinking about the future? Rather than the compartmentalized approach of the past, what is needed is a more holistic, comprehensive approach to health-linked environmental problems (Falkenmark, 1982; Bennett, 1986; Wisner, 1988: 89-119, 282-285).

IV. What Is To Be Done?

A. Minimal preconditions for creation of a healthy future

African women, men, workers, farmers, healers, teachers, and children, must participate in creating the conditions for a healthier future. Their organizations exist: the Federation of Collective Cooperatives of Zimbabwe, the Naam groups in the Sahel, the Greenbelt Movement in Kenya. They are presently engaged in rethinking the future of Africa, in struggling to build a healthy future. In the words of one of their leaders, "Tomorrow is built today"

(Nyathi, 1990). However, they need the space within which they can experiment and create their future.   As the UN Under-Secretary-General for Africa has put it, "Let the people put themselves first - let them seize the initiative" (Adedeji, 1990: 45).   Such political and economic 'space' for popular action requires some minimal conditions: (1) a halt to geopolitical manipulation of the continent's conflicts; (2) cancellation of foreign debt;   (3) negotiation of GATT terms that will favor African producers; (4) adjustment with much more than a 'human face.' Fiscal policy must put the needs of the people first;   (5) donor encouragement of comprehensive rather than selective primary health care; and (6) donor encouragement of projects and programs that take an intersectoral view of health.   These minimal conditions could open up a space in the economic crisis within which Africans could more freely experiment with democratic forms of defining health priorities and controlling the determinant of their health.

B. Research questions

Health research has to be totally rethought from several points of view. First, if one takes seriously the inclusion of the complementary agendas of 'experts' and ordinary people, what would health research look like? What alternative donor activities are implied? What role would the university play? What new training for undergraduates and post-graduates is implied? What role should primary and secondary teachers and their students play in generating health research information among the people?

Second, what kind of health research is needed to help countries deal with the consequences of war, environmental degradation, massive urbanization, structural adjustment and economic crisis?

Third, one must rethink the relationship between biomedical and socioeconomic research in light of the great challenges identified above.

If health research is reconsidered from these three points of view, some of the research questions for Africa might be the following:

1. How can the participation of ordinary Africans in conceptualizing and prioritizing their own health problems be maximized?

2. For each of the highly vulnerable groups identified at the beginning of this chapter, what are their major complaints, needs, frustrations? How are these linked to health? In each case what are the available local material resources and human skills? What forms of organization exist among these

people?   What are the obstacles to utilizing such resources, skills, organizations to improve health?

3. What are the precise connections between socio-cultural oppression of women, their changing economic role, their health status and the well being of their children?

4. What is the significance of continued high fertility (e.g. 6-8) among African women in the face of survey results that suggest they actually want completed families of four children?

5. What are the precise connections between external shocks such as petroleum price rise, drought, price decline for export commodity (e.g. copper, coffee, cotton) and the health of specific groups of persons?   What systems in various African countries amplify these shocks?   What systems buffer or reduce them?

6. What would a "peace dividend" be like in various African countries, and how should it be spent in the health sector?

7. What is financially sustainable and what is not in all the various campaigns and other externally funded health activity in Africa today?

8. Are there forms of "cost sharing" or "community financing" that are both equitable and efficient?

9. What is the optimal combination of home care, traditional community care, and western/public health service care in various parts of Africa?

10. What will the impact of global warming be on African livestock and farm production?   On food security?

11. Evidence suggests that domestic water schemes by themselves do not improve health, that irrigation water schemes may even cause ill health among tenants and workers. How do we systematically conceptualize the role of water in human health in Africa today and in the future?

12. What are the potentials and priorities of an indigenous African capacity in biotechnology applied to major health problems defined by Africans themselves?

13. What will the impact of AIDS be on Africa?   What is the likelihood of another virus or another surprising health threat emerging?

14. What are the health hazards associated with future massive urbanization in Africa and how can they be avoided?

15. What are the most appropriate forms of U.S./African professional collaboration in order to answer these and other questions?

16. How can one best influence the research and policy agendas of donors, the U.S. Congress and international agencies with African concerns and an African perspective? How can Africans best secure space and time to form an image of their own future?

17. What are the positive lessons for U.S. and European health and health care we need to learn from Africa?

Endnotes

1. Quoted in Paul Lewis, "World Leaders Endorse Plan to Improve Lives of Children." *New York Times* (1 October 1990), p. A13.

2. Country experience and attempts to sort out the chain of causes that link foreign debt and national economic and fiscal policy with health are found in Jolly & Cornia, 1984; UNICEF, 1985a; Cornia et al, 1897; Haq & Kirdar, 1987; Wisner, 1988; Nafziger, 1988; Packard et al., 1989; Onimode, 1989.

3. Quoted in the *New York Times* (1 October 1990), p. A13, "Excerpts from Remarks by Leaders at Summit for Children." Brogan, 1990, pp. 568-576 lists 27 wars in Africa between 1948-1988 which claimed the lives of more than 5 million persons. He also lists 68 coups d'etat and revolutions from 1960 until June of 1989 (compare more detailed list of regime changes in Folz & Bienen, 1985, 197 ff). Apart from the direct casualties that resulted, enormous numbers of people have been forced to flee their homes as refugees (Kibreab, 1985). Social infrastructure including health care and sanitary facilities has been destroyed. The resulting emphasis on military budgets has skewed investment away from social sectors (including health care) and has contributed to foreign debt that adds further stress on the common person's livelihood, hence health status and life changes. On the frequency of violent conflict in Africa also see Van der Wusten, 1985.

4. On the basic needs approach to development and, in particular, the indivisibility of basic needs, see Wisner, 1988, chapters 1 & 5; Stewart, 1985, chapters 1 & 2; and various authors in Coate & Rosati, eds., 1988.

5. For instance, Swantz, 1970; Janzen, 1978; Chavunduka, 1978; Ulin & Segal, 1980; Comaroff, 1981; Stock, 1985c; Sargent, 1985; Feierman, 1985; Makinde, 1988.

6. Wood gives a number of examples of large urban hospitals trying to integrate more effectively with their surrounding communities in prevention of disease and promotion of health. This also spreads the benefit of such costly investments.

7. For text of draft convention on the rights of the child, see Ennew & Milne, 1989, pp. 200-216.

8. Edwards and Lyon, 1983, on Sierra Leone; Wisner, 1988, pp. 76-86, on Kenya; Walt & Melamed, 1984, on Mozambique.

9. On successes and potential in Zimbabwe and the other SADCC countries, see Prah, 1988; Dag Hammarskjöld Foundation, 1987; Seidman, 1991. On successes and potentials in Kenya, Kiriro & Juma, 1989; Downing et al, 1989. On the strength of small holder farming in Nigeria and its ability to adjust and cope with risk: Richards, 1985; ILO, 1981, pp. 79-100; Abumere, 1978; Mortimore, 1978; Mortimore, 1989.

10. On Malawi: Lindskog & Lundquist, 1989; on Nigeria: Tomkins, 1978; on Lesotho: Feachem, 1978; on Tanzania: Kreysler, 1970.

Bibliography

Abdalla, R. 1982. *Sisters in Affliction: Circumcision and Infibulation of Women in Africa.* Trenton: Africa World Press.

Abumere, S. 1978. "Traditional Agricultural Systems and Staple Food Production." In J. Oguntoyinbo et al., Eds. *A Geography of Nigerian Development.* Ibadan: Heinemann. 208-225.

Adedeji, A. 1990. *The African Initiative: Putting the People First.* Addis Abeba: UNECA.

Agarwal, A. et al. 1981. *Water, Sanitation, Health—For All?* London: Earthscan.

Agarwal, B. 1986. *Cold Stoves and Barren Slopes.* London: Zed.

Aluko, G. & Alfa, M., 1985. "Marriage and Family." In S. Bappa et al., Eds. *Women in Nigeria Today.* London: Zed. 163-173.

Anonymous. 1989. *International Rehabilitation Review.* 40, 1, June. 6.

Anon, 1988. "The Incalculable Cost of AIDS," *The Economist.* March 12. 48.

African Network for the Prevention and Protection Against Child Abuse and Neglect (ANPPCAN), 1988. *Children in Situations of Armed Conflict in Africa*. Nairobi: ANPPCAN/ UNICEF/R dda Barnen.

ANPPCAN. 1989. *The Rights of the Child*. Nairobi: Initiatives.

Banugire, F. 1989.   "Employment, Incomes, Basic Needs and Structural Adjustment Policy in Uganda, 1980-87." In B. Onimode, ed., *The IMF, the World Bank and the African Debt: The Social and Political Impact*. Vol. 2. London: Zed. 95-110.

Bennett, F. 1989.   "The Dilemma of Essential Drugs in Primary Health Care." *Social Science and Medicine*. 28, 10. 1085-90.

Bennett, F. 1986.   "Introduction: Health Revolution in Africa?" *Social Science and Medicine*. 22, 7. 737-740.

Blaikie, P. 1990.   Personal communication, University of East Anglia, School of Development Studies.

Breman, J. & Campbell, C. 1988.   "Combatting Severe Malaria in African Children." *Bulletin WHO*. 66, 5.

Brennen, T. 1987.   *Uprooted Angolans: From Crisis to Catastrophe*. Washington D.C.: U.S. Commission for Refugees.

Brogan, P. 1990. *The Fighting Never Stopped*. New York: Vintage.

Brown, J. 1978.   "Maternal Mortality: A Survey of Maternal Deaths Occurring During 1976." *Central African Journal of Medicine*. 24, 10. 212-214.

Campbell, B. et al. Eds. 1989.   *The Save Study: Relationships Between the Environment and Basic Needs Satisfaction in the Save Catchment, Zimbabwe*.   Harare: University of Zimbabwe Publications.

Carney, J. 1988.   "Struggles Over Crop Rights and Labour Within Contract Farming Households in a Gambian Irrigated Rice Project." *Journal of Peasant Studies*. 15, 3. 334-49.

Chandler, W., 1985.   *Investing in Children*. Washington, D.C.: World Watch Institute.

Chavanduka, G., 1978.   *Traditional Healers and the Shona Patient*. Gwelo: Mambo.

Chirimuuta, R.C. & Chirimuuta, R.J. 1989. *Aids, Africa and Racism*. 2nd ed. London: Free Association Books.

Christensen, H. 1985. *Refugees and Pioneers: History and Field Study of a Burundian Settlement in Tanzania*. Geneva: UN Research Institute for Social Development.

CIMADE et al. 1986. *Africa's Refugee Crisis*. London: Zed.

Cliff, J. & Noormahomed, A. 1988. "Health as Target: South Africa's Destabilization of Mozambique." *Social Science and Medicine*. 27, 7. 717-722.

Clyde, D. 1987. "Recent Trends in the Epidemiology and Control of Malaria." *Epidemiologic Reviews* 9.

Coate, R. & Rosati, J. Eds. 1988. *The Power of Human Needs in World Society*. Boulder, CO: Rienner.

Comaroff, J. 1981. "Healing and Cultural Transformation." *Social Science and Medicine*, B. 15,3B. 367-78.

Commission on Health Research for Development, 1990. *Health Research: Essential Link to Equity in Development*. Oxford: Oxford University Press.

Conroy, C. & Litvinoff, M. 1988. *The Greening of Aid: Sustainable Livelihoods in Practice*. London: Earthscan.

Cornia, G. et al. Eds. 1987. *Adjustment with a Human Face*. 2 Vols. New York: Oxford University Press.

Crowther, C. 1985. "Management and Pregnancy Outcome in Eclampsia at Harare Maternity Hospital." *Central African Journal of Medicine*. 31, 6. 107-109.

Cutrufelli, M. 1983. *Women of Africa*. London: Zed.

Dag Hammarskjöld Foundation, Ed. 1987. *Another Development for SADCC*. Serowe, Botswana: Dag Hammarskjöld/FEP.

Dankelman, I. & Davidson, J. Eds. 1988. *Women and Environment in the Third World*. London: Earthscan.

De Muylder, X. 1986. "Maternal Service in a General Hospital." *Central African Journal of Medicine*. 32, 10. 240-243.

Dey, J. 1981. "Gambian Women: Unequal Partners in Rice Development Projects?" *Journal of Development Studies*. 17, 3. 109-122.

Downing, T. et al. Eds. 1989. *Coping with Drought in Kenya*. Boulder: Westview.

Duggan, M. et al. 1986. "The Nutritional Cost of Measles in Africa." *Archives of Diseases in Childhood*. 61. 61-66.

Eastman, S., 1987. *Vitamin A Deficiency and Xerophalmia*. Assignment Children 1987-3. New York: UNICEF.

Edwards, N. & Lyon, M. 1983. "Community Assessment: A Tool for Motivation and Evaluation in Primary Health Care in Sierra Leone." In: D. Morley et al. Eds. *Practicing Health for All*. Oxford: Oxford Univ. Press. 101-113.

Ellis, F. 1984."Relative Agricultural Prices and the Urban Bias Model." In: J. Harris & M. Moore. Eds. *Development and the Rural-Urban Divide*, London: Cass. 28-51.

Ellis, R. 1987. "The Revenue Generating Potential of User Fees in Kenyan Government Health Facilities." *Social Science and Medicine*. 25, 9. 995-1002.

Ennew, J. & Milne, B. 1989. *The Next Generation*. London: Zed.

Evans, T. G. & Murray, C. L. 1987. "A Critical Reexamination of the Economics of Blindness Prevention Under the Onchocerciasis Control Programme." *Social Science and Medicine*. 25, 3. 241-249.

Evans, T., 1989. "The Impact of Permanent Disability on Rural Households: River Blindness in Guinea." *IDS Bulletin*. 20, 2. 41-48.

Falkenmark, M. Ed. 1982. *Rural Water Supply and Health*. Uppsala: Scandinavian Institute of African Studies.

Feachem, R. et al. 1983. *Sanitation and Disease*. Chichester: John Wiley & Sons.

------. 1978. *Water, Health and Development: An Interdisciplinary Evaluation*. London: Tri-Med.

Feierman, S. 1985. "Struggles for Control: The Social Roots of Health and Healing in Modern Africa." *African Studies Review*. 28,2/3. 73-147.

Folta, J. & Deck, E. 1987. "Rural Zimbabwean Shona Women: Illness Concepts and Behaviour." *Western J. Nursing Research*. 9, 3. 301-16.

Folz, W. & Bienen, H. 1985. *Arms and the African: Military Influences on Africa's International Relations*. New Haven: Yale University Press.

Green, R., 1989. "The Broken Pot: The Social Fabric, Economic Disaster, and Adjustment in Africa." In: B. Onimode. Ed. Op. cit. 31-55.

Haaga, J. et al. 1984. *An Estimate of the Prevalence of Child Malnutrition in Developing Countries*. Ithaca: Cornell University/Nutrition Surveillance Program.

Hadjor, K. 1987. *Transforming Africa*. Trenton: Africa World Press.

Hansen, E. Ed. 1987. *Africa: Perspectives on Peace and Development*. London: Zed.

Harrison, P. 1987. *The Greening of Africa*. London: Penguin.

Haq, K. & Kirdar, U. Eds. 1987. *Human Development, Adjustment and Growth*. Islamabad: North South Roundtable.

Hay, M. & Stichter, S. 1984. *African Women*. London: Longman.

Hellinger, S. et al. 1988. *Aid for Just Development*. Boulder: Rienner.

International Labor Organization (ILO). 1981. *First Things First: Meeting Basic Needs of the People of Nigeria*. Addis Ababa: ILO/Jobs and Skills Programme for Africa (JASPA).

-----. Ed. 1984. *Rural Development and Women in Africa*. Geneva.

Janzen, J. 1978. *The Quest for Therapy in Lower Zaire*. Berkeley: University of California Press.

Jolly, R. and Cornia, G. Eds. 1984. *The Impact of World Recession on Children*. Oxford: Pergamon.

Jones, C., 1986. "Intra-Household Bargaining in Response to the Introduction of New Crops." In J. Moock Ed. *Understanding Africa's Rural Households and Farming Systems*, Boulder: Westview. 105-123.

Kanji, N. 1989. "Charging for Drugs in Africa" *Health Pol. & Plan.* 4, 2, 110-120.

Kibreab, G. 1985. *African Refugees.* Trenton: Africa World Press.

Kiriro, A. & Juma, C. 1989. *Gaining Ground.* Nairobi: ACTS Press.

Kisseka, M. Ed. 1981. *Children in Kaduna State, Nigeria.* Zaria: Ahmadu Bello University/Dept. Sociology.

-----. 1990. Remarks during presentation at Hampshire College, Amherst, MA, USA, May, 1990.

Kreysler, J. 1970. "Health, Water Supply and Self Reliance in Mayo Village." *Journal of Tropical Pediatrics.* September, 1970. 116-23.

Leach, G. & Mearns, R. 1988. *Beyond the Woodfuel Crisis.* London: Earthscan.

Lindskog, P. & Lundquist, J. 1989. *Why Poor Children Stay Sick: The Human Ecology of Child Health and Welfare in Rural Malawi.* Uppsala: Scandinavian Institute of African Studies.

Lipton, M. 1977. *Why Poor People Stay Poor.* New York: Praeger.

Loewensen, R., 1986. "Farm Labour in Zimbabwe." *Health Policy & Planning.* 1, 1. 48-57.

Loewenson, R., Sanders, D. & Davies, R. 1990. "Challenges to Equity in Health and Health Care: A Zimbabwean Case Study." Paper presented to the First African Regional Conference of Social Science and Medicine. Mombasa, Kenya.

Mabogunje, A. 1980. *The Development Process.* New York: Holmes & Meier.

McGregor, Ian. 1984. "Epidemiology, Malaria and Pregnancy." *Tropical Medicine and Hygiene.* 33, 4.

McKenzie, J. 1990. "Facing the Crisis." *Africa South.* 6. 5-6.

Mafeje, A. 1987. "Food Security and Peace in the SADCC Region." In E. Hansen. Ed. *Africa: Perspectives on Peace and Development.* London: Zed. 183-212.

Makinde, M. 1988. *African Philosophy, Culture, and Traditional Medicine*. Monographs in International Studies, Africa Series 53. Athens, OH: Ohio University.

Mbilinyi, M. 1990. "'Structural Adjustment', Agri-business, and Rural Women in Tanzania." In H. Bernstein et al. Eds. *The Food Question: Profits Versus People?*. London: Earthscan. 111-124.

Mburu, F. 1986. "The African Social Periphery." *Social Science and Medicine*. 22, 7. 785-790.

Morgan, R. 1988. *Social Welfare Programmes and the Reduction of Household Vulnerability in the SADCC States of Southern Africa*. Development Economics Research Programme No. 25, London School of Economics, Suntory-Toyota International Centre for Economics.

Mortimore, M. 1978. "Livestock Production." In J. Oguntoyinbo et al. Eds. *A Geography of Nigerian Development*. 240-260. Ibadan: Heinemann.

Mortimore, M. 1989. *Adapting to Drought*. Cambridge: Cambridge University Press.

Muntemba, D. 1989. "The Impact of IMF-World Bank Programmes on Women and Children in Zambia." In: B. Onimode. Ed. Op. cit. 111-124.

Mwabu, G. & Mwangi, W. 1986. "Health Care Financing in Kenya" *Social Science and Medicine*. 22, 7. 763-67.

Mwangi, W. & Mwabu, G. 1986. "Economics of Health and Nutrition in Kenya." *Social Science and Medicine*. 22, 7. 775-80.

Nafziger, E. 1988. *Inequality in Africa*. Cambridge: Cambridge University Press.

Navarro, V. 1986. *Crisis, Health, and Medicine*. New York: Tavistock.

Nyathi, A. 1990. *Tomorrow is Built Today*. Harare: Anvil.

Nzongola-Ntalaja et al. 1987. *Africa's Crisis*. London: IFAA.

O'Keefe, P. 1988. "Toxic Terrorism." *Review of African Political Economy*. 42. 84-90.

Onimode, B. Ed. 1989. *The IMF, the World Bank, and the African Debt*. Vol. 2. London: Zed.

Otolorin, E. et al., 1988. "Maternity Care Monitoring: A Contrast at Two Levels of Health Care." *International Journal of Gynaecology and Obstetrics.* 26, 3. 367-73.

Packard, R. 1989a. "Industrial Production, Health and Disease in sub-Saharan Africa." *Social Science Medicine.* 28, 5. 475-96.

Packard, R., 1989b. *White Plague, Black Labor: Tuberculosis and the Political Economy of Health and Disease in South Africa.* Berkeley: University of California Press.

Packard, R. et al. Eds. 1989. "The Political Economy of Health and Disease in African and Latin America." Spec. Issue, *Social Science Medicine.* 28, 5.

Panos Institute. 1989. *AIDS and the Third World.* London: Panos.

Parkipuny, M., 1979. "Some Crucial Aspects of the Maasai Predicament." In: A. Coulson, ed., *African Socialism in Practice.* London: Spokesman. 136-57.

Pinstrup-Andersen, P. et al., 1987."The Impact on Government Expenditure." In G. Cornia et al. Eds. op. cit. 73-89.

Pietil , H. & Vickers, J. 1990. *Making Women Matter.* London: Zed.

Prah, K. Ed. 1988. *Food Security Issues in Southern Africa.* Southern African Studies. Ser 4. Institute of Southern African Studies. Roma: National University of Lesotho.

Prost, A. 1986. "The Burden of Blindness in Adult Males in the Savanna Villages of West Africa Exposed to Onchocerciasis." *Transactions of the Royal Society for Tropical Medicine and Hygiene.* 80. 525-27.

Ransom, R. 1990. "Training for Self and Group Employment Creation in Africa." *International Rehabilitation Review.* 40, 1. 4-5.

Raikes, A. 1989. "Women's Health in East Africa." In R. Packard et al. Eds. op. cit. 447-460.

Richards, P. 1985. *Indigenous Agricultural Revolution.* London: Hutchinson University Press.

Rifkin, S. & Walt, G. Eds. 1988. "Selective or Comprehensive Primary Health Care?" Spec. Issue: *Social Science and Medicine.* 26, 9.

Sargent, C. 1985. "Witches, Merchants and Midwives." In B. Du Toit & I. Abdalla, eds., *African Healing Strategies*. Owerri/New York/London: Trado-Medic Books (Division of Conch Magazine). 96-107.

Satterthwaite, D. & Hardoy, J. 1989. *Squatter Citizen*. London: Earthscan.

Scrimshaw, N. et al. 1968. *Interactions of Nutrition and Infection*. WHO. Monograph 27. Geneva: WHO.

Scrimshaw, N. 1987. "Adjustment Policies that Increase Poverty." In K. Hag & U. Kirdar. Eds. Op. cit. 192-207.

Seidman, A. et al. Eds. 1991. *Transforming Southern African Agriculture*. Trenton: Africa World Press.

Smith, S. 1990. *Front Line Africa*. Oxford: Oxfam.

Snow, R. 1984. "Famine Relief: Some Unanswered Questions from Africa." In B. Currey & G. Hugo. Eds. *Famine as a Geographical Phenomenon*. Dordrecht: Reidel.

Sommer, A. 1982. *Nutritional Blindness*. New York: Oxford University Press.

Spencer, H. et al. 1987. "Community-based Malaria Control in Saradidi, Kenya." *Annals of Tropical Medicine and Parasitology*. 81, Supplement 1. 13-23.

Stewart, F. 1985. *Planning to Meet Basic Needs*. London: Macmillan.

Stock, R. 1985a. "Health Care For Some: A Nigerian Study of Who Gets What, Where, and Why." *International Journal of Health Services*. 15. 469-84.

Stock, R. 1985b. "The Social Impacts of Differential Access to New Health Programs in Nigeria." In W. Derman & S. Whiteford, Eds. *Issues in Social Impact Analysis and Development*. 216-239.

Stock, R. 1985c. "Islamic Medicine in Rural Hausaland." In: B. du Toit & I. Abdalla. Eds., Op. cit. 29-46.

Stock, R. 1976. *Cholera in Africa*. London: International African Institute.

Swantz, M.L. 1970. *Ritual and Symbol in Transitional Zaramo Society (with special reference to women)*. Uppsala: Gleerup/ Almquist & Wiksells.

Tadesse, Z. 1982. "The Impact of Land Reform on Women: The Case of Ethiopia." In: L. Bener2a. Ed. *Women and Development.* 203-222. New York: Praeger.

Timberlake, L. 1988. *Africa in Crisis.* 2nd ed. London: Earthscan.

Tomkins, A. et al. 1978. "Water Supply and Nutritional Status in Rural Northern Nigeria." *Transactions of the Royal Society of Tropical Medicine and Hygiene.* 72. 239-43.

Trenchard, E. 1987. "Rural Woman's Work in Sub-Saharan Africa and the Implications for Nutrition." In J. Momsen & J. Townshend. Eds. *Geography of Gender in the Third World.* 153-172. London: Hutchinson.

Turshen, M. 1989. *The Politics of Public Health.* New Brunswick: Rutgers University Press.

Ulin, P. & Segal, M. Eds. 1980. *Traditional Health Care Delivery in Contemporary Africa.* Syracuse: Maxwell School African Series 35.

United Nations, 1985. *Estimates and Projections of Urban, Rural and City Populations, 1950-2000.* New York.

United Nations Development Programme/World Bank (UNDP/ WHO). 1990. *End of Decade Report.* Geneva: WHO.

United Nations Economic Commission on Africa (UNECA). 1990. *Economic Report on Africa 1990.* Addis Ababa, UNECA.

United Nations Children and Education Fund (UNICEF). 1989a. *The State of the World's Children 1989.* New York: UNICEF/Oxford University Press.

------. 1989b. *Children on the Front Line.* New York. UNICEF.

UNICEF, 1988. *Situation Analysis of Women and Children in Kenya.* Nairobi: UNICEF/ Republic of Kenya.

------. 1987. *Progress Review of the Child Survival and Development Revolution 1983-1986.* New York.

------. 1985a. *The State of the World's Children 1985.* New York: UNICEF/Oxford University Press.

------. 1985b. *Children and Women in Zimbabwe: A Situation Analysis.* Harare: UNICEF/ Republic of Zimbabwe.

------. 1985c. *Universal Child Immunization by 1990*. New York. UNICEF.

------. 1984. *Urban Basic Services: Reaching Children and Women of the Urban Poor*. Occas. Pap. Ser. 3. New York. UNICEF.

Van der Wusten, H. 1985. "The Geography of Conflict Since 1945." In D. Pepper & A. Jenkins. Eds. *The Geography of Peace and War*. London: Basil Blackwell. 13-28.

Van Ginneken, J. & Muller, A. Eds. 1984. *Maternal and Child Health in Rural Kenya*. Beckenham: Croom Helm.

Vaughan, J. 1980. "Barefoot or Professional? Community Health Workers in the Third World." *Journal of Tropical Medicine and Hygiene*. 83: 3-10.

Waddington, C. & Enyimayew, K. 1989. "A Price to Pay: The Impact of User Charges in Ashanti-Akim District, Ghana." *International Journal of Health Planning and Management*. 4. 17-47.

Walt, G. & Melamed, A. Eds. 1984. *Mozambique: Towards a People's Health Service*. London: Zed.

Wang'ombe, J. & Mwabu, G. 1987. "Economics of Essential Drugs Schemes: The Perspective of the Developing Countries." *Social Science and Medicine*. 25,6. 625-30.

Warner, D. 1977. "The Village Health Worker: Lackey or Liberator?" Hesperian Paper. Palo Alto: The Hesperian\Foundation.

Watts, M. Ed. 1986. *State, Oil, and Agriculture in Nigeria*. Berkeley: Institute of International Studies.

White, G. et al. 1972. *Drawers of Water: Domestic Water Use in East Africa*. Chicago: University of Chicago Press.

Wisner, B. 1988. *Power and Need in Africa: Basic Human Needs and Development Policies*. London: Earthscan.

Wood, C. 1990. "Can We Afford Hospitals? *Amref News* (Jan-Mar). 10. Nairobi: Afr. Med. Research Foundation.

World Bank. 1989. *Sub-Saharan Africa: From Crisis to Sustainable Growth*. Washington, D.C. The World Bank.

------. 1988. *World Development Report 1988*. New York: Oxford University Press.

------. 1981. *Accelerating Development in sub-Saharan Africa*. Washington, D.C. The World Bank.

World Health Organization (WHO). 1986.   *WHO Expert Committee on Malaria. 18th Report*. WHO Technical Series 735. Geneva.

World Resources Institute. 1990.   *World Resources 1990-1991*. New York: Oxford University Press.

Chapter 6

Facing Africa's Ecological Crisis

By Calestous Juma and Richard Ford
in consultation with Wanjiku Mwagiru

Dealing with Africa's current ecological crisis requires an approach that takes into account the importance of institutional innovation in long-term socioeconomic transformation. Further, despite the seemingly desperate ecological situation, at least as reflected by macro-economic indicators, local communities are engaged in a wide range of social experiments which involve integrating ecological improvements into local economic development activities. This Chapter aims to bring lessons from these experiences to bear in the design of research to meet the challenges of national and regional development. Attainment of this goal requires:

1. Review, analysis, and development of research to consider the appropriateness and potential effectiveness of a variety of locally-based and participatory models that are achieving ecologically sustainable development;
2. Examination of these experiences to identify policy-options that can be incorporated into and contribute to national and regional development plans.

Models based on community development take different forms in different ecosystems and socio-cultural settings. They offer promise, but they are rarely scrutinized by external agents, nor have their organizers had the opportunity to share with one another the strengths and weaknesses of their respective experiences. This underscores the potential benefits for collaborative between research teams and local leaders and institutions to contribute directly to assessing, disseminating and improving models of ecologically sustainable development.

The chapter first reviews the scope, impact and causes of Africa's ecological crisis; then examines the consequences of macro- and micro-level responses; and finally suggests the implications for the initial research program to be undertaken by the Task Force Environmental task group.

I. Africa's Ecological Crisis: A Review

Africa is currently experiencing major interlinked economic and ecological problems. While agricultural output has declined in most countries in recent decades, industrial output has only marginally contributed to economic growth. Twenty years ago, Africa was self-sufficient in food production. Now the continent imports 20 percent of its cereal requirements. Over the 1970-1980 period, cereal imports increased threefold; the cost of these imports multiplied 600 percent. Overall, since 1970, Africa's annual agricultural output has grown at an average rate of less than 1.3 percent, less than half the 3.0 percent rate of population growth. From 1970 to 1984, Africa's per capita production of food fell by 13 percent. Africa is the only region in the world where nutrition levels have declined over the last two decades.

While the agricultural system's current productive capacity is reaching limits, it is experiencing increasing pressures to produce more. About 70 percent of Africa's population of 500 million live in rural areas where agriculture remains the primary economic activity. These rural areas not only must meet subsistence needs; they must also produce food for the continent's growing urban populations and export markets. Between 30 and 60 percent of African countries' Gross National Product derives from agriculture. The level of technology, agricultural inputs and management skills available in rural areas remains too low to simultaneously provide the food required for the growing population and generate income for increasing monetary needs.

In recent decades, two major interrelated factors introduced far-reaching technological and ecological consequences in Africa. First, the 1973-74 oil price increases mainly multiplied the costs of African efforts to increase productivity. Taking advantage of the new microelectronics possibilities, industrialized nations rapidly introduced new technologies that revolutionized all aspects of industrial and social organization. Unfortunately, in contrast, African countries experienced difficulty in adapting resource-efficient technologies and non-polluting innovations. For them, the increased cost of oil essentially boosted to unprecedented levels the cost of all technological innovation.

Secondly, and closely associated with the import of oil and technologies from industrialized countries, African countries experienced a rapid growth of external debt.[1] In an effort to generate revenues and foreign exchange to repay said debt, governments adopted programs to accelerate their competitive efforts to expand raw materials exports. These further marginalized the cultivation of food crops as well as the lives of the people—more than two thirds of them women—who grew them.[2]

In Africa, any new investment activities must rely largely on the ecological base for their expansion and maintenance. Nowhere else is human survival so dependent on the integrity of the ecosystems. A United Nations assessment underscored the deeply imbedded and interrelated characteristics of economic and ecological elements manifested in Africa's crisis when it emphasized that   African countries are:

"all characterized by very low income per head, the majority of the population living at below minimum acceptable standards in basic needs and predominantly in the subsistence sector; extremely low agricultural productivity and weak agro-support institutions; the low share of manufacturing in GDP; inadequate levels of exploitation of natural resources, especially of minerals and energy, because of lack of knowledge and energy, finance and skills; low per capita export levels and even with aid flows, very little absolute availability of imports; acute scarcity of skilled personnel at all levels; weak institutional and physical infrastructure, especially in the areas of transport and communications, and major geographical and/or climatological handicaps such as a land-locked situation, insularity, drought and desertification'"(UNCA, Regional Assessment: 1).

Past research has suggested three clusters of explanations for Africa's ecological plight. The first cluster includes external factors, some of which go back many generations: the impact of the slave trade and the colonial experience; the current terms of trade which some argue reflect continued colonial dependency; the debt crisis and negative financial transfers which afflict many African nations; the nature of development design and management planned without involving the users of investments or their products; and inappropriate technologies.

The second cluster of explanations identifies factors internal to individual African states. These include: weak, ineffective government institutions; internal civil and military unrest; personal political ambitions; land tenure systems and limited land access; corruption; and weak infrastructure, especially in the areas of financial management, communications and transport.

Beyond these internal and external causes of the crisis, a range of pressures run parallel to and aggravate the impact of the crisis. These include events such as drought and climate change; the population explosion of the last three decades; gender issues; diet change; psychic changes in attitude leading to a preference for urban, rather than rural life; and growing income and class differentials.

Undoubtedly, in Africa as elsewhere, modernization strategies have aggravated aspects of the continent's environmental deterioration, especially in urban areas. In specific circumstances in particular countries, these include:

1. Industrial wastes: As urbanization and industrialization take place, disposal of toxic wastes threaten both water and air quality of Africa's larger cities. In addition to locally produced wastes, dumping from external sources (both Europe and North America) poses a potentially serious hazard.

2. Inadequate government regulation: Environmental Impact Assessments, planning, design, monitoring, and regulation have proved incapable of limiting the negative environmental impacts of some of the larger commercial and industrial investments.

3. Agricultural and chemical inputs: Petro-chemicals are causing great harm to sustainability in parts of the continent, requiring development of an overall policy on, for example, pesticide management.

4. Wildlife: In many countries, especially in Eastern and Southern Africa, wildlife compete with people for the same land, aggravating problems confronting local inhabitants seeking to improve their levels of life.

These environmental hazards will probably intensify as African nations accelerate their efforts to industrialize. Nevertheless, at this stage in their development efforts, African nations confront as their primary challenge the necessity of introducing innovative policies and institutions capable of surmounting the overwhelming economic and ecological problems that threaten the already substandard conditions of life of Africa's still-rural majority. For this reason, this Chapter primarily focuses on assessing the consequences of current African responses to this challenge.[3]

II. Responses to Africa's ecological crisis

In the post-colonial era, both national and international institutions operating on the macro-level, and local communities responded to the complex interrelated threats to Africa's rural environment. This section reviews those responses, concluding that involving local communities in devising strategies in the context of their own resources and constraints, appears more successful in achieving ecologically sustainable development.

A. Macro-level programs:

Initial post-independence optimism and growth oriented policies led to a number of economic problems. The industrial sectors experienced over-investment, while agricultural production was maintained by heavy subsidies. Excessive government investment fostered monopolies and unnecessary protection. Although in some countries some of these policies helped promote local industrial growth and the expansion of smallholder farms, they too frequently led to the choice of inefficient productive units and major distortions in the economy.

Recently, mostly under structural adjustment programs promoted by the World Bank and the International Monetary Fund (IMF), more African governments have introduced policies aimed at restructuring their economies. Aimed primarily to improve balance of payments and ease the burden of debt, these typically introduced short term measures dealing with immediate problems such as budgetary allocation, improving foreign reserves and debt servicing.

Sustainable development, on the other hand, requires long-term planning and involves variables difficult to quantify. Conventional notions relating to allocative efficiency prove inadequate for dealing with long-term environmental questions. To supplement this short-term orientation, governments need to emphasize long-term conservation, environmental education and technical training related to ways to solve interrelated ecological and economic problems.

Preliminary research[4] indicates that the new 'conventional wisdom' of structural adjustment may actually accelerate African ecological deterioration. On the one hand, increased attention to market prices by-passes the rural and urban poor who participate only marginally in market-oriented production. Impoverished people constitute a high proportion of the population in countries with per capita incomes below US$180, like Ethiopia, Somalia, Zaire, Chad, Tanzania, Mozambique and Malawi. Yet focus on privatization of production most often brings rewards to those who already have access to productive resources and disadvantages those who do not. Furthermore, market-driven pricing does little to bring resources or official attention to marginal ecological systems or the marginalized people who live in them. Because much of the decline in resources and degradation of the environment takes place in these marginal zones which spread across upwards of three fourths of the African continent, such macro-level programs may endanger further deterioration of soil, water and tree cover, causing still further declines in productivity.

Some individual fiscal and monetary features of IMF and World Bank programs have had further unintended negative implications for the environment. By worsening income disparities, elimination of some subsidies have forced poorer members of society to pursue survival strategies, like chopping down trees for low cost fuel and construction purposes, that aggravate ecological degradation. Financial management policies aimed at government budgets deficits have reduced essential funds leaving numerous conservation programs, planned in the mid-1980s, unimplemented. Lack of funds has also hindered local authorities, previously acting on behalf of central governments, from undertaking conservation projects.

An emphasis on short term profit-maximization has led directly to neglect of environmental consequences. For example, prices of farm produce often have excluded the costs of soil erosion, soil acidification, pesticide pollution, and other environmental damage. The pricing of amenities, like those associated with tourism, have frequently failed to reflect environmental costs. Tourism, for example, not only depends on nature for its existence, but also may utilize the natural environment as a sink for its wastes; yet programs to encourage tourism do not even reach the majority of African peoples, far less take into consideration the industry's potential damage to their environment.

Although in many countries resource constraints have limited programs adopted to those endorsed by the World Bank and the International Monetary Fund (IMF), numerous national and even international institutions have proposed socioeconomic experiments in an effort to improve the environment. In 1981, the United Nations introduced its Substantial New Programme of Action (SNPA) for the least developed countries. Over the next decade, as the continent's economic situation worsened, the numbers of countries eligible rose from twenty-one to twenty-eight. In 1985, under the auspices of the Organization of African Unity (OAU), African countries adopted Africa's Priority Programme for Economic Recovery, 1986-1990 (APPER).

Nevertheless, although in most African countries the threats to sustainable development lay deeply rooted in long-term interrelated economic and ecological factors, most of these programs, too, dealt primarily with short-term symptoms. Essentially all of them revolved around efficient macro-economic management, resource mobilization, enlargement of financial assistance, commodity stabilization and the alleviation of the external debt burden.   Even the UN Economic Commission for Africa (ECA) recommended similar measures although, drawing on the Lagos Plan of Action, it incorporated additional dimensions, involving a more comprehensive set of policies directed towards internal as well as external transformation.

These programs did emphasize the need to strengthen the internal economic demand of African countries.   This entailed "substantial expansion of capabilities at the national, sub-regional and regional levels for identification, evaluation, extraction and management of natural resources and raw materials for processing to meet domestic needs" (UNDP, : 4).   In general, however, most of these macro-level programs tended to neglect the danger of planning economic expansion without major changes in the handling of issues related to the environment.

Neither the World Bank nor the Lagos Plan of Action devoted much attention to policies and institutions required to meet the continent's environmental challenge.   While the World Bank recognized the issue's importance, its experts seldom considered its implications in terms of alternative conceptual formulations. The Lagos Plan[5] and other ECA policy documents still apparently viewed environment as a sectoral issue.[6] Too often, national and international experts blame Africa's environmental crisis solely on persistent droughts, the unfavorable international economic climate and increased external debt (and its related costs).[7]   They tend to neglect the increasing evidence that environmental degradation would, more likely, thwart efforts to attain long-term sustainable development. Too often, they fail to recognize that overcoming the causes of environmental hazards must constitute a central focus of the process of economic production itself.

In particular, experts concerned with economic development tended to ignore the essential link between environment and technology. In contrast, claiming technology constituted a major source of environmental degradation, some environmentalists urged a reduction in the pace of technological advance. Others equally concerned with conservation criticize that view as mistaken on two grounds. First, environmental degradation in Africa largely reflects constraints on development options imposed by technological limitations of existing production systems. Increasing productivity requires changing the technological base. The solution, they held, lies not in halting technological change, but in deciding which technologies will most suitably serve Africa's needs. Secondly, solution of Africa's most persistent environmental problems also necessitates changes in the continent's technological base. New biotechnologies, for example, might accelerate reforestation to provide local inhabitants with low-cost fuel while protecting steep hillsides against erosion.

In short, despite a growing awareness of environmental dangers, most national and international approaches to economic development too frequently incorporate measures that not only prove inadequate to attain ecologically sustainable development, but even threaten to undermine it still further.

B. Local level community models

Given findings that the earlier development style of centrally or externally planned and managed projects could not attain sustainability, the search for alternatives has become more important. Over the last decade, especially in the Sahel and other semi-arid and marginal environments, a number of groups have been developing models for local level sustainable development. In Kenya, the National Environment Secretariat within the Ministry of Environment and Natural Resources, Clark University, Egerton University and the World Resources Institute have launched a collaborative research effort into the nature of the environmental crisis as it has affected production, and what the Kenyan government and non-governmental agencies (NGOs) could do about it.[8] That research underscores the findings, outlined above, that large, multifaceted and interrelated factors have caused Africa's ecological crisis. No single, simple solution exists. At the same time, however, the research has identified several entry points that appear to offer promise. Given additional investigators, field testing, revisions and adaptations, these may prove helpful in returning productivity to at least some of Africa's degraded areas.

In Kenya, over three years of field experimentation, a strategy began to emerge that started with rural communities rather than with macro-scale institutions. It places the burden of analysis, planning and implementation with local institutions rather than external or national agents. It identifies local leadership and rural organizations as the most effective units to undertake rehabilitation of Africa's degrading ecosystem and to launch truly sustainable development.

The methodology that has evolved thus far in Kenya resembles local and participatory planning tools employed by a number of agencies and organizations in Africa and elsewhere. A brief description may help to suggest how and why it has worked effectively in communities where it has been tested.

Known as Participatory Rural Appraisal (PRA), the Kenya approach builds on the premise that individual rural communities reside in discrete ecosystems or micro-zones—rainfall, soils, elevation, vegetation, etc.—and require particular and unique combinations of farm, health, soil, water and woodland/grassland management. As a result, popular participation introduces a fundamental ingredient in project planning, helping to devise locally maintained institutions and technologies, as well as sustainable economic, political and ecological inputs, more likely to achieve a reversal in Africa's decline.

The Participatory Rural Appraisal approach recognizes that, although community residents have a good working knowledge of ecological and development needs, they do not necessarily have the means to systematize this information or mobilize the community to take action. It brings multi-sector teams together with village members to assess village needs and priorities and then create village resource management plans. The plan becomes the basis for action in the rural community and enables local institutions, government units and NGOs to cooperate. PRA draws upon knowledge and skills already in the village; it creates a setting in which local residents exchange information with one another and the local technical officers. It provides a structure for the expression and implementation of local aspirations and goals. It facilitates a ranked listing of village project activities that funding agencies can support. In sum, it sets in place a plan that village members and institutions can implement and sustain (Thomas-Slayter, 1989).

The research team that carried out the pilot Participatory Rural Appraisals consisted of a social scientist with extensive agricultural experience, who served as team leader, a biologist, another social scientist, and specialists in health, nutrition and environmental information. The team worked closely with extension officers who provided technical assistance, particularly relating to water resources. The team also drew heavily on the energy and assistance of local members, including formal leaders such as Assistant Chiefs, and informal leaders such as heads of women's groups.

The Participatory Rural Appraisal model involves eight clearly defined steps, though the procedures may vary greatly, depending on local needs and preferences of the team members. These steps, which all require extensive community participation, include:

1. Site selection, and clearance of the proposed appraisal with the assistance of local administrative officials;
2. A preliminary site visit to meet the village leaders and members and formulate an initial identification of environmental problems;
3. Collection of data relating to four aspects of the community's environmental problems: a) spatial; b) time-related; c) social; (d) technical;
4. Synthesis and analysis of data;
5. Setting the problems in priority order and exploring opportunities for resolving them;
6. Ranking the opportunities by priority and feasibility and formulating them into a Village Resource Management Plan (VRMP);
7. Community adoption of the proposed plan;
8. Implementation of the plan, including monitoring the results, by local institutions.

In summary, the Participatory Rural Appraisal methodology functions effectively by engaging the rural community itself. It serves to <u>mobilize community institutions</u> around issues of sustainable development by raising awareness of what can be accomplished as well as how local groups can do it. It <u>systematizes rural participation</u> by helping local communities to define their own problems and identify potential solutions to them. It enables villagers to <u>rank solutions</u>, based on local priorities, feasibility, ecological sustainability, and cost effectiveness. It <u>sets out priorities</u> in a community-based plan for resource management. It offers <u>prompt turn-around</u>, requiring an average of only six days field work and three days to organize priorities. It is <u>cost effective</u> because it uses technical officers who are already assigned to the field site.

To date, in the participating communities, this approach has accomplished increased local food production and sustainability as well as reduced soil loss, water decline and deforestation. Given the encouraging local level responses, a broadly based effort is underway to disseminate the findings and methods of these rural appraisals to training institutions, policy groups, and implementing agencies throughout Kenya and in a growing number of other African nations.

Equally promising approaches have appeared in other parts of Africa. These community projects would benefit from a systematic participatory assessment which, as an important first step in tackling Africa's rural environmental degradation, could identify local communities' potential role in contributing to resolving Africa's rural environmental problems.

III. Proposed research

Producing for sustainability requires substantially more information than is presently available. In the first stage, scarce research resources should focus on assessing the advantages and limitations of four different themes relating to policy-formulation and implementation: (1) self-reliant community efforts; (2) community efforts developed through external intervention; (3) local participation in regional resource management; and (4) policies of government and donor agencies.

In respect of each of these themes the researchers should first conduct a thorough literature search.[9] Then participatory research teams should explore each theme in terms of specific issues such as relevant institutional characteristics, leadership, technology, outside help (if any), economic incentives, the role of political entities, cost benefit formulae, gender characteristics, land tenure patterns and marketing systems. In the process, teams should seek to identify in detail the elements that have contributed to the effectiveness of actions directed to attaining ecologically sustainable development.

In the process, participatory research teams should seek to improve methods of tracking the progress of different kinds of community strategies. Where possible, these should incorporate comparable quantitative data sets. Careful descriptive write-ups of the negative as well as positive features of the models studied will help generate important insights into which methods work in specified sets of circumstances, and which do not.

Environmental research must take into account the range of problems communities encounter in their efforts to formulate and implement local level ecologically-sound development strategies. These should be specified in some detail, accompanied by the community members' own concrete suggestions for making their efforts more effective. If, for example, a need exists for improved community mobilization or strengthened leadership, how do local community members suggest this might happen? What do leaders in the region suggest that might help? If additional resources were made available, in what form would they prove most useful? If the effort requires changed infrastructure, what kinds and why? What would community members, themselves, be willing to do to make these changes possible?

In the same way, the research should discover what regional NGOs and administrative/extension officers have to say about community needs. Do they view community participation as an important contribution or simply a waste of time? To what extent have local and regional officers been involved in the planning and implementation processes? Does the issue of majority vs. minority affect the community's efforts to improve its resource management? Have social class conflicts been at issue?

This kind of participatory evaluation, centering on the causes of difficulties encountered, as well as accomplishments, will serve to engage the community in a systematic analysis that in itself, will strengthen their capacity for self-reliance. At the same time, building up a comparable data base and writing up the findings will provide a powerful tool for deepening the insights gained at seminars devoted to policy issues; making recommendations to local and national governments; and devising improved regional and national policies.

In more detail, the proposed participatory evaluation will consider the following kinds of information relating to each of the four parallel research themes:

1. Self-reliant communities: The research team will seek better knowledge of local systems and community institutions already in place and functioning in terms of their traditional resource use, institutions and land management practices. The research will aim at understanding what elements have made sustained resource use possible and how the communities have preserved them over the years.

2. Communities developed via external intervention: The research team will seek to understand how some communities have achieved sustainable production by incorporating new ideas, institutions, and technologies or systems into their community management systems. To what extent has local participation assisted in importing these new elements? What institutions have most successfully fostered acceptance of the new ideas (government extension agencies, NGOs, private agencies, commercial organizations, church groups, locally-generated participation, or others, like Kenya's PRA)?

3. Local participation in regional resource management: Individual communities, acting in isolation from each other, will find they cannot maintain sustainable production over extended periods of time. Groups require support, assistance, guidance, and inspiration from institutions beyond their

borders.   Regional economic, infrastructural, employment, marketing, and services issues require analysis. Most African nations already have or are developing regional plans for delivery of health, education, transport, extension and other services. Yet too often they develop these in isolation from the people whom they aim to serve. The research teams will evaluate means whereby the sustainability achieved by participation can be multiplied and incorporated into participatory regional plans. These include new methods, already utilized in some areas, like regional information systems based on spatial integration of technical and socioeconomic data; regional collectives of NGOs and governments; regional associations of extension officers designed to integrate sectoral efforts and stimulate local participation; and popularly-based committees of farmers and resource users, like those emerging in parts of the Sahel. The research teams should help to take inventory, categorize, describe and analyze these approaches in order to suggest ways they may contribute more effectively to regional ecologically sustainable development.

4.   Policies for government and donor agencies: While it seems premature at this early stage to consider what national policies and programs will look like, the research teams should seek to assist in their eventual formulation. For this, they will need to recognize the need for national backing, clearance, and information. They should keep people, both in the government and political positions, informed of the nature of the research and ways it might facilitate formulation of longer term national programs. In like manner, donor agencies of various types and at different levels may prove interested and helpful. On the one hand, some donor organizations themselves have accumulated information from which the research will benefit. At the same time, they also continually seek new insights into the causes of ecological degradation of the kind the research may provide. On the other hand, the research process will require financial resources that the donors may contribute. If the village appraisal program catches on, rural funds might make small blocks of money available to women's groups and other rural institutions to implement projects such a locally-based water, forestry, agricultural and soil control. Eventually, too, the research teams should publish their findings to make them available to the participants, to other researchers, and

more widely in the form of guidelines and manuals. Orientation seminars and training programs, as well as more permanent establishment of an on-going participatory evaluation program will help to extend the evaluation process to a number of widely differing communities. All these should contribute to an on-going deepening and extension of community-level, regional, national and even continent-wide efforts to link environmental improvements to macro-level programs for attaining sustainable development. All of these, too, will cost money. In short, while the immediate task of the research teams will be to engage in participatory evaluation of local and regional community efforts, these may both benefit from and contribute to national institutional support and policy will.

IV. Conclusion

Sustainable production in the context of sound ecological policies is not a hopeless cause. Elements already exist to help make it happen. A review of the current state of research suggests that macro-level programs for economic development too often focus on short-term objectives without attention to long-term implications for the environmental conservation essential to sustainability. On the other hand, technologies, local institutions, methodologies for community participation and mobilization, and development resources are essentially known and available. The first stage of research here proposed, by helping to enable rural communities to learn from present examples, can not, alone, surmount the obstacles blocking attainment of ecological sustainability. In conjunction with macro-level initiatives, however, they may provide a missing link that in the past has precluded donors, NGOs, and government agencies from reversing Africa's decline.

Endnotes

1. See United Nations Development Programme, Orientation and Areas of concentration. By the end of 1985, Africa's external debt was estimated at US $150 billion. Of this, 40 percent was owed by four North African countries. Sub-Saharan Africa owned US $90 billion. Low income countries owed $30 billion, equal to about 55 percent of their combined GDPs. For all of Africa, debt as a share of GDP reached about 35 percent.

2. Chapter 2, "Towards a new economic strategy for sustainable African development" explores in more detail the impact, the alternative explanations, and the range of possible solutions of the causes of Africa's economic crisis.

3. Chapter 5, "Africa: Health of the future, the future of health," discusses the impact of growing industrial and urban hazards for the health of urban dwellers, especially for women, children and youth. The Health Task Group proposes to focus its initial participatory research efforts to explore the causes interrelated economic and environmental factors causing these hazards to lay the basis for recommending improved policies and institutions in this area.

4. See Chapter 2, above, for details.

5. See the 1979 Lagos Plan of Action and the 1980 Final Act of Lagos.

6. In his address to the 1989 ASA Annual Meeting in Baltimore, Dr. Adebayo Adediji, head of the ECA, spelled out in great detail the dangers that threatened Africa's environment, calling for more direct efforts to address this important issue in the context of an overall strategy for transformation in Africa.

7. See UNDP, Orientation and Areas of Concentration.

8. The many publications and documents resulting from this research are available from Kenya's National Environment Secretariat, the International Development Program at Clark University and the World Resources Institute.

9. ASA members in the U.S. with access to materials and documents relating not only to Africa but other Third World regions (not available in Africa), could make an important contribution to this search.

Bibliography

Baum, W.C. and S.M. Tolbert (1985), *Investing in Development: Lessons from World Bank Experience*, Oxford University Press, New York.

Belshaw, B. (1980), "Taking Indigenous Knowledge Seriously: The Case of Intercropping Techniques in East Africa," in Brokensha D., Warren, D.M. and Werner, O., (eds.), *Indigenous Knowledge Systems and Development*, University Press of America, Washington, DC.

Blaikie, P. and H. Borrkfield (1987), *Land Degradation and Society*, Methuen, New York.

Brown, Janet Welsh (ed.), 1990. *In the U.S. Interest: Resources, Growth, and Security in the Developing World*, Boulder: Westview Press.

Brown, L. (1963), *The Development of Semi-arid Areas of Kenya*, Ministry of Agriculture, Nairobi.

Cernea, Michael M., 1988. *Nongovernmental Organizations and Local Development*, Washington D.C., World Bank.

_____, (ed.) 1985. *Putting People First: Sociological Variables in Rural Development*, New York: World Bank/Oxford University Press.

Chambers, Robert, 1983. *Rural Development: Putting the Last First*, London; New York: Longman.

_____, 1985. *Managing Rural Development: Ideas and Experience from East Africa*, West Hartford, CT: Kumarian Press.

_____, 1989. *Farmer First: Farmer Innovation and Agricultural Research*, London: Intermediate technology Publications.

_____, 1990. *To the Hands of the Poor: Water and Trees*, Boulder, Colorado: Westview Press.

Chambers, R. and M. Leach (1986), "Trees to Meet Contingencies: Savings and Security for the Rural Poor," *IDS Discussion Paper No. 228*, Institute of Development Studies, University of Sussex, UK.

Clark, N. and C. Juma (1987) *Long-Run Economics: An Evolutionary Approach to Economic Growth*, Pinter Publishers, London.

_____, 1991. *Biotechnology for Sustainable Development: Policy Options for Developing Countries*, Nairobi, Kenya: Acts Press, African Centre for Technology Studies.

Conway, Gordon R. and Edward B. Barbier, 1990. *After the Green Revolution: Sustainable Agriculture for Development*, London: Earthscan Publications, Ltd.

Hansen A. and D.E. McMillan (eds.), 1986. *Food in Sub-Saharan Africa*. Boulder Colorado: Lynne Rienner Publishers, Inc.

Hardin, G., 1968. "The Tragedy of the Commons," Science 162 (13 December): 1243-1248.

Hyden, G., 1983. *No Shortcuts to Progress: African Development Management in Perspective.* London: Heinemann.

Juma, C., 1987. *Long Run Economics: An Evolutionary Approach to Economic Growth,* London; New York: Printer Publishers.

_____, 1989a. *The Gene Hunters: Biotechnology and the Scramble for Seeds,* Princeton, NJ: Princeton University Press.

_____, 1989b. *Biological Diversity and Innovation: Conserving and Utilizing Genetic Resources in Kenya.* Nairobi: African Centre for Technology Studies.

Kabutha, C. and R. Ford, 1989. "Using Rapid Rural Appraisal to Formulate A Village Resource Management Plan: Interim Report." Mimeo, Nairobi, Kenya: Notes on RRA and a Meeting (4 August 1988) of The National Environment Secretariat (NES), Mbusyani Women's Groups and Division Technical Officers.

Kituyi, M. 1990. *Becoming Kenyans: Socio-Economic Transformation of the Pastoral Masai.* Nairobi: Acts Press.

Korten, David C. 1980. "Community Organization and Rural Development Learning Process Approach," *Public Administration Review,* Sept-Oct., pp. 480-510.

Korten, David C. and Felipe B. Alfonso (eds.), 1983. *Bureaucracy and the Poor: Closing the Gap,* West Hartford, CT: Kumarian Press.

Korten, David C. and Rudi Klauss (eds.), 1984. *People-Centered Development: Contributions Toward Theory and Planning Frameworks,* West Hartford, CT: Kumarian Press.

Korten, David C., 1990. *Getting to the Twenty-First Century: Voluntary Action and the Global Agenda,* West Hartford, CT: Kumarian Press.

Leonard, D.K., 1977. *Reaching the Peasant Farmer: Organization Theory and Practice in Kenya,* Chicago, IL: University of Chicago Press.

Leonard, D.K, and D.R. Marshall, (eds.) 1982. *Institutions of Rural Development for the Poor: Decentralization and Organizational Linkages,* Berkeley, CA.: Institute of International Studies, University of California Berkeley.

Mountjoy, Alan B. and David Hilling, 1988. *Africa, Geography, and Development*, London: Hutchinson; Totowa, NJ: Barnes and Noble.

Okoth-Ogendo, H.W.O., 1991. *Tenants of the Crown: Evolution of Agrarian Law and Institutions in Kenya*, Nairobi, Kenya: Acts Press, African Centre for Technology Studies.

Pala, A., 1974. "The Role of Women in Rural Development: Research Priorities," Discussion Paper No. 203, Nairobi, Kenya: Institute for Development Studies, University of Nairobi.

Paul, Samuel, 1987. *Community Participation in Development Projects: The World Bank Experience*, Washington, D.C., World Bank.

Richards, P., 1980. "Community Environmental Knowledge in African Rural Development", in Brokensha, D., Warren, D.M. and Werner, O. (eds.) *Indigenous Knowledge Systems and Development*, Washington, DC: University Press of America.

Richards, P., 1983. "Ecological Change and the Politics of African Land Use", *African Studies Review* 26(2): 1-72.

Shaikh, Asif, et al (eds.), 1988. *Opportunities for Sustained Development: Successful Natural Resources Management in the Sahel*, Volume I/Main Report, Washington, D.C., USAID, Office of Technical Resources and Sahel Office, Bureau for Africa.

Thomas-Slayter Barbara P. "Implementing Effective Local Management of Natural Resources: How Much Can NGOs Accomplish?" Paper presented at the African Studies Association meeting, Atlanta, November, 1989.

Timberlake, Lloyd, 1986. *Africa in Crisis: The Causes, the Cures of Environmental Bankruptcy*, edited by Jon Tinker, Philadelphia: New Society Publishers.

_____, 1987. *Only One Earth: Living for the Future*, London: BBC Books; Earthscan.

UNCA

UNDP

Uphoff, Norman, 1986. *Improving International Irrigation Management with Farmer Participation: Getting the Process Right*, Boulder: Westview Press.

World Bank, 1989. *Sub-Saharan Africa: From Crisis to Sustainable Growth*, Washington, D.C.: World Bank.

World Commission on Environment and Development, 1987. *Our Common Future*, Oxford; New York: Oxford University Press.

Chapter 7

Gender Relations and Development: Political Economy and Culture

By Brooke Grundfest Schoepf[1]

I. Introduction

The study of gender relations is the study of interrelated, significant, persistent inequalities. Interacting with inequalities between nations in the global economy, with inequalities of national 'racial,' class and ethnic hierarchies, gender inequalities permeate contemporary societies at all levels (WIN, 1985; Ramphele, 1989; Antrobus, 1990; Tinker, 1990). Throughout the world, women have borne the brunt of the economic crisis (Cornia et al, 1987; Joekes, 1987; Sen and Grown, 1987).

A. A gendered perspective

This chapter reviews issues of African development from a gendered perspective. It explores other subject areas of the Task Force, asking how institutions structure the social roles, responsibilities and identities of women and how they are affected by relations between women and men. It considers the following issues:

•What is generally agreed upon with respect to gender inequality in the development process—about the causes, consequences and ways to move forward?

•What debates remain to be resolved and what types of research are needed to advance toward their resolutions?

•What types of collaborative, participatory strategies would be useful in capacity-building research?

The subject of women and development, barely two decades old, already has given rise to an astonishingly rich literature (See Staudt, 1988; Wipper, 1988; Stichter and Parpart, 1988; Stamp, 1989; Johnson-Odim and Strobel, 1990). Several shifts evident in the WID discourse indicate the distance travelled. The subject was never an exclusively, nor even a predominantly Western preoccupation. African women engaged in anti-colonial struggles and following independence, articulated their concerns in pan-African and regional associations, as in scholarly work. Few doubted that they were "fighting two colonialisms."[2] Critique of 'developmentalist' assumptions by Third World women scholars has been crucial in orienting the field (See Wellesley Editorial Committee, 1977; Okeyo, 1980; Seidman, 1981; AAWORD, 1982; Sen and Grown, 1985; Steady, 1987). African women formed associations which reshaped discourse and practices; several developed new forms of participatory research.[3] Their insistence upon understanding the international and structural dimensions of women's inequality impelled many western women to rethink the approach based on adding women to development.[4]

Much recent work by African and Africanist scholars illuminates the complexity of women's subordination. Rather than neglecting theory or using it as a rigid mold, detailed case studies provide data that "...are used to elaborate and comment on theory—to make theory comprehensible, part of daily life and scholarship, not disembodied truths in which women's experiences float"(White, 1988:361, original italics). The need for grounded theory is widely acknowledged in development studies. Since researchers' perspectives frame their methodological choices, research is not neutral, and data are not 'just facts.' Rather, social facts contain within them interpretations arising from the social positionings of the researchers, who are social actors in their own right.[5] Research on gender is informed by the understanding of knowledge as power and the ability of those in power to create and define knowledge (Ifeka in Rohrlich-Leavitt, 1975: 559-566; Sutton et al, in ibid: 580-600 Stamp, 1989). This understanding was culturally shared in many hierarchically organized precolonial societies. African gnosis also has been shaped in the context of relations between Africa and the West (Houtondji, 1983; Mudimbe, 1988).[6] The need to listen to voices from 'within' and 'below' has been theorized, and interest in personal documents renewed as a source of information on relationships of structure and agency (Shostak, 1983; Kariuki, 1985; Geiger, 1986; Marks, 1987; Romero, 1988; Hay, 1988; Davison, 1989; Mbilinyi, 1989; Mizra and Strobel, 1989; D.E.H. Russell, 1989).

There is another perspective which views empirical data as neutral collections of facts. However, the methodological icons conventionally recognized as science, for example graphs, tables and statistical manipulations, do not insulate empirical data from social context, including the conditions of their production. For example, women's labor and produce have been ignored in agricultural production and other economic statistics (Beneria, 1981; Guyer, 1981, 1988). This is in part a consequence of the notion that the domestic sphere in which women operate is separated from the public sphere; that women's labor merely reproduces the family and that social reproduction can be subsumed in that of the household. Such notions trivialize women's roles and responsibilities (Schoepf and Mariotti, in Rohrilich-Leavitt, 1975; 389-419; Beneria and Sen, 1986).

B. Plan of this chapter

This chapter reviews several major collections and articles published in the past 20 years on women in Africa to see what new light has been cast on old issues and what new problems have been identified. It starts with the gender-and-households debate, and goes on to summarize an historical perspective. The rest of the chapter discusses the main issues affecting gender relations in Africa today. Agricultural development is central; the majority of sub-Saharan women continue to cultivate, process, transport and market crops. Since cities are places of refuge and opportunity for many rural women, the chapter then examines urban survival strategies, including AIDS prevention, a health-and-gender issue that cross-cuts urban-rural and class divisions. The newer area of gender, class and state formation links these themes. The last section presents an example of a participatory action-research method. The conclusions and recommendations are based on discussion by participants in 1990 Task Force workshops.

C. Gender and Households

The initial designation of the working group on women as 'Gender and Households' was broadened to reflect understandings widely shared during the 1980s. First, the epistemological status of the household as a category is problematic. Households—however they are defined—are not 'natural units' (Guyer, 1981, 1988). Although they are often conceived as such by neoclassical microeconomists, households, like genders, are socially produced and culturally constructed; their structures, and the interrelationships of their members result from wider socio-cultural forces. They are endowed with meanings both by the wider institutions and by the individuals whose negotiated interaction shapes their everyday life (Guyer and Peters, 1987). Because households are socially constituted, their composition, attributes and functions have changed over time.

Second, the assumption that gender relations within households are governed by 'altruism,' or that resources are pooled and shared for the common good of all members is invalid for many societies throughout the world; in Africa men and women generally keep separate accounts (Hay, 1976; Safilios-Rothschild, 1980; Guyer, 1981; Muntemba in Bay, 1982: 72-l04; Bruce and Dwyer, 1988). Therefore, instead of taking the household as a unit of analysis, we treat it as a point of departure, asking how membership in a particular type of household affects people's access to resources, their obligations to others, their understanding of their options and their ability to negotiate their roles and positions (Berry, 1984; Moock, 1986).

Third, focus on the household may obscure women's contributions to culture-building. Most African women are active in the wider world beyond the household (Okonjo in Rohrlich-Leavitt, 1975: 31-40; Sudarkasa, 1976; Sacks, 1979; Afonja in Robertson and Berger, 1980). They produce food and other crops for sale as well as for family consumption; and engage in wage work, petty commodity production, trade and other informal sector occupations. Women are also important social actors in kin groups, religious organizations and voluntary associations. Their ability to give gifts is a form of social support that enhances the quality of community life (Guyer, 1981; Cloud, 1986). Women's positions in the wider society may be even more important in determining their life chances than the fact of being a sister, mother, daughter, wife, mother-in-law or grandmother. For example, the relationship of small peasant producers to the state is crucial in the lives of most villagers, women and men. The same is true with respect to employment and trade. However, in state-society relations, too, 'gender makes a difference' (Muntemba in Bay, 1982: 72-l04; Afshar, 1987; Parpart, 1988; Staudt, 1988; Parpart and Staudt, 1989; Obbo in Tinker, 1990: 2l0-222).

For historic reasons that have only partly to do with their subordinate status within families today, women have generally been affected differently than men by economic and social change (Boserup, 1970; Wipper, 1972; Mullings in Hafkin and Bay, 1976; Mullings, 1976; Etienne and Leacock, 1980; Obbo, 1980; Hay and Stichter, 1984; Davison, 1988; Staudt, 1988; Johnson-Odim and Strobel, 1990). At the same time, the character of women's social participation, including their work, is indelibly stamped by their status within households (Paulme, 1963; Wipper, 1975; Bay, 1982; Moock, 1986; Stichter and Parpart, 1988, 1990; Wipper and Lyons, 1988). This set of understandings is now fairly well agreed-upon in the field.

II. Interpreting the Past[7]

Historians and anthropologists have explored both the underlying patterns and the tremendous diversity of women's experience in African societies. There is increasing agreement with respect to the variability and mutability of gender roles, social relations and ideologies that have determined the status of women historically and today. That diversity is testimony to the resilience of cultures and the power of human inventiveness. Notions of seamless patriarchy in which elder men everywhere controlled the labor of juniors and women, of timeless, un-changing "tradition," have succumbed to new research. Studies reveal both complementary and oppressive domestic relations and the agency of women as historical subjects in families, communities and states. Nevertheless, divergent interpretations persist.

It has been difficult to penetrate colonial constructions which portrayed women as powerless, dependent minors, relegated to strictly domestic roles. Nevertheless, if the notion of African women as passive victims of fate (of men, or of patriarchal states) has been cast aside, so has the notion that by their own efforts, as individuals and collectivities, women can surmount all manner of adversity. Women's circumstances have varied with their age, condition and class: royals, priestesses, warriors and traders; free cultivators and slaves; respected elders and young, unmarried women; sisters and wives. Whatever their class, women's opportunities have varied with the state of their societies: expanding prosperity; conquest and disruption; stagnation and poverty. Women make history under conditions that often escape their control.

In the 1980s new attention was brought to relationships between women, men and the state (Hay and Wright, 1982; Afshar, 1987; Parpart and Staudt, 1989). Colonial rule instituted new structures of oppression which in many areas reinforced indigenous forms of male dominance. Nevertheless, in some cases, women were able to use new opportunities in production and trade to advance their interests (Bujra, 1975; Stichter and Parpart, 1988). In other areas women chiefs were removed and the social, religious and economic supports of women's former autonomy and power eroded (Leboeuf, 1963; Van Allen, 1972; Rousseau in Rohrlich-Leavitt, 1975: 41-52; Okonjo in Hafkin and Bay, 1976: 31-40; Awe, 1977; Conti, 1979; Afonja, 1980; Poewe, 1981; Arhin, 1983; Mandala, 1984, 1990; Schoepf 1987).

Colonialism brought new, often brutal, ways to control labor and extract 'surplus' produce.   Specific colonial and post-colonial institutions have had different impacts upon women and men variously situated in their societies (Robertson and Berger, 1986; Berger and White, 1990). These include new economic institutions, courts and the law, agricultural bureaucracies, health services, churches, community development agencies, credit organizations, and so on. For the vast majority, the result was loss of status, both as members of dominated communities and as members of the second sex.

Although Boserup (1970) characterized African hoe cultivation as 'female farming systems,' the gender division of labor varied greatly in precolonial societies. However, it suited colonial rulers to assert that removing men from food production made no difference. Taxation forced men to seek wage employment far from home or to engage in export crop production. Women remained tied to social and biological reproduction; their increased labor subsidized the accumulation of capital by firms that paid men wages below the cost of their daily reproduction (Boserup, 1970; White, 1990).

Periods of crisis in colonial economies triggered efforts by states and male elders to control women's labor. Local courts codified (and sometimes invented) custom, making divorce difficult, taxing independent women and legislating sexual morality (Okeyo, 1980; Ault, 1983; Chanock, 1985, and in Hay and Wright, 1982: 53-67; Parpart, 1986). Commoditization of bridewealth fostered a view of women as instruments of production. At the same time, elder women in matrilineal communities lost access to male labor as sons-in-law took to sending money (which wound up in the control of their husbands or brothers) instead of performing bride-service (Wright, 1983; Schoepf, 1987). Patterns of fertility were affected as birth intervals were shortened; labor burdens increased; and new diseases introduced and spread (Retel-Laurentin, 1974; Molnos, 1973 and Oppong, 1983, 1987; Turshen, 1991). Often the result was to increase women's disguised contributions to capital accumulation by settlers and transnational firms, local elites and traders (Savanne in Mook, 1986: 124-132).

In regions of European plantations and settlement, large territories were expropriated. Africans experienced growing scarcity of fertile land and restricted market access. Where land became a private resource held mainly by men, women family members could no longer count on use rights. Commodity production gave rise to new forms of inequality, as class differences emerged and domestic communities that formerly had protected women's access to resources no longer functioned (Pala, 1976; Bukh, 1979; Etienne and Leacock, 1980; Bryceson and Mbilinyi, 1980; Agbessi-Dos Santos in Michel et al, 1981: 93-116; Muntemba in Bay, 1982: 72-104; Oppong, 1983; Chanock in Hay and Wright, 1982: 53-67; Wright, 1983; Nasimiyu, 1985; Geffray, 1989; Mikell, 1989). Where cash cropping increased the value of women's labor, high bridewealth was used to justify elder males' control of women's work and produce (Kitching, 1980). In areas of heavy male labor migration, during periods of crisis, lack of labor, new cropping patterns, and tax obligations could undermine women's ability to meet family subsistence needs even where land was not an issue (Poewe, 1989; Schoepf, 1987; Mandala, 1990). Many forms of inequality ascribed to 'tradition' actually arose from colonization (Afonja, 1980; Wilson, 1982).

The colonially instituted 'double patriarchy' of state and elder males was not simply accepted by women.[8] In Nigeria, some two million women joined the Igbo Women's Wars in a general protest against taxation of women (Okonjo, 1975; Van Allen in Hafkin and Bay, 1976: 58-86). Other anti-colonial revolts were spearheaded by women (Isaacman, 1990). Women have taken part in everyday resistance, sometimes acting individually in an attempt to influence men's decision-making and sometimes collectively to improve their position in relation to markets, states and husbands. Since open resistance could be dangerous, peasant women's individual strategies also included accommodation and silent struggles (Mandala, 1990). Across the continent, women in groups applied collective sanctions to men who abused their wives (Van Allen, 1972; Wipper, 1988). Women's daily activities—even cooking—could be transformed into symbols of resistance to colonialism (Okonjo in Rohrlich-Leavitt, 1975: 31-40).

Emergent class systems of the post-independence period brought new opportunities for some women but increasing disadvantage for the majority. New studies confirm that poor women bear the brunt of the prolonged economic crisis (Mikell, 1984; Pittin, 1989; Bujra, 1990, and in Robertson and Berger, 1986: 117-140; World Bank, 1989; Gladwin, 1991). Some scholars view women as 'more vulnerable' to the effects of crisis, almost as a natural given. This points to the need to deconstruct the category 'women' and the notion of 'vulnerability'. Since all women are not equally vulnerable, we examine structures and policies that increasingly disadvantage poor women and ask: Who benefits from their disadvantage?

III. The main issues

A. Gender issues in agriculture

New studies continue to document African women's extensive contributions to agriculture. Producing an estimated 60 to 80 percent of crops, they are also the primary processors and marketers of food supplies consumed within Africa (Kongstad and Monsted, 1980; Okeyo, 1985; Trager 1985; WIN, 1985; Moock, 1986; Guyer, 1987). Today, women's lack of land for food production is of increasing concern (contributors to Davison, 1988). The equity issue is embedded in that of efficiency (Lewis, 1981; Cloud and Knowles in Davison, 1988). Food crops are often produced and processed by women as cash crops (Newbury and Schoepf in Parpart and Staudt, 1989). If women producers lack resources, then food supplies cannot keep pace with expanding population.

The notion persists from colonial agricultural officials' practice and discourse to the effect that women are 'conservative traditionalists,' refractory to change. In some areas women have indeed resisted changes that they perceived would increase their labor while depriving them of control of their produce or lessening family food security (Dey, 1981; Schoepf, 1987; Jones in Moock, 1986: 105-123; Staudt, 1987). They also have been quick to take advantage of new opportunities where they could, adopting new crops, storage techniques, processing mills, and so on (Hay in Hafkin and Bay, 1976; Guyer, 1981). Across the continent rural and urban women producers express their need for labor-saving, yield-enhancing technologies in fields and households. Yet, given the demonstrated effects of new technologies on the social relations of production, it is crucial to ensure that, when innovations are introduced, women are able to keep or gain control over resources: land, labor, produce and cash.

Even where they are acknowledged as household heads, women's land and labor resources may be too low to meet the input requirements of the technological 'packages' designed on agricultural stations. These are seldom either scale- or gender-neutral. Some schemes continue to ignore women because they define men as the farmers, and assume that male 'household heads' will mobilize the labor of their wives and daughters (Schoepf, 1987). At the same time, planners have sought for decades to increase the labor provided by 'lazy' peasant men. These considerations suggest the need to be on the look-out for ideological elements underlying development projects that continue to work to women's disadvantage (Rogers, 1980; Lewis, 1981; Amadiume, 1987; Newbury and Schoepf 1989; Stamp, 1989; Hunt, 1990).

B. Gender and technology transfer [9]

Increasing agricultural production to provide food, industrial and export crops is an urgent need across the continent. Since extending present cultivation practices to new land areas is neither ecologically sound nor economically efficient, new productive technologies are essential. However, like the research process, technology transfer incorporates social relations. Consequently, agricultural development projects generally have beneficial effects for some and not for others. Women may be doubly disadvantaged by loosing control of both land

and labor even as their work increases (Cloud and Knowlesin Davison, 1988: 250-264; Roberts in Stichter and Parpart, 1988: 97-114). Economic analysis can use gender as an indicator and still neglect crucial issues that determine the effects of development projects on women.

A case study serves to illustrate the consequences of adopting different methodologies for project evaluation. A recent report evaluates six agricultural development projects to discover if the change from 'semi-subsistence' cultivation with few purchased inputs to more technology-dependent, market-oriented farming systems had brought corresponding benefits to producers (von Braun, et al 1989). The report makes no reference to earlier literature assessing these and similar projects.[10] It evaluates benefits in terms of reported aggregate family income, land and labor productivity, total calories available and the nutritional status of household members. It found incomes of participating households had risen significantly, except in the Kenya project, where expropriated cultivators had less land than before and 13 percent were made landless. Land productivity at least doubled; labor productivity also was higher everywhere but in Rwanda, described as a 'labor surplus' area.[11]

Total family food consumption was used as a 'proxy' for welfare; in all projects it rose slightly. More calories were available and some families with larger land holdings shifted their purchases to meat and more prestigious calorie sources. Most people, and especially young children, did not get enough food to meet their full energy needs. Since undernourishment in children under three years remained high in most schemes, and no changes in women's health status were discernable, it may be that men were the primary consumers of the more prestigious foods.

Supplies of other nutrients are not assessed. The report fails to mention whether the projects left women with adequate land or labor-time to cultivate gardens that provide essential dietary ingredients. Nor is there mention of food preparation, digestibility or length of time between preparation and consumption—factors found to be relevant to nutrient availability and bacterial loads in earlier studies made near the project sites in The Gambia (Barrell and Rowland, 1979). In some projects—mainly in wealthier families—women's agricultural labor inputs declined. Since domestic labor-time is not reported, we do not know whether these women spent more hours processing crops or cooking for hired laborers.

In the Gambia rice project, the development scheme expropriated land that women had used for crop production. "Individual women farmers lost rice land previously cultivated on their own account, when it became redefined as communal for the compound as a whole"(von Braun et al, 1989:84). Although this project was supposed to have overcome past failures, reduction in women's resource control resulting from the project is not defined as an issue.

The report does not refer to earlier project evaluations that showed complex interrelations between women's resource access, autonomy and labor mobilization (Dey, 1981; Carney in Davison, 1988: 59-78). Yet failure of earlier irrigation schemes was due "...as much to social as to technological factors"(Carney in Davison, 1988:73). Redefinition of the women's plots as 'communal' holdings had enabled compound heads to increase their claims on dependents' labor (Carney and Watts, 1990). Senior men centralized rice production, storage, sales and the economic benefits therefrom under their control, in the process greatly increasing their power and accumulation possibilities. Although married women did not immediately become more impoverished by this new dependency, there are legitimate concerns in need of investigation (Moock, 1986; Stamp, 1989). Without this, the project's technological potential "...may well become irrelevant"(Carney in Davison, 1988:73). Predictably, when women could no longer control their produce, they withdrew their labor (Carney and Watts, 1990).

Survey methods can discover these relations—so long as investigators are looking for them. Listening to women's voices helps. For example, using two-day recall interviews in North Cameroon, Jones (in Moock,1986: 165-123) found that women whose husbands gave them little money after the rice harvest were subsequently likely to withhold their labor. Cost-benefit analysis of women's cropping strategies showed that where land was not a constraint, those who headed their own households earned more for their labor. This quantitative study was informed by a sophisticated understanding of gender issues that the report by von Braun and colleagues lacks.

Why does it matter? Many studies find that women and men not only keep separate accounts, but allocate their resources differently (Hill, 1969; Afonja in Robertson and Berger, 1980; Guyer, 1981; Schoepf and Schoepf in Davison, 1987: 106-130; Goheen in Davison, 1988: 90-105; Pankhurst and Jacobs in Davison, 1988: 202-227; Hongoke, 1990). Since responsibility for raising children is central to women's social role, their incomes are more likely to be used for this purpose (Obbo, 1980; Smith and Stevens, 1988). Women who are widowed or repudiated are likely to find themselves destitute unless they have founded a successful business or accumulated capital in land, houses or other assets to which they have exclusive claim (Bryceson and Mbiliny, 1978; Obbo, 1980; selections in Potash, 1986).[12] Depriving women of resources makes it likely that they and children will suffer. Women's striving for incomes and autonomy are so strong that they often prefer employment at very low wages rather than supply unremunerated labor to husbands or other kinsmen (Jackson, 1978; Hongoke, 1990).

Commercialization of agriculture does not necessarily bode ill for women. The record is variable. When women retain control, their labor burdens are eased, prices are favorable and cropping strategies are designed to minimize risk, results can be encouraging. Nevertheless, since numerous case studies document long-term negative effects of increasing commodity production over the long term, it is necessary to seek deeper understanding in order to foresee and prevent them (Stamp, 1989; Wisner, 1989).

The Gambia example suggests a research strategy for the future. Development projects, extant and proposed, need to be examined by researchers familiar with the social and technical issues in collaboration with the designated 'beneficiaries.' Rapid surveys are likely to be inadequate for understanding complex issues of resource control, dependency, nutrition and health. An historical focus is important since many projects are contemporary iterations of previous schemes. Research that collects data solely on quantitative indicators—using recall interviews, measurements of produce, agricultural labor time and anthropometry[13]—is methodologically inadequate, for it may be misleading. Even if local field enumerators are trained and supervised by anthropologists, such 'empirical' studies are apt to ignore contextual analysis of production relations which case studies of women and development have shown to be crucial.

Recognized or not, methodological choices involve ethical issues (Stavenhagen, 1971). Understanding past successes and failures may help to prevent unforeseen consequences that could have been foreseen. Ethical research practice must include methodologies and conceptual frameworks that build upon earlier studies; listen to what women, variously situated socially, already know about their life circumstances; and foresee the conflicts that socioeconomic changes bring to gender relations. 'Production politics,' as Carney and Watts term such conflicts, are not simply about intra-household resource allocation. They express women's resistance to "...the appropriation of their product by the international commodity market through the agency of their husbands...it is a resistance to dual exploitation."(Stamp, 1989:83.)

As illustrated in the Gambia rice project, transformation of women from autonomous producers into unpaid workers could bring unfortunate effects for both women and men. Continuing participation in the project depends upon delivering stipulated quantities of rice.   If women withdraw their labor and men are unable to meet production quotas set by the project management, men could lose their access to land, title to which is now held by the scheme. It is not difficult to imagine a future in which many men will have become wage laborers on land they now occupy. This suggests that it is in the interests of both men and women not to accept the new definitions of rights and entitlements structured into this development project.   Rather than collaborating in the immediate disenfranchisement of women for illusory gains which may turn into losses, most peasant men probably have a stake in promoting community-based planning and management. Collaborative research using a participatory, problem-solving approach might discover a way to use the same resources to increase not only rice production, but food security and community welfare—including women. Action-research can be used not only to transfer planning and evaluation skills, but to foster new value consensus in support of change (Hope, Timmel and Hodzi, 1984).

C. Gender and structural adjustment

The decade of the 1980s opened with widespread recognition that Africa's agrarian crisis is a general one not limited to areas struck by drought or insect pests. Agrarian crisis is a symptom of the general crisis affecting externally oriented, raw materials producing economies enmeshed in a world recession with declining terms of trade (Lawrence, 1986; Amin, 1989). The subject of continuing policy negotiations between African leaders, multilateral agencies and Western governments, mounting debt and economic stagnation have given the institutions of international finance enormous policy-making leverage. One set of policy prescriptions, contained in the "Berg Report," (World Bank, 1981) has been implemented under the leadership of the IMF. Summarized as "reliance on market forces" and "getting prices right," the stated premise of structural adjustment is that free market capitalism can be instituted and will lead to development in Africa.

The ills for which structural adjustment is prescribed are real. They result from the combined effects of inherited economic distortions, with declining terms of trade and continuing capital drain, unproductive national accumulation strategies and widening inequality (UNECA, 1989).   However, the question: Development for whom? is central. African intellectuals and many others, as well, have argued that by ignoring the international political and economic causes of crisis, the fiscal prescriptions of structural adjustment programs (SAPs) do not offer hope of transformation or renewal. Instead, they place the burdens of crisis more firmly on the backs of the continent's poorest producers (Onimode, 1989; Adedeji, 1989, 1990).

The Berg Report's gender blindness does not render SAPs gender neutral: poor women and children have been most negatively affected (Newbury and Schoepf in Parpart and Staudt, 1989: 91-110; Pittin, 1989; Bujra, 1990; Gladwin, 1991). The consequences were not unexpected; they were delineated in advance of the report's publication (Safilios-Rothschild, 1980, cited in Staudt, 1988). Throughout the continent, the repercussions of structural adjustment have been exacerbated by women's subordination within the household, by continuing constraints on peasant productivity, and mass unemployment.

Structural Adjustment measures have been mediated by the state in many ways that could have been foreseen. Fiscal reforms contained in IMF guidelines have been directed at reducing both budget deficits and the taxes levied on large firms. This is accomplished by redistributing the burden downward to local levels through 'decentralization.' Regional and local officials have been directed to raise new revenues for their own operations as well as for the governments, while services such as health and education are supported primarily by user fees—rendering them inaccessible to poor women and girls.[14] New taxes have been levied on traders who pass them on to peasants by holding down producer prices. In the face of monopsonist markets (many sellers and one or few buyers), especially in areas where poor roads make rural markets difficult to reach, decontrolling producer prices does not create lasting incentives for small producers.

In Zaire, local authorities imposed other ways of collecting revenues, including fines for violation of the myriad regulations governing village life; work on obligatory crops, building latrines and dish-drying racks, owning radios and dogs, keeping livestock, hunting, cutting wood, carrying party cards and baptismal certificates, ad infinitum (Schoepf and Schoepf, 1984).[15] New programs of supervised cultivation have been instituted for peasants and some urban workers. Agricultural agents levy fines on those who fail to report for work. Women bear the brunt of the new coercion for, as one chief stated: "Women are easier to round up and control, while men run away." (Schoepf, Walu, Russell and Schoepf in Gladwin, 1991: 162)[16] Local officials in Bandundu recently devised a new wrinkle on the cultures obligatoires persisting from the colonial period. Only women whose marriages are actually registered at the collectivité now are considered to be married. Women for whom bridewealth has been paid—who thus are recognized in the community as married women—have been designated by officials as 'unmarried household heads.' As 'free women,' they are taxed at higher rates than legal spouses and held responsible for corvée labor. Since most do not have cash to pay additional fines and taxes, they constitute a vast unremunerated labor force.

Extra-economic measures are part of an entrenched system operating at local, regional and national levels. Women's subordination within the family is used by officials to fuel the process of capital accumulation. Since women have the least control over their labor in family or community, most of the resources extracted from the rural areas are generated by women. The new resources have not been used to lighten women's workloads by means of new technology, but to augment the wealth and prestige of officials. Administrative coercion, used as a primary accumulation strategy by the state and by officials (many of whom are traders), places poor women at increased disadvantage. Sometimes women's groups can obtain redress; nevertheless, the heavy hand of the state remains (Newbury, 1984).

Zaire can be dismissed as a worst-case scenario (Cloud and Knowles in Davison, 1988: 250-264). However, removing price controls does not create 'free' markets elsewhere, either. Under conditions of unequal access, competition generates its own forms of controls (Berry, 1986). The overall thrust of current policy advice is to encourage commercialization of agriculture at all levels. Credit, input supply and resources of development projects are directed mainly to large and medium-scale landowners producing export and industrial crops (Schoepf and Schoepf in Davison, 1988: 106-130; Newbury and Schoepf in Parpart and Staudt, 1989: 91-110). Although some women are among the owners of large farms and plantations, most are men or trans-national corporations with useful political connections. Large producers generally possess their own trucks and are able to market in quantity. Thus either they are unaffected by monopsonist markets, or they actually profit from them by purchasing peasants' crops for resale. As a result, while some women are able to benefit from higher farm prices, most cannot. They have limited access to and control over productive resources, including fertile land and labor, or to project inputs such as credit, improved seeds, fertilizer and extension information. Even apparently well-intentioned policies, such as land redistribution to farming cooperatives, can reduce women's autonomy and control over strategic resources by increasing the power of elder men who head kin groups, local political bodies and non-governmental organizations (Brain in Hafkin and Bay, 1976: 265-282; Tadesse, 1982; Jacobs in Parpart and Staudt, 1989: 161-184; Poluha, 1989; Wisner 1989).

Liberalization and privatization may work to most women's further disadvantage (Bujra, 1990; selections in Gladwin, 1991).

Policy decisions are choices about class and gender relations. Since peasant women are the main producers of food for mass consumption, decisions unfavorable to them are detrimental to the majority of the population as consumers and to national development. Although raising consumption levels of poor rural and urban families to create internal markets has not been a priority of the 1980s, it is a necessary condition of balanced growth. Liberalization—or hiding behind the market—is a political process in which new wealth can be garnered to enhance the economic power and patronage resources of those already in place. The examples presented in this section underscore the centrality of political process. Decentralization is no solution without democratic participation to safeguard the rights of poor women, and ensure the accountability of officials.

D. Women in cities

Experiences of women in the cities of sub-Saharan Africa vary by region, historical period, color, class and ethnicity. In East, Central and Southern Africa, colonial governments and male elders tried to keep African women in the rural areas to perform agricultural labor on peasant holdings, white settler farms and plantations. Wives were not wanted in the cities in the early years. Some women who came were detached from their kin groups (as ex-slaves, infertile women or those accused of witchcraft); some fled unhappy marriages; and some came to garner capital with which to help their families purchase food, land or livestock. Barred from waged jobs, most women resorted to petty trading, peri-urban agriculture, illegal brewing and commercial sex work. The relative success of some sex workers should not be exaggerated; the majority lived short, desperately poor, unhealthy lives. By the 1950s a few women found industrial jobs in food processing and textiles, while some were trained for low level teaching, nursing and clerical posts. However, African petty bourgeois men joined states and Christian missions in promoting the domestication of women (Boserup, 1970; Schuster, 1979; Obbo, 1980; Yates in Bay, 1982: 127-152; Wilson in Bay 1982: 153-170; Dickerman, 1984).

In many areas of West Africa, women were renowned as traders from the eighteenth century. Elsewhere, they moved into trade in the twentieth century as men turned to the professions (Clark, 1990). Some have done extremely well and enjoy both economic independence and social power, progressing from market stalls and itinerant hawking to shops, wholesale and long-distance ventures, and contributing to the vitality of the economy (Sudakarsa, 1976; Trager, 1985, 1987; MacGaffey in Robertson and Berger, 1986; in Stichter and Parpart, 1988).[17] The outstanding success of many women traders has become legendary. Today, with few jobs available and access to education so difficult, most urban women are self-employed as traders and artisans. While some trade continues to be highly profitable, most traders are reduced to eking out a meager living (Robertson, 1984, 1988; Vidal and LePape, 1986; Dennis, 1988; Clark and Manuh in Gladwin, 1991: 217-236). They appear to be no better off than most women in East and Southern Africa, for whom trade is a survival strategy rather than a profit-making enterprise, and who often face harassment by police (Bujra, 1975, 1978; Muchena, 1980; Gaidzanwa, 1987).[18] However, under some conditions, women's informal economic activities, particularly when they are organized in cooperatives and other associations, offer women spaces for political participation (Newbury and Schoepf in Parpart and Staudt, 1989: 91-110; Tripp, 1990).

Economic crisis severely limits the opportunities for women in the formal sector. Even those with secondary or university-level education have limited prospects in stagnant or retrenching economies. In most sub-Saharan nations, women constitute 4 to 10 percent of formal sector wage workers outside of agriculture (ILO, 1985; Stichter, 1990).[19] Yet these are the only jobs which offer even limited job security and benefits. As casual, often invisible, workers, women without choices are highly exploited (Michel et al, 1981; Mbilinyi, 1985: Loewenson in Turshen, 1991: 35-50). The double day of income-generating and domestic labor is most taxing for poor women without amenities or home appliances, while adequate food and health services are beyond their means (Okeyo, 1979; Muchena, 1980; Hansen, 1980; Cock, 1989). Domestic workers are the most exploited, but many middle class women are overtaxed by the responsibilities of large extended families, even when they have household and child care help (Fapohunda, 1982; Oppong, 1983; Parpart, 1990; Schoepf and Walu in MacFaffey, 1991).

African states have been vehicles for capital accumulation and class formation since the colonial period. In the post-independence period many states have been used (to varying degrees) by the officials who staffed them to amass wealth and establish themselves in commerce, industry, farming and finance. The role of the informal sector, or 'off-the-books' trade, including smuggling, in the total economy is much debated. Some believe that liberalization will make it possible for states to regulate and tax these activities which currently escape control, thereby generating new sources of revenue. Others (Kitching, 1980; MacGaffey in Robertson and Berger, 1986;

Hansen in Parpart and Staudt, 1989: 143-160) believe such entrepreneurship is creating a new class which will challenge the practices of those currently in power.   Further research will show whether they can dynamize the economy by creating new means of production capable of redressing existing structural distortions.

The extent to which major irregular sector operators remain independent of the state and separate from the formal sector is also at issue. Many of the largest operators are men with capital, credit access and well-placed international political and business connections, who can continue to avoid taxation and controls (Fatton, 1989; Rukarangira and Schoepf in MacGaffey, 1991).   Since smaller operators include low-paid civil servants and the plethora of unemployed, many of whom dream of growing wealthy, the safety-valve function is manifest.

In this, too, gender makes a difference. Gender is being used to consolidate and mask the closing gates of class mobility. While some women have grown wealthy in informal sector trade, most operate on a very small scale, 'breaking stones' to feed their dependants, thereby relieving the pressure on (more politically volatile) men. Yet female traders have been targeted by campaigns against high food prices, smuggling and illegal currency transactions (Dennis, 1987; Schoepf and Schoepf in Davison, 1988: 106-130; Clark, 1990; Hansen in Parpart and Staudt, 1989: 143-160).[20] Market women's political protests have stressed rising wholesale prices and their solidarity with other urban women unable to feed their families; in some countries they have been violently repressed.

Women also have been scapegoated as the cause of AIDS. The next section looks at AIDS as a gendered development issue.

E. Gender, crisis and AIDS [21]

Although AIDS has caused fewer deaths than malaria, diarrheal and respiratory diseases, it is becoming a significant public health and development problem.   AIDS is the leading cause of death among adults in the high prevalence belt of Central Africa, and infection rates are rising elsewhere. At this time there is no cure and no vaccine. The principal mode of infection is through heterosexual relations. Blood transfusions, injection syringes and other skin piercing instruments also can infect people when they are contaminated with the HIV virus which causes AIDS.

Cities contain the highest concentration of people diagnosed with AIDS and of people with antibodies to the HIV virus; in some areas, the populations of market towns and rural villages are seriously affected. Young women between the ages of fifteen and thirty are most at risk and 6 to 40 percent of mothers delivering in Central African cities were infected in 1990. About 30 to 40 percent of babies born to HIV-infected women also will get AIDS. In the high prevalence areas, AIDS has increased mortality in children under five by about 15 to 25 percent.

In periods of crisis, disease epidemics often break out. Gendered differences in power, wealth and ideology contribute to the spread of AIDS. Most women are unable to negotiate safer sex practices with their partners; many men are reluctant to do so. Moreover, poverty forces many women to use sex with multiple partners to ensure their own and family survival, and restricts access to treatment for other sexually transmitted diseases which increase risk of AIDS. In the presence of a new virus, the economic crisis has turned a survival strategy into a death strategy.

Commercial sex workers are most at risk, but even faithful wives are at risk if their husbands have had sex with multiple partners without using condoms. Since the HIV infection can be transmitted to others for ten years or more before a person becomes sick, a healthy appearance is no guarantee of safety. Ideological blinders hinder AIDS prevention.   Women traders, perceived by many men to be 'promiscuous,' also are blamed for the spread of AIDS. Yet both formal and informal sector economic and political activities furnish wealthy men with access to multiple partners who cannot afford to dispense with their patronage.

Research findings from Project CONNAISSIDA in Zaire indicate that community-based, participatory non-formal education can empower people to make informed risk-assessments. Limiting sexual transmission requires sensitive inquiry into intimate relations and attention to the structures and meanings that produce gender subordination in economy, society and households. In addition, socioeconomic changes that provide greater economic opportunity, social autonomy and equality for women are needed to reduce the spread of infection (Schoepf, 1988; Standing and Kisekka, 1989). The prevalence of AIDS lends urgency to the search for sustainable development strategies that promote gender equality and put an end to the grinding poverty that prevails throughout the continent. The methodology used in research on prevention was adapted from a participatory social change strategy based on small group dynamics. An example of the method in another setting follows.

IV. Participatory research methodologies

Participatory methods allow researchers to collaborate with people who have had limited formal education to reflect critically upon problems, to generate new knowledge and to act on that knowledge to change society. The action-research method described here is based on concepts of non-formal education (Freire, 1972; Hope, Timmel and Hodzi 1984; Schoepf, Walu, Rukarangira, Payanzo and Schoepf in Tunshen, 1991: 187-203). The example is taken from a 1983 leadership seminar with urban women leaders of the Women's League of a national political party.[22] All were married to artisans and clerical workers, all had children; only one had more than a few years of primary schooling. Their goal for the weekly workshop was to: "Learn how to better help our families." The sub-text, that women need to be able to support themselves and dependents in the event that husbands die or leave them, was not articulated. Likewise, the idea of public leadership was muted.[23] Participants also stated emphatically their expectations about the learning process: "We do not want to be lectured to like in school."[24]

Officials of the Women's League also sought to identify income generating activities. The social inquiry fieldwork that is part of the 'experiential' or 'process training' method would be used to seek feasible activities. The next step would be for participants to organize these in their communities. A private voluntary organization representative had agreed to provide seed money for small projects.

Discussion in earlier sessions had shown that participants tended to frame their attitudes toward poor rural and urban women in moralistic terms, dismissing them as 'lazy and ignorant.' A role play was used to help participants think about poverty in a different way, rather than blaming the victims. The exercise used a situation based on ethnography from another country (LeVine, 1979): While the husband is absent, working in the capital, his wife raises crops on land he has inherited from his patrilineage. The husband's widowed mother lives adjacent, and does some of the gardening, cooking and childcare. Surplus maize is sold through the producers' cooperative, which sends the money to the husband, "because it is his land." This year, as for several years past, the wife has not received any remittance money. She wants to get money for school fees.

Six characters were assigned:
- Wife
- Husband
- Husband's mother
- Town wife (the youngest participant)
- Party Chairman (the most authoritative)
- Women's League leader

No instructions were given about how to interpret the roles or how to play the scene. The following drama was enacted:

The wife laments to her mother-in-law: There is no money for school fees, the children have no uniforms, the last baby is sick and there are no medicines. Where is my husband? The elder woman sympathizes: My grandchildren are suffering!

Together they decide to visit the husband in town to put the problem before him. They walk to the highway and flag the inter-city bus. Arriving hot and dusty at the man's lodging, they find another woman who keeps them standing at the door. The husband/son appears, but still the women are kept outside. He listens to his wife's complaints, distracted by the interruptions of his 'town wife.' His mother tries to interject her support; the town wife replies in cheeky fashion and moves in front of the husband to close the door. The two country women find themselves out in the street, hot, thirsty and utterly amazed! Returning to the village, they put the problem to the Party Chairman, who is also head of the husband's patrilineage. The elder promptly decides: This is a problem for the Women's League. The WL leader listens to their story sympathetically, but tells the women that they must work harder to make a cash income, since it is true, the land belongs to the husband.

Participants ended their drama at this point, leaving the peasant women to 'redouble their efforts,' a solution that would not upset the status quo of gender and property relations (See Bujra in Robertson and Berger, 1986: 117-140). Each woman knew how to play her role, which she embellished with vivid details. Enthusiastic responses from observers indicated that the play was experienced as true-to-life.

In this learning method, a 'processing cycle' follows the structured experience. The first step is sharing reactions. Participants tell what they have seen, heard and felt during the exercise. There are no 'wrong' answers. Everyone's contribution is valued and different perspectives complete one another. Some 'far out' perceptions provide new ways of looking at problems. At the same time that each person's participation is acknowledged and written on newsprint,[25] facilitators can emphasize responses they find particularly appropriate and ask for elaboration.[26]

In the next phase, a facilitator reads back the responses, and asks questions leading to interpretation, such as:
- How did you feel when the town wife was cheeky to the mother?
- Why do you think she did that?
- Why didn't the husband react? What do you think he was feeling?
- Why didn't he bring his country wife and children to town?

Responses to the exercise were used to teach complex concepts of land ownership, labor markets, social reproduction, surplus and commodity production, international terms of trade, capital accumulation and so on. Discussion should be built upon the shared experience so that it remains concrete.

Several older participants acknowledged that their hostility to the pretty, young town wife resonated with their own fears of abandonment. This brought out a deeper meaning of the goal articulated in the first session which was "to learn how to better help our families." Women were able to redefine their need to obtain economic independence so that they could care for their families 'just in case.'[27] Having ended their play in an impasse, the women showed that they had not yet begun to envisage practical solutions to problems of women and development. The facilitators probed for their perception of contemporary village politics: Would not the Party Chairman, in his capacity as head of the husband's patrilineage have called the elders together to find a way to send the children to school?

> No, he would not. You see even in our villages, today it is not the whole big family that men look out for, even when they are grandfathers. Anyway, he's a man and he would not want anyone to challenge what he did with his money. Men stick together.

Although their portrayal was far removed from the official portrayal of community solidarity, the group agreed that the play was correct. Individualism and commodity relations have increased women's responsibilities without offering them new ways to meet them. Implicitly, they did not regard the political party as a force for changing gender relations.

The final phase of the experiential cycle involves applying new insights to real life situations. Workshop participants chose the most socially acceptable option to improve women's economic position: a cooperative. They suggested vegetable gardening, basket-making, bread baking and sewing school uniforms. How could we discover if such activities would be worthwhile? By what criteria should they be judged?

The group decided that if the woman could earn enough to meet their essential expenses and replenish their stocks that would be a measure of success. They did not mention labor time. This created an opportunity to discuss the economists' view that women's labor is without opportunity cost. We agreed to go out in small teams to examine some functioning cooperatives and ask the women to share their experiences. The best ones would provide a starting point; the worst ones would serve as lessons in 'how not to.' Although the workshop was halted,[28] the example suggests the potential of participatory action-research using empowering learning strategies.

The scene that participants had enacted was played out in real life two months later at an interministerial conference on "Women and Land." There representatives of a rural women's cooperative told of their members' inability to control the fruits of their labor because the land belonged to their husbands. Former workshop participants who were present commented privately: "We saw all that in our workshop with you!" Empathizing with the village women, they nonetheless remained silent while Government community development agents admonished the women farmers: "Go home and settle these problems with your husbands within your households. These are problems of the couple, not of society." The rural women retorted: "Since when, in Africa, are problems of the couple not problems of the community?" Their voices were silenced; intrahousehold gender issues were ignored. As in the role play, women were urged to 'redouble their efforts.' Both State and Party refused to hear poor women's voices. [29]

This example dates from 1983. Soon afterward, urban women were scapegoated and many free women were run out of the capital. However, political climates are in flux, and in some countries democratization may open spaces for dialogue on intrahousehold gender inequalities. Where political space exists, action-research which begins with people's felt needs offers a method for personal and social change (Muchena, 1980).[30]

V. Conclusion

Poor women and children have been made to pay with their work and health for past and present policies. Social scientists often point to the unforeseen consequences of policies as they are actually implemented. Sometimes policy failures are more properly viewed as undeclared goals. Neglecting to incorporate knowledge of gender differences cannot be attributed to ignorance. Thus, we must assume that structural adjustment was intended to continue debt reimbursement and other capital transfers in part by mobilizing more labor from working women. This suggests that hiding behind reliance on the market, international and bilateral agencies have attempted to rationalize the process of extracting resources, upward from women producers to officials and traders, and outward from Africa to the West.

Gender ideology and the conditions it justifies are crucial to this accumulation, for they promote continuing inequality in access to resources. Gender inequality will continue to provoke conflict within households. Such conflict is political as well as personal, for it serves to deflect attention from the structures and ideology that keep the vast majority of men and women subordinated as a low-cost labor force in the interest of capital accumulation. Taken together, these considerations indicate that ending gender inequality should be an urgent development priority for men, as well as for women.

Many development professionals regard basic research as a luxury and theory as a waste of time. However, three decades of policy, program and project failures point to the need for theoretical perspectives and methodological approaches adequate to reformulate strategies that will lead to African renewal. These must incorporate textured understandings of gender relations, including the ways that these have been restructured during the colonial period and the recent past.

Policy-makers who rely on policies derived from neoclassical macro-economics continue to reproduce, justify and strengthen economic and socio-political inequality. Linking macro-economics to micro-level studies with a gendered focus highlights the need for a transformation of societal structures in a manner quite different than that involved in improving the performance indicators of existing economic institutions. The experience of poor rural and urban women shows that political democracy, with effective accountability of officials at all levels, is an integral part of any sustainable development strategy.

The Task Force Gender Workshop participants decided upon a two-pronged strategy to implement the action-research aims. First, to ensure the centrality of African women's concerns and perspectives in all other Task Force research, experienced women scholars will take part in the activities of these groups. In addition, this working group will undertake gender-centered research projects with community-based AIDS prevention as the initial focus. Perceived as an urgent health problem, it has drawn men into research on gender relations. Members of the Pan-African Action-Research Network have organized country teams to conduct participatory research. They will test the hypothesis that confronting AIDS has the potential to generate wide awareness of the need for development strategies that alter social structures, material conditions and ideologies that determine gender relations. Specific strategies to test this assumption will be designed during a workshop to be held in August, 1991. Country teams will adapt the participatory methodology and develop collaborative research proposals. The network is open to others who organize teams to investigate problem-solving approaches to preventing AIDS by changing political economy and culture.

Endnotes

1. Revised version of a working paper prepared for the 1990 Task Force Workshop on "Gender and Households." Many people contributed to the perspective it presents; special thanks are extended to Gracia Clark, Mitzi Goheen, Mere Kisekka, Marjorie Mbilinyi, Catharine A. Newbury, Susan Namfukudza, Alice Nkhoma, Christine Obbo, Jane Parpart, Ann Seidman, Lillian Trager and Walu Engundu. The errors are mine.

2. A phrase used by women in Guinea Bissau (Urdang, 1979).

3. For example, Women in Nigeria (WIN), and Women Research and Development Project (WRDP) in Tanzania.

4. Prof. Jane Parpart calls this the "add women and stir" approach.

5. Despite the dominance of logical positivism, critical perspectives have a long tradition in western science.

6. Interrogations of male dominance, as well as general critiques of colonial anthropology were informed by this perspective.

7. While Hay (1988) separates anthropological from historical perspectives— especially with respect to the fiction of an "ethnographic present," this construct was criticized by several anthropologists (Leacock in Rohrlich-Leavitt, 1975). Much newer work is transdisciplinary, with anthropologists doing historical studies.

8. The term is from Dickerman, 1984.

9. See Stamp (1989) for a comprehensive review.

10. Other case studies appear in the cited collections.

11. Actually, land shortages in Rwanda result in high labor requirements to maintain soil fertility. "Labor surplus" appears to be a euphemism for "overpopulation."

12. Otherwise, at best, they will be reduced to the status of dependents in the households of relatives (Schoepf and Walu in MacGaffey, 1991)

13. These include measurements of height, weight, and arm circumference used to determine nutritional status.

14. Meena (in Gladwin, 1991: 169-190) provides figures for Tanzania.

15. Fiscal decentralization has had similar effects in Sierra Leone (Zack-Williams, 1990).

16. Fines are substantial for poor people—equivalent to a chicken or two.

17.There are also exceptions: In some areas of the Sahel male-dominant ideology stigmatizes women's participation or limits them to trading from their homes. In Northern Nigeria even the latter is under attack from Islamic fundamentalists (Pittin, 1990).

18 Some writers (not those cited here) apply the term 'profit' to these earnings without first deducting compensation for labor time. This practice appears to rest upon the unstated assumption that since women have few alternatives, their labor time is without 'opportunity cost.'

19. Comparison of figures provided in World Bank tables (1989, pp. 270-271) indicates that countries with the highest rates of female employment (and incomes), also report the highest rates of contraceptive prevalence and the lowest maternal mortality.

20. Although small-scale female operators in the trans-border trade "are only the tip of the iceberg," (*Elmina* August 25, 1986; March 4-5, 1988), attacking the tip (women) was safer than revealing illegal activities of politically powerful men.

21. References to the biomedical literature can be found in Schoepf, 1988; Bassett and Mhloyi, 1991.

22. Contrary to several readers' assumptions, this example does not come from Zaire.

23. The skills that they already possessed were quite adequate to fulfilling their assigned political tasks. These were to mobilize women to turn out for rallies and to collect old clothes for distribution to a distant rural area.

24. Generally, the school experience of most people is oppressive. Freire (1972) terms this "banking education," in which teachers pour facts into their heads rather than opening new vistas of experience and reflection.

25. Even when many participants do not read, posting their contributions for all to see further acknowledges their value. Other techniques, such as popular theater (Lihamba 1986), can be incorporated in this methodology.

26. This leaves room for manipulation by facilitators and must be guarded against (cf. Mbilinyi, 1984).

27. This generalization later was used as part of a new exercise.

28. Male Party leaders decided that the lead facilitator was importing western feminism and ended the seminar.

29. The keynote speech drafted for the Assistant Minister for Women's Affairs had not included this issue. This amnesia indicates the extent to which the facilitator had been silenced by political pressure and had repressed consciousness of this silencing. It further demonstrates the need for women's support groups within bureaucracies as well as in communities.

30. Other forms of popular culture, such as stories, riddles, proverbs and plays (see Lihamba, 1986) can be incorporated into this process.

Bibliography

AAWORD. 1982. "The Experience of African Women for Research and Development." In *Another Development with Women*. Proceedings of a seminar held in Dakar, June 1982, *Development Dialogue* 1, No, 2. pp.101-113.

Adedeji, Adebayo. 1989. *Towards a Dynamic African Economy*. London: Frank Cass.

_____. 1990. "Development and Ethics: Can Africa Put Itself on the Road to Self-reliant and Self-sustaining Process of Development?" Plenary address, annual meeting of the African Studies Association, Baltimore. November 1-4.

Afonja, Simi. 1980. "Current Explanations of Sex Roles and Inequality." *Nigerian Journal of Economic and Social Studies* 22, No. 1:85-105.

Afshar, Haleh. Ed. 1987. *Women, State and Ideology: Studies from Africa and Asia*. Albany: State University of New York.

Amadiume, Ifi. 1987. *Male Daughters, Female Husbands: Gender and Sex in African Society*. London: Zed Books.

Amin, Samir. 1989. *La Faillite Du Developpement en Afrique et dans le Tiers-Monde: Une Analyse Politique*. Paris: Editions l'Harmattan.

Antrobus, Peggy. 1990. "Women's Worlds: Realites and Choices." Presentation at the Fourth Interdisciplinary Congress on Women, New York. June 3-7.

Ault, James. 1983. "Making 'Modern' Marriage 'Traditional': State Power and the Regulation of Marriage in Colonial Zambia." *Theory and Society* 12: 181-210.

Awe, Bolane. 1977. "Iyalode in the Traditional Yoruba Political System." In Schlegel, Alice. Ed. *Sexual Stratification: A Cross-cultural View*: 140-160. New Haven: Yale University Press.

Barrell, R.A.E. and Rowland, M.G.M. 1979. "Infants Foods as a Potential Source of Diarrheal Disease in Rural West Africa." *Transactions of the Royal Society of Tropical Medicine and Hygiene*. 73, No. 1: 85-90.

Bassett, Mary T. and Mhloyi, Marvellous. 1991. "Women and AIDS in Zimbabwe: The Making of an Epidemic." *International Journal of Health Services* 21, No. 1: 1433-156.

Bay, Edna G. Ed. 1982. *Women and Work in Africa*. Boulder, CO: Westview Press.

Beneria, Lourdes. 1981 "Conceptualizing the Labour Force: The Underestimation of Women's Activities." *Journal of Development Studies* 17, No. 3 : 10-27.

Berger, Iris and White, Frances E. 1990 (1988). "Women of Sub-Saharan Africa." In *Restoring Women to History: Teaching Packets*. Revised Ed. Bloomington: Association of American Historians.

Berry, Sara. 1984. "The Food Crisis and Agrarian Change in Africa: A Review Essay." *African Studies Review*. 27, No. 2:59-112.

Boserup, Ester. 1970. *Women's Role in Economic Development*. New York: St. Martin's Press.

Bruce, Judith and Dwyer, Daisy. Eds. 1988. *A Home Divided: Women and Income in the Third World.* Stanford, CA: Stanford University Press.

Bryceson, Deborah and Mbilinyi, Marjorie. 1980. "The Changing Role of Tanzanian Women in Production." Uppsala: Scandinavian Institute of African Studies. *Jipemoya* 2: 85-116.

Bujra, Janet M. 1990. "Taxing Development: Why Must Women Pay? Gender and Development Debate in Tanzania." *Review of African Political Economy.* 47: 44-63.

Bukh, Jette. 1979. "Village Women in Ghana." Uppsala: Scandinavian Institute for African Studies.

Carney, Judith and Watts, Michael. 1990. "Manufacturing Dissent: Work, Gender and the Politics of Meaning in a Peasant Society." *Africa* 60, No. 2: 207-241.

Chanock, Martin. 1985. *Law, Custom and Social Order: The Colonial Experience in Malawi and Zambia.* Cambridge: Cambridge University Press.

Clark, Gracia. 1988. *Traders Versus the State.* Boulder, CO: Westview Press.

_____. 1990. "Class Alliance and Class Fractions in Ghanaian Trading and State Formation." *Review Of African Political Economy.* 49: 73-81.

Cloud, Kathleen B. 1985. "Women's Productivity in Agricultural Systems: Considerations for Project Design." In Overholt, C., Anderson, M.B., Cloud, K. and Austin, J.F. Eds. *Gender Roles in Development Projects:* 17-56. West Hartford, CT: Kumarian Press.

Cock, Jacqlyn. 1989 (1984). *Maids and Madams: Domestic Workers Under Apartheid.* London: Women's Press.

Conti, Anna. 1979. "Capitalist Organization of Production Through Non-capitalist Relations: Women's Roles in a Pilot Resettlement in Upper Volta." *Review of African Political Economy.* 15/16:75-92.

Cornia, G.A., Jolly, R. and Steward, F. Eds. 1987. *Adjustment with a Human Face: Protecting the Vulnerable and Promoting Growth.* 2 Vols . Oxford: Clarendon Press for UNICEF.

Davison, Jean with the Women of Mutira. 1989. *Voices from Mutira: Lives of Rural Gikuyu Women.* Boulder, CO: Lynne Reiner.

Davison, Jean, Ed. 1988. *Agriculture, Women, and Land: The African Experience*. Boulder and London: Westview Press.

Dennis, Carolyne. 1988. "Women in African Labour History." *Journal of Asian and African Studies* 23, Nos.1-2: 125-140.

Dey, Jennie. 1981. "Gambian Women: Unequal Partners in Rice Development Projects." *Journal of Development Studies*. 17, No. 3: 109-122.

Dickerman, Carol W. 1984. "City Women and the Colonial Regime: Usumbura, 1939-1962." *African Urban Studies*. 18 (Spring): 33-48.

Etienne, Mona and Leacock, Eleanor, Eds. 1980. *Women and Colonization: Anthropological Perspectives*. New York: Praeger.

Freire, Paulo. 1972. *The Pedagogy of the Oppressed*. Middlesex (UK): Penguin Books.

Gaidzanwa, Rudo B. and Women's Action Group. 1987. "Operation Clean-Up." In Davies, Miranda. Ed. *Third World, Second Sex*. Vol.2. pp. 225-229. London: Zed Press.

Geffray, Christian. 1989. "Les Hommes Au Travail, les Femmes Au Grenier" and "Les Hommes Pique-Assiettes et Femmes Amoureuses." *Cahiers des Sciences Humaines*. 25, 3:313-324; 325-337.

Geiger, Susan. 1986. "Women's Life Histories: Method and Content." *SIGNS: A Journal of Women in Culture and Society*. 11, No. 2: 334-351.

Gladwin, Christina. Ed. 1991. *Structural Adjustment and African Women Farmers*. Gainesville: University of Florida Press.

Guyer, Jane. 1981. "Household and Community in African Studies." *African Studies Review*. 24, No. 2-3:87-137.

_____. Ed. l987. *Feeding African Cities*. Bloomington: University of Indiana Press.

_____. 1988. "The Multiplication of Labor: Historical Methods in the study of Gender and Agricultural Change in Modern Africa." *Current Anthropology*. 29. No. 2:197-213.

_____. and Peters, Pauline. 1987. "Introduction to Conceptualizing the Household: Issues of Theory and Policy in Africa." *Development and Change*. 18, No. 2:247-272.

Hafkin, Nancy and Bay, Edna. Eds. 1976. *Women in Africa: Studies in Social and Economic Change*. Stanford: Stanford University Press.

Hansen, Karen Tranberg. 1984. "Negotiating Sex and Gender in Urban Zambia." *Journal of Southern Africa Studies*. 10, No.2:219-238.

_____. 1989. *Distant Companions: Men, Women and Domestic Service Zambia*, 1900-1985. Ithaca: Cornell University Press.

Hay, Margaret Jean and Stichter, Sharon. Eds. 1984. *African Women: South of the Sahara*. London: Longman.

_____. and Wright, Marcia. Eds. 1982. *African Women and the Law: Historical Perspectives*. Boston: Boston University Papers on Africa, No. 7.

_____. 1988. "Queens, Prostitutes and Peasants: Historical Perspectives on African Women, 1971-1986." *Canadian Journal of African Studies*. 22, No. 3:431-446.

Hongoke, Christine. 1990. "Cultural Conflicts Faced by Women Roadmakers in Tanzania." Paper prepared for IV International Interdisciplinary Congress on Women, Hunter College, New York, June 3-7.

Hope, Anne, Timmel, Sally and Hodzi, Peter. 1984 Training for Transformation: *A Handbook for Community Workers*. 3 Vols. Gweru, Zimbabwe: Mambo Press.

Houtondji, Paulin J. 1983 (1976). *African Philosophy: Myth and Reality*. Bloomington: Indiana University Press.

Hunt, Nancy Rose. 1990. "Domesticity and Colonialism in Belgian Africa: Usumbura's Foyer Social, 1946-1960." *SIGNS* 15, No.3: 447-474.

International Labor Organization (ILO). *L'Emploi des Femmes en Afrique. Rapport de synthese dans six pays francophones*. Addis Ababa: ILO, Jobs and Skills Programme for Africa.

Isaacman, Allen. 1990. "Peasants and Rural Social Protest in Africa." *African Studies Review*. 33, No. 2:1-120.

Jackson, Cecile. 1978. "Hausa Women on Strike." *Review of African Political Economy*. 13:21-36.

Joekes, Susan. 1987. *Women in the World Economy*. New York: Oxford University Press for INSTRAW.

Johnson-Odim, Cheryl and Strobel, Margaret. 1990 (1988). Introduction. In *Restoring Women to History: Teaching Packets*. Revised ed. Bloomington: Association of American Historians.

Kariuki, Priscilla. 1985. "Women's Aspirations and Perceptions of Their Own Situation in Society." In Were, Gideon S. Ed. *Women and Development in Africa*: 22-29. Nairobi: Gideon Were Press.

Kitching,Gavin. 1980. *Class and Economic Change in Kenya: The Making of an African Petty Bourgeoisie*. New Haven: Yale University Press.

Kongstad, Per and Mnsted, Mette. 1980. *Family, Labour and Trade in Western Kenya*. Uppsala: Scandinavian Institute of African Studies.

Kruks, Sonya and Wisner,Ben. 1984. "The State, the Party and the Female Peasantry in Mozambique." *Journal of Southern African Studies*. 11, No. 1: 106-128.

Lawrence, Peter. Ed. 1985. *The World Recession and the Food Crisis in Africa*. London: James Currey.

LeVine, Sarah. 1979. *Mothers and Wives: Gusii Women of East Africa*. Chicago: University Chicago Press.

Lewis, Barbara C. Ed. 1981. *Invisible Farmers: Women and the Crisis in Agriculture*. Washington, DC: USAID/Office of WID.

Lihamba, Amadina. 1986. "Health and the Africa Theatre." *Review of African Political Economy*. 36 (Health Issue):35-42.

Loewenson, Rene. 1991. "Harvests of Disease: Women at Work on Zimbabwean Plantations." In Turshen, M. Ed.: 35-50.

MacGaffey, Janet. Ed. 1991. *The Real Economy in Zaire*. London: James Currey.

Mandala, Elias. 1984. "Capitalism, Kinship and Gender in the Lower Tchiri Valley of Malawi, 1860-1960." *African Economic History*. 13:137-170.

_____. 1990. *Work and Control in a Peasant Economy: A History of the Lower Tchiri Valley in Malawi 1859-1960*. Madison: University of Wisconsin Press.

Marks, Shula. Ed. 1987. *Not Either an Experimental Doll: The Separate Worlds of Three South African Women*. Bloomington: Indiana University Press.

Mbilinyi, Majorie. 1984. "'Women in Development' Ideology: The Promotion of Competition and Exploitation." *The African Review* 2, No. 1:14-33.

_____. 1985. "The Changing Position of Women in the African Labor Force." In Shaw, Timothy M. and Aluko, Olajide. Eds. *Africa Projected*: 170-186. New York: St. Martins Press.

_____. 1989. "'I'd Have Been a Man': Politics and Labor Process in Producing Personal Narratives." In Personal Narrative Group, Eds. *Interpreting Women's Lives*: 204-227. Bloomington: University of Indiana Press.

Michel, Andree, Agbessi-Dos Santos, Helene and Diarra, Fatoumata-Agnes. Eds. 1981. *Femmes et Multinationales.* Paris: Editions Karthala. 93-116.

Mikell, Gwendolyn. 1984. "Filiation, Economic Crisis, and the Status of Women in Rural Ghana." *Canadian Journal of African Studies.* 18, No. 1:195-218.

_____. 1989. *Cocoa and Class in Ghana.* New York: Paragon House.

Mizra, Sarah and Strobel, Margaret. Eds. 1989. *Three Swahili Women: Life Histories fron Mombassa, Kenya.* Bloomington: University of Indiana Press.

Moock, Joyce Lewinger. Ed. 1986. *Understanding Africa's Rural Households and Farming Systems.* Boulder, CO: Westview.

Mudimbe, V.Y. 1988. *The Invention of Africa: Gnosis, Philosophy and the Order of Knowledge.* Bloomington: Indiana Press.

Muchena, Olivia. 1980. *Women in Town: A Socioeconomic Survey of Women in Highfield Township Salisbury.* Salisbury: University of Zimbabwe, Centre for Applied Social Science.

_____. 1985. "Zimbabwe: It Can Only Be Handled by Women." *Sisterhood is Global*, edited by Robin Morgan. New York: Anchor Books.

Muntemba, Dorothy C. 1987. "The Impact of the IMF/World Bank on the People of Africa with Special Reference to Zambia." Paper No.7 presented at IFAA conference on the impact of the IMF/World Bank policies on the People of Africa, London. September 7-10.

Nelson, Nici. 1979. "How Women and Men Get By: The Sexual Division of Labour in the Informal Sector of a Nairobi Squatter Settlement." In *Casual Work and Poverty in Third World Cities*, edited by R. Bromley and C. Gerry. London: Gordon Wiley.

Nelson, Nici, Ed. 1981. *African Women in the Development Process*. London: Frank Cass.

Newbury, Catharine. 1984. "Ebutumwa Bw'Emiogo: The Tyranny of Cassava: A Women's Tax Revolt in Eastern Zaire." *Canadian Journal of African Studies*. 18, No. 1:35-54.

Nkhoma-Wamunza, Alice. 1987. "Beer-brewing in Utengule-Usansu Village." In Koda, B., Mbilinyi, M., Muro, A., Nekebukwa, U., Nkhoma, A., Tumbo-Masaba, R. and Vuovela, U. Eds. *Women's Initiatives in the Republic of Tanzania*. Geneva: ILO.

Nomvete, N. 1984. "The Participation of the Female Working Class in Trade Unions and in Labour Struggles in South Africa from 1950." Occasional Papers No.6. Edinburg University: Centre of African Studies.

Obbo, Christine. 1980. *African Women, Their Struggle for Economic Independence*. London: Zed Press.

_____. 1989. "Sexuality and Economic Domination in Uganda." In Yuval-Davis, N. and Anthas, F. Eds. *Women-Nation-State*: 79-91. London: Macmillan.

Oboler, Regina. 1985. *Women, Power and Economic Change: The Nandi of Kenya*. Stanford, CA: Stanford University Press.

Okeyo, Achola Pala. 1980. "Definitions of Women and Development: An African Perspective." *SIGNS* 3, No. 1:9-13.

_____. 1985. "Toward Strategies for Strengthening the Position of Women in Food Production: An Overview and Proposals on Africa." "Study on the Role of Women in International Economic Relations." Santo Domingo: INSTRAW.

Onimode, Bade. Ed. 1989. *The IMF, Word Bank and the African Debt*. 2 Vols. London: Zed Press.

Oppong, Christine. Ed. 1983. *Female and Male in West Africa*. London: George Allen and Unwin.

_____. Ed. 1987. *Sex Roles, Population and Development in West Africa*. London: James Currey.

Parpart, Jane L. and Staudt, Kathleen A. Eds. 1989. *Women and the State in Africa*. Boulder, CO: Lynne Reiner

Parpart, Jane L., Ed. 1989. *Women and Development in Africa: Comparative Perspectives*. Lanham, MD: University Press of America.

Paulme, Denise. 1963 (1960). "Introduction." In Paulme, Denise Ed. *Women of Tropical Africa*: 1-16. Berkeley and Los Angeles: University of California Press.

Pearce, Tola, O., Kujore, O.O., and Agboh-Bankole, V.A. 1988. "Generating an Income in the Urban Environment: The Experience of Street-Food Vendors in Ile-Ife, Nigeria." *Africa*. 58, No.4: 385-399.

Pittin, Rene. 1989. "Women, Work and Ideology in a Context of Economic Crisis: A Case Study." *Women, History and Development* WP. 11. The Hague: Institute for Social Studies

Poewe, Karla. 1990. *Religion, Kinship and Economy in Luapula, Zambia*. Lewiston, NY: Edwin Mellen Press.

Poluha, Eva. 1989. "Central Planning and Local Reality: The Case of a Producer's Cooperative in Ethiopia." *Studies of Social Anthropology*. (Stockholm), 23.

Potash, Betty. Ed. 1986. *Widows in African Society: Choices and Constraints*. Stanford: Stanford University Press.

Ramphele, Mamphela. 1990. Address, African Studies Association, Women's Caucus Breakfast. November.

Retel-Laurentin. 1974. *Infecondite en Afrique Noire*. Paris.

Robertson, Claire C. 1984. *Sharing the Same Bowl: A Socioeconomic History of Women and Class in Accra, Ghana*. Bloomington: University of Indiana Press.

_____. and Berger, Iris. Eds. 1986. *Women and Class in Africa*. New York: Africana Publishing Company.

_____. 1988. "Invisible Workers: African Women and the Problem of the Self-employed in Labour History." *Journal of Asian and African Studies*. 23(1-2):180-198.

Rogers, Barbara. 1980. *The Domestication of Women: Discrimination in Developing Societies*. New York: Tavistock Publications.

Romero, Patricia. Ed. 1988. *Life Histories of African Women*. London and Atlantic Highlands, NJ: Ashfield Press.

Rohrlich-Leavitt, Ruby. Ed. 1975. *Women Cross-Culturally: Challenge and Change*. The Hague: Moutton.

Rowland, M.G.M., A. Paul, A.M. Prentice, E. Muller, M. Hutton, R.A.E. Barrell, and R.G. Whitehead. 1981. "Seasonality and the Growth of Infants in a Gambian Village." In Chambers, R. Longhurst, R. and Pacey, A. Eds. *Seasonal Dimensions of Rural Poverty*: 164-175. London: Frances Pinter.

Russell, Diana E.H. 1989. *Lives of Courage: Women for a New South Africa*. New York, Basic Books.

Safilios-Rothschild, Constantina. 1980. "The Role of the Family: A Neglected Aspect of Poverty." *In Implementing Programs of Human Development*: 313-372. Washington, DC: World Bank.

Schmidt, Elizabeth. 1988. "Farmers, Hunters and Gold-Washers: A Reevaluation of Women's Roles in Precolonial and Colonial Zimbabwe." *African Economic History*. 17:45-80.

Schoepf, Brooke G. 1987. "Social Structure, Women's Status and Sex Differential Nutrition in the Zairean Copperbelt." *Urban Anthropology* 16, No. 1: 73-103

_____. 1988. "Women, AIDS and Economic Crisis in Central Africa." *Canadian Journal of African Studies* 22, No.3: 625-644.

Schoepf, Brooke G. and Schoepf, Claude. 1984. "State, Bureaucracy and Peasants in the Lufira Valley." *Canadian Journal of African Studies*. 18, No. 1:89-93.

_____. Walu, Engundu, Rukarangira, wa Nkera, Payanzo, Ntsomo and Schoepf, Claude. 1991b (1988). "Community-based Risk-reduction Support." In Berkvens, Reit. Ed. *AIDS Prevention Through Health Promotion: Changing Behavior*. Geneva: World Health Organization. Forthcoming.

Schuster, Ilsa. 1979. *The New Women of Lusaka*. Palo Alto, CA: Mayfield.

Seidman, Ann. 1981. "Women and the Development of 'Underdevelopment': The African Experience." In Dauber, R. and Cain, M.L. Eds. *Women and Technological Change in Developing Countries*: 199-206. AAAS Symposium Papers No.53. Boulder, CO: Westview.

Sen, Gita, and Caren Grown. 1985. *Development Crises and Alternative Vision: Third World Women's Perspectives*. New York: Monthly Review Press.

Shostak, Marjorie. 1983. *Nisa: the Life and Words of a !Kung Woman*. New York: Vintage.

Smith, Charles D. and Stevens, Lesley. 1988. "Farming and Income-generation in the Female-headed Smallholder Household: The Case of a Haya Village in Tanzania." *Canadian Journal of African Studies*. 22, No. 3: 552-566.

Stamp, Patricia. 1989. *Technology, Gender, and Power in Africa*. Technical Study 63e. Ottawa: International Development Research Centre (IDRC).

Standing, H., and M.N. Kisekka. 1989. *Sexual Behavior in Sub-Saharan Africa: A Review and Annotated Bibliography*. Glasgow, U.K.: Overseas Development Administration.

Staudt, Kathleen. 1978. "Agricultural Productivity Gaps: A Case Study of Male Preference in Government Policy Implementation." *Development and Change*. 9, No. 3:439-437.

Staudt, Kathleen. 1987. "Uncaptured or Unmotivated? Women and the Food Crisis in Africa." *Rural Sociology*. 52, No. 1: 37-55.

_____. 1988. "Women Farmers in Africa: Research and Institutional Action, 1972-1987." *Canadian Journal of African Studies*. 22, No. 3: 567-582.

Stavenhagen, Rodolfo. 1971. "Decolonializing the Applied Social Sciences." *Human Organization*. 30, No. 4:333-357.

Steady, Filomena Chioma. Ed. 1987. "African Feminism: A Worldwide Perspective." In Terborg-Penn, Rushing and Harley, Eds. Washington, DC: Howard University Press.

Stichter, Sharon and Parpart, Jane L. Eds. 1988. *Patriarchy and Class: African Women in the Home and Workforce*. Boulder, CO: Westview.

_____. and Parpart, Jane L. Eds. 1990. *Women, Employment and the Family in the International Division of Labor*. Philadelphia: Temple University Press.

Strobel, M. 1982. "African Women (Review Essay)." *SIGNS: A Journal of Women in Culture and Society*. 1(8): 109-113.

Sudarkasa, Niara. 1976. "Female Employment and Family Organization in West Africa." In McGuigan, Dorothy. Ed. *New Research on Women and Sex Roles*. Ann Arbor: University of Michigan, CCEW,

Swantz, Maria-Luisa. 1985. *Women in Development: A Creative Role Denied? the Case of Tanzania*. New York: St. Martins.

Tadesse, Zenebworke. 1979. "The Impact of Land Reform on Women: The Case of Ethiopia." *ISIS, Women, Land and Food Production*: 18-21. Geneva.

Tinker, Irene Ed. 1990. *Persistent Inequalities: Women and World Development*. Oxford: Oxford University Press.

Trager, Lillian. 1985. "From Yams to Beer in a Nigerian City: Expansion and Change in Informal Sector Trade Activity." In Plattner, Stuart. Ed. *Markets and Marketing*: 259-286. New York: University Press of America.

_____. 1987. "A Re-examination of the Urban Informal Sector in West Africa." *Canadian Journal of African Studies*. 21, No.2: 238-255.

Tripp, Aili Mari. 1990. "Responses of Urban Women to Economic Reform and Crisis in Urban Tanzania: The New Role of Women's Organizations." Paper presented at the 33rd annual meeting of the ASA, Baltimore. November 1-4.

Turrittin, Jean. 1988. "Men, Women and Market Trade." *Canadian Journal of African Studies*. 22, No.3: 583-604.

United Nations Economic Commission for Africa (UNECA). 1989. *An African Alternative to structural Adjustment Programmes: A Framework for Transformation and Recovery*. Addis Ababa: UNECA.

Urdang, Stephanie. 1979. *Fighting Two Colonialisms: Women in Guinea-Bissau*. New York: Monthly Review Press.

Van Allen, Judith. 1972. "'Sitting on a Man': Colonialism and the Lost Political Institutions of Igbo Women." *Canadian Journal of African Studies*. 6, No. 2: 165-182.

Vidal, Claudine, and Marie LePape. 1986. *Pratiques de Crise et Conditions Sociales A Abidjan 1979-1985*. Abidjan: ORSTOM Centre de Petit-Bassam.

von Braun, Joachim, Kennedy, Eileen and Bouis, Howarth. 1989. *Comparative Analysis of the Effects of Increased Commercialization of Subsistence Agriculture on Production, Consumption and Nutrition.* (Report for USAID.) Washington,DC: International Food Policy Research Institute. November.

Wellseley Editorial Committee. 1977. *Women and National Development: The Complexities of Change.* Chicago: University of Chicago Press.

White, Luise. 1988. "Gender and History." *SIGNS: A Journal of Women in Culture and Society.* 13, No. 2: 360-364.

_____. 1990. *The Comforts of Home: Prostitution in Colonial Nairobi.* Chicago and London: University of Chicago Press.

Wipper, Audrey. Ed. 1972. Special Issue on Women in Africa. *Canadian Journal of African Studies.* 6, No. 2: 329-349.

_____. 1972. "African Women, Fashion and Scapegoating." *Canadian Journal of African Studies.* 6, No. 2: 329-349.

_____. Ed. 1976. "Rural Women: Development or Underdevelopment?" *Rural Africana.* (Special Issue) 29.

_____. and Harriet Lyons. Eds. 1988. "Special Issue: Current Research on African Women." *Canadian Journal of African Studies.* 22(3).

Wisner, Ben. 1989. *Power and Need in Africa.* Trenton, NJ: Africa World Press.

Women in Nigeria (WIN). 1985. *Women in Nigeria Today.* London: Zed Books.

World Bank. 1981. *Accelerated Development in Sub-Saharan Africa: An Agenda for Action.* Washington, DC: World Bank.

_____. 1989. *Sub-Saharan Africa: From Crisis to Sustainable Growth.* Washington, DC: World Bank.

Wright, Marcia. 1983. "Bwanikwa: Consciousness and Protest Among Slave Women in Central Africa, 1886-1911." In Robertson, Claire C. and Klein, Martin A. *Women and Slavery in Africa*: 246-267. Madison: The University of Wisconsin Press.

Young, Kate, Wolkowitz, Cathy and McCullagh R. Eds. 1984. Of *Marriage and the Market.* London: Routledge and Kegan Paul.

Zack-Williams, A. B. 1990 "Sierra Leone: Crisis or Despair?" *Review of African Political Economy*. 49: 22-33.

Chapter 8

On Research on the State, Law, and the Legal Processes of Development

By Adeno Addis, Bereket Selassie and Robert B. Seidman[1]

I. Introduction

The preceding chapters emphasize that realization of Africa's great potential requires changing existing state policies and institutions. Instead of serving narrowly-based urban elites and their foreign clients or partners, these must engage the African people in participatory policy-making to attain self-sustainable development.

The past thirty years of African experience reveal two pre-eminent realities. On the one hand, in most countries, expansive centralized state structures came to dominate the scene. On the other, unless the state regimented its 'mobilization,' an apathetic civil society tended to withdraw. In this respect, Africa should not lose sight of the lessons of Eastern Europe. The unrealized democratic aspirations of African peoples require support, not in mere doctrinal principles, but through creation of new structures and procedures to apply these principles in practice, and hold state power-holders accountable.

The failure of development in Africa implies the failure of the state to implement principles of democracy in practical terms. This relates to both the kinds of institutions which comprise the state, itself; and its role in formulating and implementing appropriate policies to foster productive activities and essential services. More specifically, it implies a failure of the law-making and law-implementing systems of the legal order (Chazan & Rothchild, 1988: 325, 327). In this respect, failure refers to the inadequate use, misuse or abuse of state power. Kwame Nkrumah taught to seek first the political kingdom. As Goren Hyden tells us, however, "today Africa knows that there is nothing magical about the political kingdom" (in Wunsch and Olowu, 1990: 245, 246).

This chapter considers alternative theories purporting to explain this failure, and offers a research agenda which may enable scholars to contribute to building more democratic, participatory state structures.

Section I identifies the general difficulty implied in all the foregoing chapters: Rather than exercising state power to alleviate the poverty and powerlessness of most Africans, the post-independence governments—regardless of their stated intentions—tended to exacerbate them. This difficulty has two different but related aspects, both of which require explanation. First, all too frequently, those who gained state power exercised it, not to restructure the inherited distorted social structure, but to amass their own wealth and privilege. Section II critically reviews and discusses the dominant theories of the state—libertarianism, pluralism and Marxism—that purport to explain that aspect of the difficulty in the African circumstance. This, however, leaves a second aspect of the difficulty. Theories at the level of generality discussed in Section II may provide valid initial explanations. Nevertheless, they may prove inadequate to guide research to assist those sincerely seeking to exercise state power for the benefit of the mass. Attainment of sustainable development, as explained in the previous chapters, required massive changes in existing institutions. To make those changes, Africa's liberation movements needed to use state power to alter the laws that underpinned those institutions. Section III addresses their failure to make those necessary changes. Finally, Section IV proposes an agenda for research as a basis for using the state and legal order to implement policies and create institutions more likely ensure realization of Africa's rich potential in favor of the mass.

II. The Difficulty: The State and Law as Part of the Problem

We first discuss the general relationship between state, law and the development process; and, second, the roles and behaviors that constitute the difficulty researchers must address to ensure that the state plays a more appropriate role.

A. The state, law and the development process

The preceding chapters expose the misallocation of resources that lay at the heart of Africa's poverty and powerlessness. Those allocations did not happen by themselves. They resulted from repetitive patterns of social behaviors—that is, from institutions. For example, banks shipped investable surpluses out of Africa to metropolitan corporate bank accounts; peasants used low-level, antiquated technologies, while wealthy farmers hogged the best arable land; educators employed hierarchical, authoritarian teaching methods; and health authorities squandered funds on urban-based curative medicine for the rich. Powerlessness, too, arose out of repetitive human behaviors. Some occurred in civil society, where corporate managers gave orders, and employees obeyed; farm owners told farm laborers what to do and how much they would earn; and madams, masters and bosses dictated to houseservants. Some of these behaviors took place in the state sector: Ministers did not listen to the plaints of the working people; rather than advance the public interest, managing directors of public corporations feathered their nests; courts heeded the rich and powerful, not the powerless; and cabinets attended to the needs of transnational corporations, not of their countries' poor. All these constituted social problems which the post-independence African state failed to solve.

In its most general sense, African society—like any other—consists of interrelated, interacting individuals and collectivities. To change their modes of production and distribution of goods, allocation of material wealth, and systems of governance requires that they change their ways of interacting with each other—that is, their repetitive patterns of social behaviors. They must do so, moreover, in a new way. "[D]evelopment means that people must relate with confidence to many more people and in many more roles than are required by smaller, and less ambitious economies, societies and polities." Once this aspect of development is understood, then our stress on humans' "self-organizing capacities, and on rules and institutions can be more easily understood."(Wunsch and Olowu, 1990: 8)

Max Weber points out that states consist of more than the government. They include bureaucratic, administrative, military, police, judicial and parliamentary structures—what Alfred Stepan describes as "the continuous administrative, legal, bureaucratic and coercive systems that attempt not only to structure relationships between civil and public authority in a polity but also to structure many crucial relationships within civil society as well." (Stepan in Evans et al, 1985: 7) These structures underpin and sometimes reshape not only the relationships between private right and public power, and between civil and official society, but within civil society itself (Weber, 1968, c. 9; Evans et al, 1985: 7). In this sense, the African state comprises sets of functionaries who collectively carry out the government's several tasks. The legal order serves as the means of ordering those relationships.

No matter in what field particular social problems arise, African governments, like those elsewhere, can only use the legal order[2] to change the patterns of social behaviors (institutions) that cause them. The legal order thus plays an underbearer role as society's primary instrument for implementing any and all forms of policy intervention (Makgetla and Seidman, 1988). In Africa, no more than elsewhere can governments—as neo-classical economists recommend—simply let the market perform. Nor can they issue a fiat to the market and expect it to comply. They can only enact laws to command ministers and bureaucrats and judges to behave in certain ways with respect of market actors. African agricultural ministries cannot command the soil to yield more crops; they can only recommend that governments enact laws requiring farmers to change their practices and farm agents to change their behavior towards farmers in ways likely to bring about the new practices. The state engages in the development process ubiquitously by directing sets of people to behave in particular ways. Thus to observe that Africa still suffered poverty and powerlessness three decades after independence is to say that Africa's legal order still sustained the institutions that caused these problems. In this sense, laws contributed to causing or aggravating them.

We take as problematic the question of whether the post-colonial African state's failure to produce development-oriented laws derived from the absence of capacity of power or of autonomy. The international economic and legal order and the power of local capitalists lie at the heart of Africa's incapacities. Nevertheless, only if problem-solving, policy-oriented research can first show that the available evidence warrants its explanations as to the causes of a given social problem can it propose solutions likely to succeed.

Those explanations must meet two criteria. First, they must prove valid in the sense that after conscientious research, the available evidence does not falsify them.   Second, they must focus on factors which the national state and its constituent institutions can conceivably change, taking all other factors as conditions, not causes. In that context, at least in the short run, African government policy-makers must take as conditions factors about which they frequently can do precious little: not only geography, natural resources and climate, but transnational corporations, the world economic order and multilateral institutional agencies. Where those factors have had an adverse effect on development, the explanations must show what civil and state institutions in the African country, and which laws underpinning them, made that adverse effect possible. Only explanations with these characteristics can suggest new state institutions and laws which African governments may introduce to cope with those given realities to attain more successful development.

As another way to put it, development cannot take place in Africa until the peoples of Africa tame the state and law, making the state and law not part of the problem, but part of the solution. Even after a new liberation movement gains state power, it will still require research that addresses the state and the legal order as sets of problematic social behaviors (Azarya in Chazen and Rothchild, 1988). For this purpose, we first identify precisely what and whose behavior comprises the social problems that we suggest caused the failure of the 'state' and 'the legal order' in Africa.

B. The difficulty: The behavior of law-makers and law-implementers

That the state and law hindered development in Africa raises two sorts of questions. First, why did post-independence governments enact and implement laws that generally favored the rich and powerful?   An answer requires explication of the social behaviors of officials in the law-making and law-implementing process.   Second, even when officials subjectively wanted to alleviate poverty and oppression, why did the newly-enacted laws so often fail to help?   To answer that requires an investigation of the legal order's 'underbearer' role in fostering social behaviors that continued to cause social ills.[3]

This requires reappraisal of the classical conceptions about how government functions.   Formal statute-making (in our myths, the exclusive province of legislatures) comes only in the middle of a long chain that begins with whoever has an idea for a law, often a relatively low civil servant, and ends with the policeman, bureaucrat or judge who enforces and therefore interprets the law. In the former British colonies, for example, the list of officials who shaped the impact of any given law included:

1. the civil servants who usually first suggested the need for the legislation;

2. the Permanent Secretary and Minister who decided to study the identified difficulty;

3. the civil servants who studied the problem, generated a legislative program, contacted 'interested parties' for comments, and produced a memorandum (sometimes called a 'layman's draft');

4. the Cabinet Committee on Legislation that approved the proposal and instructed Parliamentary Counsel to draft the bill, and later would approve its final draft for Cabinet vote ;

5. the lawyers in the Office of Parliamentary Counsel, who draft not only the principal legislation but usually subsidiary legislation under it;

6. those whom they consulted—civil servants, mainly in the Ministry concerned, but frequently in related Ministries, and sometimes 'interested parties' in civil society;

7. the Cabinet that approved the bill for introduction into Parliament;

8. the legislators who formally enacted the bill into law;

9. the ministerial officials who developed memoranda concerning subordinate legislation that will give the law its effective content;

10. the Minister who actually promulgated the subsidiary legislation;

11. the judges, police and officials who interpreted the law in the course of implementing it;[4]

To understand the law-making and law-implementing processes, we must investigate these many interconnected roles and institutions.

III. Political Theory and Jurisprudence and the African Dilemma

To guide policy-oriented, problem-solving research directed to changing Africa's inherited state institutions requires first an explanation as to how those institutions hindered the development process. For the most part, theories advanced in Africa to explain the failure of the state and law proved inadequate to provide that guidance. In part, that inadequacy arose because they drew on theories based on First World experiences that remained singularly inappropriate to the African circumstance. More significantly, they explained the role of the state on a level of generality that rendered them incapable of guiding research as to the specific changes Africa's new governments should make to support development. In this section, we first discuss the particular post-independence conditions in which new African state officials functioned; and, second, the major categories of theories advanced to explain the negative impact of their social behavior: libertarianism, modernization theory, pluralism, Marxism, and, in the 1980s, the non-governance approach that seemed to abandon the state as irredeemable.

A. The African condition

African circumstances differed significantly from those of Western societies within which the dominant theories of the state arose. Africa's colonial history defined the structure and function of the

African state and conditioned the agenda for utilizing the state and law.

1. <u>Africa's diverse constituencies</u>. African countries inherited national boundaries imposed by the 19th Century European colonial powers without regard to pre-existing historical, geographical or ethnic realities. Instead of strong integrated political economies, these encompassed profoundly bifurcated societies. The mass of peasants remained impoverished and vulnerable. In most countries, distorted economic growth had generated no real industrial proletariat, and, in only a few, a semi-proletarianized agricultural and mining labor force. Trade unions remained weak, peasant organizations almost non-existent. Almost no moral entrepreneurial groups, concerned with environment, human rights, etc., had emerged. Very few black capitalists had established viable businesses. Transnational corporation affiliates and, in southern Africa, a handful of white settlers, still dominated the modern economy's 'commanding heights.' Seemingly, only minutes after independence, black elites, who organized very powerfully in informal ways, although they held little or no economic power, emerged as members of a new political ruling class (Kennedy, 1988). In some countries—as varied as Nigeria, Kenya, Ethiopia, Somalia and Rwanda—different ethnic elites waged sometimes bloody struggles for political power.

2. <u>Agenda for African governments</u>. Colonial history bequeathed to Africa agendas quite different from those in the West. The new African governments did not merely have to run a state, using well-developed institutions that had been in existence for many years; they had both to change the inherited institutions and create new ones (Glicksman in Lystad, 1965: 140).

3. <u>Institutional Frameworks</u>. The basic structure of most African governments remained the same the day after independence as the day before. They had the following characteristics: bifurcated legal systems; colonial capitalist legal orders; a legacy of authoritarianism; the absence of accountability to the poor majority; and laws that endowed officials with power to make and implement key decisions, granting them great discretion. In short, the colonial legacy did not, as sometimes claimed, bequeath democracy to the new African nations. On the contrary, those countries inherited hierarchical authoritarian institutions. The new constitutions, drafted by departing colonial powers, did not change these.

B. Libertarianism

Libertarianism, the political theory that underpinned most new African constitutions, arose in England out of the new middle classes' struggles against the aristocracy's economic and political formations. There, new entrepreneurial classes strove to throw off the aristocratic influence that, in government, granted radical discretion to officials, especially judges—discretion used mainly to favor aristocratic interests (Hay et al, 1975; Chambliss and Seidman, 1981).

1. First world origins. Libertarianism rested on an explanation for the arbitrariness, secrecy, corruption and government-by-crony that supported mercantilism and made entrepreneurial activity in a market economy almost impossible. As Lord Bryce summarized it, "Power tends to corrupt, and absolute power corrupts absolutely." To tame aristocratic power, libertarianism formulated both the normative basis for a political system, and institutions aimed at establishing it. Resonating with classical economics, it assumed the world consists of 'free' individuals endowed with 'natural' (i.e., pre-political) rights. The role of the state was seen to be one of providing a neutral framework through which rights-bearing, free individuals interact. Under the libertarian scheme, therefore, the role of the state was to be exhausted by three functions: (1) the protection of private property rights; (2) the protection of a market through which individuals can arrange and re-arrange those rights; and (3) to respect individual preferences which manifest themselves through an exchange process (Macpherson, 1977: 26-27).

Second, the libertarian assumptions that individuals are free and equal before the market is erroneous. They remain oblivious to the fact that lack of resources and opportunities systematically constrain many people from participating fully in the life of the polity.

Third, the fact that the state may formally withdraw from some spheres of life and that private groups or non-governmental organizations take over some of its functions does not necessarily mean that the state has totally withdrawn from the field. In many ways, the state continues to set the parameters, often implicitly, within which these groups continue to function, without intervention being a subject of critical commentary.

The libertarian conception of state and legal order may have an unacceptable cost in the developing countries. It may simply consecrate the unequal distribution of resources both between the elite and the masses, and between various countries and transnational entities. It tends to remain historically insensitive and institutionally imperial.

1. The African experience. The liberal agenda failed in Africa, not because there was an unacceptable level of state intervention in the area of private property, but because its inner premises contradicted African imperatives.

Three other categories of state theory arose to explain the failure of the state: modernization, with pluralism as a principal component; various versions of Marxism; and what some call 'political choice' theory and others, the 'non-governance' school. Some authors suggest these paradigms burst on the scene, briefly blazed furiously, and then declined (Chazen et al, 1988). In fact, all three coexisted, though at given times some achieved greater popularity. Here, we discuss in turn these different perspectives on the African state and law.

C. Modernization and pluralist theory

Modernization theory became especially popular among the first generation of Africanists from the West. In its normative dimension, that theory implied that to become modern, an African state should copy an admittedly modern state (with unexpressed hubris, that meant the country from which the particular Western academic hailed). In its positive aspect, modernization theory held that pluralism explained the political choices of an African state—and, as too frequently occurs with positive theory, that, too, became normative.

1. The ideology of modernization. Modernization frankly argued that an African state should copy the characteristics of a Western, industrialized, capitalist nation. Thus Marc Galanter identified the characteristics of a modern legal system, as "a cluster of features that characterize, to a greater or lesser extent, the legal systems of the industrial societies of the last century." (in Weiner, 1966: 153, 154; see also Braibanti in Weiner, 1966)

These academics apparently assumed that copying on paper the institutions of the metropole would produce modernization. When it did not, they mainly blamed the Africans, claiming they lacked the necessary 'modern' subjective values and attitudes.

Thirty years after modernization theory had gone into decline, some observers still tended to blame the evils of the predatory state on the African officials' psyche: "the constriction of the reach of government bodies in recent years is...the outcome of the conscious abandonment by state bureaucrats of economic and moral responsibility for the welfare of their citizens" (Chazen and Rothchild, 1988: 327-28).

Africans, however, stubbornly remained Africans. Whatever its powers, a government has only relatively small potential for transforming the value sets of all its people. Psychological theories of modernization could hardly serve to redirect African governments on more developmental courses.

2. The pluralist explanation. Formulated in the United States, pluralist theory sought to demonstrate that every people got the government they wanted. It explained that societies generally failed to fulfill libertarianism's democratic promises because not public interest, but the parochial claims of interest groups moved governments (eg., Carnoy, 1984: 9). The elite of society's many interest groups—government, military, labor, business, and so forth—bargain[5] with each other; the outcome constitutes the State's policies. The State is an empty vessel: "For pluralists, the State is neutral, an 'empty slate,' and still a servant of the citizenry—of the electorate—but the common good is defined as a set of empirical decisions that do not necessarily reflect the will of the majority" (Ibid: 37).

The neutral state corresponds to the minimal value-consensus to which pluralism still clings. Despite the conflicts in society, all right-thinking people agreed at least that society must continue. That required a neutral state to contain conflict and to determine which conflicting view would emerge as public choice. Just as state interference in bargaining in the economy made efficiency impossible, so in the bargaining between elites it resulted in outcomes that did not genuinely reflect the power balances between the various interest groups those elites represented. In pluralist theory, the state no longer functioned as representative of a mythical value-consensus on substantive issues. Instead, it represented the consensus against social suicide.

Pluralists claimed their theory at once celebrated diversity and, through neutral state structures, contained it (Ibid: 37). The resulting laws represented a political analogue of economic 'effective demand'. That some people had more political power than others raised no greater moral issues than the fact that in the market some people had more dollars (and hence more 'effective demand') than others. If some groups remained so poorly organized that their leaders could not make themselves heard at the bargaining table, they received only their just deserts.[6]

Scholars early invoked the pluralist paradigm to explain Third World development failures (Kautsky, 1962: 3, 5-6). Superficially, pluralism seemed adequate to explain Africa's predicament. Transnational corporations, political elites and organized ethnic groups had the most cohesive organization and bargaining power, and African policies tended to favor them. At the end of the day, however, pluralism failed to provide a sufficient explanation since it viewed the

Third World state and its officials as themselves a rapacious gang devouring civil society. These scholars tended to perceive the state as captured by the officials who nominally served as its agents and servants.

> "From this perspective the managerial class has monopolized resources for its own private use and purposefully prevented major portions of the population from gaining access to public resources. The constriction of the reach of government bodies is therefore not random; it is an outcome of the conscious abandonment by state bureaucrats of economic and moral responsibility for the welfare of their citizens."(Chazen in Chazen and Rothchild, 1988: 325, 327)

From that explanation no solution could flow except a call to throw the rascals out—but the rascals controlled the state structures, and were not about to acquiesce to their own demise. Even if they did, these theorists seemed to offer nothing likely to prevent reoccurrence of the phenomenon.

2. <u>Marxism, dependency and the development of underdevelopment</u>. Like the other theories examined, Marxist theory of the state focussed on the questions: Why did the law represent the interests and values of this group and not that one? Why did this group and not another obey the laws? Like other theorists, Marxists, too, disagreed among themselves. One school, widely expressed in academic circles, claimed to have a clear answer. Using class as a primary category for analysis, it explained that, in the developed capitalist world, the state and its system of laws facilitated the systematic exploitation of workers by capitalists. Whatever its seemingly democratic facade, in the last analysis, the state stood with the capitalists against the workers. In support of this explanation, this version of Marxism adopted a simplistic metaphor. The 'base,' the mode of production, determined the 'superstructure,' ideas and culture, including the legal order (Marx and Engels, 1969: 503-04).[9] Since the capitalist class dominates the mode of production in that system, their ideas and their law will dominate the culture and the legal order. The state becomes the executive committee of the ruling class (Milliband, 1969).[10] No matter how much it enshrined one person, one vote as its underlying principle, bourgeois democracy concealed the inequality of worker and capitalist behind a facade of equality before the law. The laws the state enacted and implemented tended to reproduce and strengthen the class relations of production. Necessarily, that enhanced the power and privilege of those already on top of the heap. Thus the colonial state served to strengthen colonial capitalist modes of production, and therefore the

power and privilege of the colonial capitalists. Far from protecting individual autonomy, the liberal state protected the power of the economic ruling classes, and ensured the powerlessness—Marxists called it 'alienation'—of the mass. Though not all Marxists agreed,[11] those adopting this metaphor seemed to imply, like the pluralists, that state officials behaved entirely in response to external demands, that is, that they had no independent motivations.

Some Latin American scholars early drew on Marxist theory to explain that world capitalist structures remained so powerful that, whatever they subjectively desired, local political elites could not change institutions or resist; instead they became mere henchmen for foreign interests, enacting local laws and creating political institutions that fostered underdevelopment. In Africa, Walter Rodney (1972) and others tended to blame external powers as the primary source of Africa's poverty and powerlessness. After his ouster, Ghana's former president, Kwame Nkrumah (1972), emphasized the emergence of classes that sought to block state efforts to achieve social transformation. Many leaders of southern African guerilla movements explicitly acknowledged their debt to Marxist theories in their struggles to win state power. Samir Amin (1990) and world systems theorists (eg, Wallerstein, 1986) emphasized that international capitalist penetration had undermined pre-existing social systems, aggravating the continent's external dependency, and called for further study of the state. Increasingly, theorists adopting a Marxist perspective discussed dependency theory in ways that took the power of foreign capital as a given, explaining that African governments enacted and kept in force laws which permitted that power to ravage African polities (eg, Makemure et al, 1986). Nzongola-Ntalaja emphasized this point when he said (1987: 75),

> "the crisis of the post-colonial state has to do with the betrayal of the revolution by the neo-colonial ruling class, on the one hand, and the failure of revolutionary movements to transform the economy and the state in a radical way because of their own shortcomings and the counter-revolutionary challenge by imperialism, on the other. In both cases, the post-colonial state has failed to adopt a people-oriented strategy of development."

E. Responses in the 1980s

By the 1980s, these conflicting theories had generated four sets of explanations for Africa's crisis of governance: two variant reaffirmations of liberalism, an abandonment of politics, and an institutionalist position that followed one version of Marxism.

1. <u>Liberalism renascent</u>. Some, including experts in USAID, the World Bank and IMF, re-introduced libertarianism all over again. As Peter Anyang' Nyong'o observed, they saw "the political crisis as that of a state that has bitten off more than it can chew: instead of engaging in economic activity through parastatals, the state should withdraw and confine itself to those activities it is most traditionally qualified to undertake in a free-market economy, those of providing and running the physical and social infrastructure, maintaining law and order and guaranteeing a sound policy framework for capital accumulation" (Anyang' Nyong'o, 1987: 14, 16; Huntington, 1968: 2). In other words, their solution for the failure of African governments to move towards development seems to require them to abandon the effort.

2. <u>Basic needs</u>. Viewing small entrepreneurs in agriculture and the informal sector as central potential development agents, basic needs theorists called for democratic participatory state structures that would devote resources to their aid within a basic market framework. Who should participate, and how, remained unanswered questions (eg, World Bank, 1989: 147).

3. <u>The abandonment of politics</u>. Some theorists viewed the state as captured by the officials who nominally served as its agents and servants (Chazen in Rothchild and Chazen, 1988: 325, 327). That perspective led them to abandon the study of the state as hopelessly incapable of reform. They began to focus, instead, on the non-state sector, studying how people cope in the face of a predatory state (Chazen and Rothchild, 1988; Hyden, 1980; Korten, 1989).

4. <u>Institutionalism</u>. All these theories operated on a very high level of generalization. In effect, they only identified the difficulty that lawmakers, seeking to attain sustainable development, had to analyze in order to develop adequate institutions and laws to resolve the difficulty. Pluralism, for example, only raised the issue of why in Africa some groups and not others had access to the bargaining that pluralism holds lies at politic's heart. Marxism only raised the question, how and why did the ruling class, and not other groups, continue to control government.

What we call Institutionalism held that social behavior results from choices people make within the institutional structures of society.

Those structures, themselves, however, are human constructs. "Structure does not exist independently of human beings. It is not merely like a wall that puts limits on what can be achieved. Structure is both the medium and outcome of the practices which constitute social systems....Structure and actor are interdependent." (Hyden in Wunseh and Olowu, 1990: 245, 251)

In this view, to explain Africa's failure of development we must closely examine its institutional structures and the repetitive patterns of social behaviors of the host of actors which constitute those institutions. This calls for a theory that focuses not on broad explanations, but one which would explicitly help new African governments to use law to make appropriate changes in inherited institutions. To explain why some groups had disparate power over the outcomes of government decision-making, they needed not generalized propositions, but detailed, 'middle level' propositions to explain how state institutions funnelled private power into public decision-making. They needed not generalized assertions of the power of the bureaucratic bourgeoisie, but detailed explanations about how the existing state and the legal order facilitated the behavior that led to the rise of that class. They did not need a generalized explanation for the weakness of African states in terms of variables with which African governments could not deal directly, like capitalism, the bloody-mindedness of politicians, or the inevitable gap between 'want' and 'get.' Instead, Africa needed detailed explanations for the social behaviors of relevant actors that led to governments' failure in terms of the variables which those actors had some power to manipulate. In short, it needed a theory which would generate detailed, 'middle level' propositions to explain the failure of development in terms of the only instrument that lay readily to the hand of the new governments, the state and the legal order. It needed a theory of law as underbearer to the development process.

IV. Law's Underbearer Role: Law and Institutional Change

"Rules are the 'nuts and bolts' which organize the complex behaviors involved in self-organization and development. They are the human-created mechanisms which guide, facilitate and strengthen humans' ability to work together: Rules are the midwives of organization. Rules establish understandings with which men and women organize their relationships to deal with the perplexities and limits of the human condition: to cope with fear, vulnerability,, human uncertainty and error; to satisfy the need for trust and restraint to produce costly human, social and political capital; to efficiently allocate resources; to make, legitimate and promulgate collective choices; to retain the experience of past and present, and to pass experience on to new generations; to train new role occupants; and so on." (Wunsch and Olowu, 1990: 10)

The rules of law enacted by African governments—like all others—constitute the most formal and most coercive of all the rules in the social order. The legal order consists, of course, not only of the rules, but also the institutions and their members which make and implement those rules. The legal order constitutes society's most formal and coercive normative system, with rules and their creation and implementation at its very core. It touches every important human interaction, sometimes slightly, sometimes with overwhelming impact. Law becomes government's basic tool for shaping social behaviors that comprise all societal institutions, and therefore society itself.

That implies a contradiction. Law has an inherently hierarchical, centralizing characteristic. It usually emanates from a central government; it depends for enforcement upon centralized, bureaucratically-organized structures. It breathes hierarchy. As we have seen, a whole gaggle of political scientists now explain Africa's difficulties in terms of centralization and the state. How can a law, with its inherent centralizing tendencies tame a state whose basic difficulty lies in over-centralization? How can a tool with those tendencies generate rules likely to favor the mass of the population, rather than the elite that manipulate the legal order?

At best, law constitutes a very blunt tool. It operates mainly through bureaucratically-organized institutions (courts, police, government departments, public corporations). These suffer all the ills of bureaucracy: rigidity, relative incapacity to learn from experience, compartmentalization (Seidman, 1978). Law may change some behaviors relatively easily (for example, a law that requires wills to bear two witnesses), but others hardly at all (for example, laws purporting to limit the number of children a family may bear). An adequate theory to guide the use of law in its underbearer role requires that it take account of law's limits.

Given law's underbearer role as society's primary instrument for social change in every field, from the economy to education to gender relations, Africans who are sincerely dedicated to attaining sustainable development must, when they gain state power, pass new laws to change the patterns of undesirable social behavior (the inherited institutions) that cause mass poverty and powerlessness. To lay the foundation for more effective development policies, they require research to identify middle level propositions that explain how and why existing rules of law led to particular patterns of counterproductive social behavior. To guide their investigations they need a research agenda, a set of categories.

Whether a law can successfully contribute to overcoming the obstacles to development turns on whether those who misbehave choose to obey that law. In this section, we propose a research agenda to help improve law's role as underbearer in the development process. We discuss, first, a general model of the legal order, and, second, some more specific categories for analyzing behavior in the face of a rule of law.

A. A general model of the legal order

The milieu in which particular individuals—here termed 'role occupants'—act may contain many factors likely to influence them to choose to behave in ways that may cause social problems. Researchers lack the resources to examine all of these. To decide what facts to investigate, they need <u>categories</u> to identify the primary constraints and resources in the role-occupant's milieu. The categories of possible hypotheses must of course have enough specificity to enable researchers to distinguish in general terms what data seems promising or useful to explain the social problem addressed, and what does not. In each category, researchers may then generate more detailed explanatory hypotheses as to how the critical factors shape the role-occupants' choices. Those hypotheses guide the investigation of the relevant data required to falsify them. Once proven consistent with all the available data, those hypotheses logically may suggest laws embodying policies likely to change the role occupants' behavior in ways more consistent with the development process.

Following Fredrick Barth (1966),[12] the simplest model of action consists of individuals and collectivities making choices in a physical, social, economic and psychological context made up of constraints and resources affecting their activity, their 'arena of choice' (see Fig. 8-1).

By describing that milieu, we 'explain' behavior. If we describe the constraints and resources affecting a group of farmers' milieu—for example, the availability of credit, the nature of their land, the climate, the water available, the market for different sorts of crops, the relative cost of growing them, the government programs available,

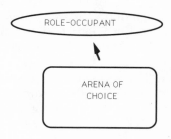

Fig. 8-1

the technology used, the farmers' expertise, their mind-sets, local customs, and so forth—we 'explain' why those farmers grow soy beans instead of wheat or cotton, and their relative productivity.

The legal order, together with its commands and opportunities, appears to its addressees (a set of primary role occupants) as one of many factors shaping their milieu: Something that perhaps they can work around, perhaps something they must obey, but always something that to some degree or another they must take into account. Whenever they enact a law, law-makers proclaim a norm that either commands the addressees' obedience (as in the case of tort law or criminal law), or offers them an opportunity to obey (like contract law or most of corporation law). Simultaneously, the law-makers address related directives to appropriate implementing agencies (administrators, courts, police, and so forth) to behave in ways that support the role occupants' appropriate behavior, or punish them if they behave inappropriately (See Rubin, 1989: 369, 375ff; H.L.A. Hart, 1961) (See Fig. 8-2).

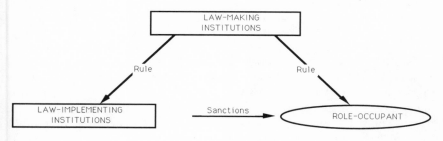

Fig. 8-2

A law's addressees may comprise all members of society ("Thou shalt not commit murder"); a defined class of non-officials ("A director of a corporation incorporated in Booga-Booga shall hold citizenship in Booga-Booga."); an official ("The Minister shall select settlers for participation in the Settlement Scheme. . . . ."). We may combine the behavioral insights of Barth's model and the formal structures of Hans Calcine's (see Fig. 8-3) to show that in deciding how to act in the face of a rule of law, role occupants take into account all the constraints and resources of their arena of choice, including the strictures of the law itself, and the potential for sanctioning behavior by the implementing agency.

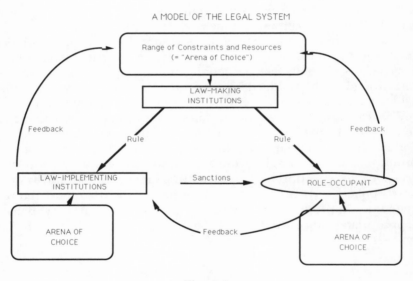

A MODEL OF THE LEGAL SYSTEM

Fig. 8-3

Ministerial or departmental behavior, too, consists of a series of choices made by relevant officials in light of their arenas of choice which include the rules addressed to them. The model thus incorporates directives addressed to both lay persons and officials to induce them to behave in ways appropriate to carry out the law's purpose. In both cases, some sort of an implementing agency administers conformity-inducing measures.

To explain the legal order's impact on behaviors that cause social problems, the model suggests the researcher ought to enquire about the content of the norm addressed to the role-occupant; the arena of choice of the role-occupant, the norm addressed to the implementing agency (including the conformity-inducing measures it empowers the implementing agency to employ); and that agency's arena of choice (Rubin, 1989: 408). These constitute the primary categories those proposing to change the legal order must investigate.

Most sociological jurisprudents (eg, Ehrlich, 1936) and American legal realists (eg, Llewellyn, 1931; Hale, 1952) agree with the model pictured in Fig. 8-3. It points attention to the primary rules and the behavior of the primary role occupants, the rules addressed to the implementing agency and that agency's behavior, the sanctions actually imposed, feedback mechanisms, and the social surroundings within which these several actors play out their roles. However, the model leaves as a formless residuary category the elements that define any particular set of the role occupants' arena of choice. On these, the realists' descendants differed strenuously.

B. Analyzing behavior in the face of a rule of law.

Three competing sets of theorists propose quite different explanations for the behavior of role occupants—African or otherwise—in the face of a rule of law: (1) the sociological school; (2) law and economics; and (3) institutionalism.

1. The sociological school. Sociologists early asserted that in general people behaved in accordance with their subjective values and attitudes (Sumner, 1906; cf. Cranston, 1978: 875). Only those laws that matched people's values and attitudes could change their behavior. With President Eisenhower (Branch, 1989), for example, they predicted that desegregation laws would not induce changed white behavior until white attitudes towards blacks changed (Roche and Gordon). Lawrence Friedman (1969) postulated that in general people's legal culture, commonly-accepted values and attitudes, determine which laws they should or should not obey.

Values and attitudes, however, seem inadequate as the sole determinant of behavior because of their circularity and their lack of supporting evidence. First, to urge that behavior responds to values and attitudes usually rests upon the same empirical basis as the perception of the same behavior. For example, some have explained the relatively slow spread of new technologies among African peasants by their supposedly conservative social values. The warrant for that 'explanation' usually consists of the evidence of the difficulty; that is, that many African peasants seem slow to adopt new technologies.

Second, as the psychological theory of cognitive dissonance

predicted (Festinger, 1957), the facts show that people do change their behavior in the face of a rule of law, although frequently not as the law requires. For example, in most African countries people pay income taxes, even though when the income tax laws first appeared, most people had no conforming values or attitudes. The extreme sociological position, that people will only obey laws that conform to their values and attitudes seems empirically false and logically incomprehensible.

2. Law and Economics (Posner, 1986; Kitch: 184).[13] Although Law and Economics has two clearly defined wings, conservative and liberal, with one exception, both explain choices people make by a single factor: self-interest. In the tradition of neo-classical economics, the conservatives insist that pursuit of one's own interests constitutes a powerful regularity in human behavior (Posner, 1986: 77). Since self-interest finds free expression only in a free, competitive market, the ideal organization of every aspect of human society—even those, like the family and adoption of children, that do not seemingly relate to economic concerns—resembles that market (See Stokey and Zeckhauser, 1978). In that sense, all social problems constitute market failures. Distributional considerations distinguish liberal Law and Economics from the conservative wing (Calabresi and Melmud, 1089; Markowitz, 1969). To guide their prescriptions for African law, the IMF (1985) followed conservative law and economics, while the World Bank was guided by liberal law and economics (Berg, 1982).

The Law and Economics methodology and categories seem unduly restrictive. First, in Africa today, every economy contains large areas of non-market relationships. Because it contains no relevant categories, Law and Economics cannot guide research looking to influence those relationships. Second, many, probably most human relationships—like love and family—take on a market-like cast only by ignoring their most human aspects. Third, the notion that people behave only in terms of wealth-maximization seems trivial, if not empirically false (eg, see Ellickson, 1986): people maximize what they most value. It also becomes circular. People behave as they do because they value what they do; we know they value what they do because they so behave.

C. Institutionalism

(Seidman, 1978b: 47; Allott, 1981; Burman and B.E. Harrell-Bond, 1978; Evan in Gouldner and Miller, 1965): Both the sociological school and the Law and Economics movement mainly seek a single, overriding motive for behavior ('values and attitudes', wealth-maximization). By contrast, the model proposed here—call it 'Institutionalism'—

suggests that, in making choices, people take into account a multitude of factors. These include the formal law and the conformity-inducing measures ('sanctions') imposed by implementing agencies. This section discusses these in turn.

1. <u>The rules.</u>

People make choices within a whole framework of existing laws and implementing agencies. For example, water polluters act not only in light of the sort of laws conventionally labelled "water pollution law", or "environmental law". They also act within a framework of property law, contract law, the laws concerning streams and rivers, tax law, constitutional law, etc. Every legal system embraces the maxim, that which the law does not forbid, it permits. Unless the property law or some other law forbids landowners from polluting a stream that runs through their property, they have a legal right to pollute it. Moreover, since the legal order includes not only the texts of the rules, but implementing agencies, if environmental agencies do not adequately enforce anti-pollution laws, the polluter will take that into account.

In short, role occupants choose to act within—among many other (often interacting, sometimes contradictory) elements—the constraints and resources introduced by the legal order itself. Therefore, researchers must examine as their first attempt at explanation the current rules of law that purport to affect the behavior that causes the given social problem.

2. <u>The requirement of choice.</u>

Before role occupants will likely choose to obey the rule, three factors must coincide:

1. Role occupants must have the *opportunity* to choose to obey or disobey. That is, their environment must put them in a position where they have a choice to obey or disobey. For example, the existence of an open stream through landowners' property gives the landowners the opportunity to pollute it, or to obey a law prohibiting pollution. In the same sense, a court's opportunity to enforce a statute depends upon the willingness of aggrieved parties to bring lawsuits.

2. Role-occupants must have the *capacity* to behave as the law directs, that is, they must have the skills and resources to do so (Keogh v. Magistrates of Edinburgh, in Anton, 1979: 236). For example; a tax law directing a Department to collect a specified tax will fail if the Department does not have sufficient well-trained tax collectors to cope with the task.

3. The rule must be *communicated* to the role-occupants.[14] For example, if a law exists prohibiting pollution, but the landowners do not know of the law, they will obey it only accidentally (Allott, 1981: 236-37; Rubin, 1989: 408).[15]

3. Incentives.

Despite the limitations of the Law and Economics approach, material incentives plainly do constitute a powerful motive in human affairs. Researchers must, therefore, investigate whether and to what extent material interests, including the probability of punishments or rewards, influence the role-occupants' behavior.   Obviously, role-occupants consider not the paper penalty for criminal activity, but rather the probabilities of sanctions imposed by the implementing authorities. For violating a criminal law, for example, will they likely face detection, arrest, and prison?

The law may or may not explicitly prescribe the relevant authorities' sanctioning behavior. If in practice, for example, promotions to higher levels of the Agricultural Extension Service go only to extension agents who do not make or implement local rules to constrain large ranchers and timber firms from exploiting the forests, many agents may perceive it in their interest to accommodate those businesses even to the detriment of environmental concerns.[16]

4. Process.

The process by which role-occupants—whether individuals or collectivities—decide whether or not to obey a law may significantly influence their behavior. This underscores the necessity to ensure the democratic organization and participation of the poor—workers, peasants, small entrepreneurs, women, youth, intellectuals—in the shaping of new laws and institutions that will facilitate their capacity to contribute to sustainable development. Section IV-B below discusses how participatory processes may more effectively enable them learn what to do to implement new development activities proposed.

5. Subjective factors.

How people view their social environment affects their behavior in two different ways. First, their attitudes and values plainly influence their choices. In China, for example, women and men so firmly believe in the traditional values of large families that they frequently try to evade the laws aimed at limiting the number of children they may have. Second, role occupants' behavior may have different subjective meaning for them than for rule makers and implementers because of their different world outlooks (Weber, 1965), their 'domain assumptions' (Gouldner and Miller, 1965).   When one person turns over to another a thin metal disc, researchers cannot explain that behavior unless they know how the actors perceive the disc: perhaps as a medal which the recipient, a craftsman, will polish; perhaps as a religious object, and the recipient as a priest or shaman; or perhaps as money which the recipient, a tradesman, perceives as payment for goods (Winch, 1958: 1051; Weber, 1968: 7). To explain sets of role occupants choices, researchers must analyze their commonly-held beliefs about action, the socially-acquired and transmitted norms that comprise their subjective ideology to discover whether it tends to move them to conform to the new rules.

An acronym, ROCCIPI, serves to help remember these categories: **R**ule, **O**pportunity, **C**apacity, **C**ommunication, **I**nterest, **P**rocess and **I**deology. Together, they provide an agenda for generating middle-level propositions[17] that may guide fruitful investigations into possible causes for the role occupants' behavior that, in Africa, contributed to poverty and oppression. Larger theoretical perspectives will likely shape the particular focus of propositions which researchers generate in each category. The more systematically researchers consider all the hypotheses suggested by alternative paradigms, the more likely they will not neglect the most important ones. Those that prove most consistent with the available evidence logically will lead to the range of middle-level policies or institutional changes likely to alter the role occupants' counterproductive behavior.

D. **Research into implementing agencies and other complex state organizations.**

Frequently, the law does not effectively control the behavior of particular sets of role occupants because the law-making institutions do not create appropriate implementing institutions, or because the established implementing agencies—education ministries, agricultural extension agencies, marketing boards, courts, parastatals, and so forth—do not do their jobs. ROCCIPI may also provide a research agenda for generating explanations of these institutions' behavior.

People frequently purport to explain the action of the state or its agencies as though each constituted a single rational actor. Any organization, however, comprises not a single actor, but many (Allison, 1971: 32ff). To say that the football team failed to complete a pass says nothing about the causes of that failure. To help them do better next time, the coach must disaggregate the team to discover which players made what specific mistakes and why (Allport in Braybrooke, 1955: 27-29). In the same way, law cannot command a legal fiction like a public corporation, or a notional entity like a bureaucracy, to do anything.   At the end of the day, law addresses its injunctions to individuals, the key role occupants who make the critical decisions shaping the activities of these institutions. To explain the behavior of the institutions that comprise the state, itself, researchers must examine the factors influencing the decisions of particular role-occupants within the implementing agency.

To understand these, ROCCIPI suggests the kinds of questions researchers should ask about each of the several actors in the decision-making system (Allison, 1971; cf Goldberg in Majone, 1989: 100). For example, if courts do not try and punish polluters, researchers could ask about all the relevant actors (judges as well as prosecutors, private plaintiffs, etc.):   What rules control the several actors' behaviors? What opportunity, capacity, interest and ideology do they have? Has the law been communicated to the relevant actors? and so on. If the social problem consists in lack of participation by landless peasants in determining who shall become settlers in a land reform scheme, the researcher could use the ROCCIPI agenda to examine the behavior of the relevant officials who select the settlers, and perhaps even the clerks who may act as gatekeepers for the agency (Stearns, 1983: 65).

The capacity of complex state implementing agencies to make the decisions as directed by law makers, of course, frequently depends not merely on the capacity of the key role occupants involved, but the structure and processes through which they decide. A simple input-output systems model captures the institutional factors that may shape their complex decision-making processes (see Fig. 8-4).

A MODEL FOR UNDERSTANDING COMPLEX ORGANIZATIONS

Fig. 8-4[18]

This model tells us that the range of decisions of complex implementing agencies results from: (1) the sorts of inputs (issues, facts, theories, personnel) that the institution's structure and processes admit into the decision; (2) the sorts of feedback processes that inform the institution's decision-makers about the consequences of previous decisions; and (3) the conversion processes, that is, the rules and criteria that set limits on how the decision-makers consider these various elements.

It suggests researchers should enquire, not only about the factors influencing key role occupants' decisions, but more generally about the processes that filter inputs and feedbacks, and determine how the conversion processes work. These processes, too, consist of behaviors of the role-occupants who hold office in the implementing agency.[19] Researchers must ask ROCCIPI questions about these role-occupants, too. Only then can they generate middle level propositions that may fully explain the causes of inappropriate institutional behavior; and suggest new laws (rules, regulations, etc.) more likely to produce more effective agency behavior to implement development-oriented laws.

In short, to validate middle level propositions to explain the behavior of institutions that comprise the state as the basis of reforms directed towards sustainable development, researchers must ultimately investigate the behavior of all the relevant role occupants. The models outlined above suggest they should explore, not only the rules of law, including conformity-inducing measurers, but also the input, conversion and feedback processes through which those actors decide how to enforce new development laws. Using ROCCIPI categories, they generate useful middle level propositions that, if validated by evidence, should assist African policy-makers to design and implement specific new measures to improve the performance of these agencies.

The law-making process that enacts (or fails to enact) new development-oriented laws in Africa, as everywhere else, also constitutes a complex organization. Researchers may employ the ROCCIPI agenda to determine which factors influence the law-makers, themselves, in choosing to pass some laws, and not others. Presumably, as in the case of implementing agencies, they would also need to investigate the working rules and processes of the legislature and its subcommittees.

V. Towards a Research Paradigm: Law as Underbearer of Political Institutions

The development failures exposed by the preceding chapters of this book in crucial fields of African societal activity—from overall economic development to education, health, environment and gender relations—reflected the failure of the state and the legal order to perform adequately their essential underbearer role. The theories of the state prevalent in post-independence Africa disagreed as to the reasons. In this part, to assist policy-makers concerned with restructuring the state itself, we first suggest the key areas in which researchers might use the agenda outlined in part III to help resolve those debates. We then consider the special questions which such research must answer to facilitate creation of more democratic, participatory state structures to involve the African people in the creative realization of a new vision of African development.

A. Resolving the key debates.

The review of alternative theories of the state in Part II left unresolved three main areas of debate relating to:

1. <u>The state, law, and the development of class</u>. How did institutions of the state (laws, implementing agencies, etc.) contribute to the emergence of a new bureaucratic class (what some call a 'bureaucratic bourgeoisie') that exercised state power in its own interests?

2. <u>Ethnicity</u>. Why and how did existing institutions foster the politics of exclusion, be it based on ethnic, sectarian or factional grounds?

3. <u>Legality</u>: Why did new government officials too often engage in manifestly illegal activities?

While investigating the state's underbearer role in every field, researchers should simultaneously formulate and test middle-level explanatory propositions to answer these questions, thus helping to explain the counterproductive behavior of the state and the legal order, per se. They should systematically examine the categories of factors, suggested by ROCCIPI, that likely shape the behavior of the various role occupants who determine the inputs, feedbacks and conversion processes involved in law-making and implementing. By using evidence to validate relevant middle level propositions, they will provide a sound basis to assist policy makers in devising measures to transform the institutions of the state and the legal order. The result will be that they perform their underbearer role in ways more likely to attain self-sustainable development.

B. Enhancing democratic participation.

As the preceding chapters indicate, many scholars and political actors agree that, unless the mass of the African people participate in political decision-making, development in the sense of alleviating the poverty and powerlessness of the masses, will remain a chimera. How might researchers, using the ROCCIPI agenda, generate warranted middle-level propositions to explain non-participation in decision-making in government and the work place, the two most common sites of social activity governed by societal rules?

The obstacles to formal and informal participation in government and industry differ substantially at the local level from those at the national level. Existing evidence indicates that people can best participate in small groups so mass participation succeeds better to the extent that the polity can decentralize decision-making to local levels. This suggests that researchers should focus on ROCCIPI factors shaping the behavior of key role occupants that exclude ordinary citizens from the decision-making processes in local government and agricultural and industrial activities.[20]   Nevertheless, modern political economic developments pose many problems that require national decisions. These affect varied activities like planning for basic industries benefitting from economies of scale; money and banking policies that affect employment and inflation; maintenance of national educational and health standards; military and foreign policy; and constitutional affairs. Problems that plague participation in these arenas have many aspects, each worthy of study. Almost everyone agrees that political participation without some sort of representative democracy seems hard to conceive. The sort of representation and methods for selecting representatives appropriate to Africa require investigation into the conditions which have hindered the functioning of the electoral process and of the exercise of basic human rights.

Democratic liberties alone, however, hardly amount to political participation on a meaningful scale. In the United States, as Schumpeter once remarked (1974), they mainly permit citizens to vote every four years for their dictators. The search for meaningful modes of participation in deciding the national issues that continually arise between elections pose far greater difficulties. In Africa as elsewhere, people may participate in governance, not only in ways permitted by law, but also by informal channels to the decision-making centers; by demonstrations, strikes and threats of strikes; or by making government untenable without their formal and peaceful participation. To facilitate participation without disruptive protests, however, governments may pass laws that increase participation in national decision-making institutions by: (1) providing referenda on key questions; (2) ensuring that representatives stay in close touch with their constituencies and the voters' right to recall their representatives; (3) eliminating restrictive secrecy rules that hinder African citizens from obtaining the facts needed to participate intelligently; (4) and providing ordinary people with regular, institutionalized input channels, like open hearings and public debates, in decision-making processes.

To understand the impact of these and other measures, researchers should study the law-in-action, not merely the law-in-the-books. These never coincide perfectly; in practice broad divergence seems pervasive. Researchers may usefully begin by formulating middle-level propositions to explain that divergence.

Both at the local and the national level, research into obstacles to participation should explore two frequently overlapping dimensions: Participation-as-accountability and participation-for-its-own-sake. Accountability issues concern devices for ensuring that representatives and officials who actually make decisions use their powers in the interests of the people. In most societies, most institutions that purport to ensure accountability have a hierarchical structure: Courts and Ombudsmen constitute the most common ones. Researchers should conduct research to help policy-makers introduce new devices ensuring that representatives represent, not the elites, but the masses.

Participation-for-its-own-sake refers to the republican tradition in politics, that, in the very act of engaging in participatory governance, citizens come to understand issues and participate more effectively in deciding them (See Kalyalya et al, 1988, ch. 2). In this view, every delegation of power necessarily dilutes the individual's learning opportunities.

Using the models and the ROCCIPI research agenda outlined above, the remainder of this section suggests ways to conduct research to increase accountability and participation-for-its-own-sake on both local and national levels of the state and the legal order to improve performance of their underbearer role.

Case studies of how bills became law in key areas—for example, any one of those considered in the earlier chapters of this book (eg, see Seidman, 1982)—illustrate the use of ROCCIPI to study participation in the lawmaking process. Of course, how the bill became a bill constitutes a part of that study, including the factors (among them the legal system) that facilitated or hindered the political and social movements that led to its consideration. In most Anglophone African countries, a key input function consists of the process of "consultation of interested parties." This usually, but not always, takes place after the ministry presents a "layman's draft" or ministerial memorandum to the cabinet legislative committee, which furnishes the basis of Parliamentary Counsel's work. In this process, the permanent secretary serves as a key gatekeeper, or role-occupant, whose behavior researchers should investigate. The ROCCIPI categories suggest several hypotheses to explain the common exclusion of the poor from this aspect of the law-making process.

First, in most cases no formal rules call for consultation. Instead, informal but extremely strong ministerial traditions usually lodge with the permanent secretary the power to determine whom officials will consult. Formal laws concerning official secrets, however, impose severe limits on their powers to consult widely. This suggests the crucial importance of altering those laws to create a more open consultative process.

Second, the permanent secretaries' powers to initiate consultation undoubtedly have some practical limits. The category of opportunity suggests that, unless the people have organizations, civil servants cannot easily consult them. They cannot personally ask every peasant to discuss bills affecting the rural poor. Even in public hearings, individuals representing only themselves rarely have the resources to make an effective presentation. Almost invariably, inputs come from the elite, representing powerful organizations like chambers of commerce, associations of commercial farmers. What changes in the legal order might encourage effective organization of the unorganized?

Third, what factors limit the permanent secretaries' capacity to consult various groups? They likely have resources to contact organized groups in the center—again, most likely elite or upper-class groups. Could they hold public meetings in the countryside to obtain inputs from peasants? What resources and institutions could increase their capacity to consult a broader range of people?

Fourth, permanent secretaries probably know whether and what kinds of rules require consultation, but even if rules give the poor the right to express their views to the permanent secretaries, do they know about them? How might the law ensure that poor know of those rules?

Fifth, what interest do permanent secretaries have in consulting different groups? Corruption aside (although that possibility exists), senior civil servants are likely to have close personal and financial ties with members of the economic elite. These would be people they meet at the Club, with whom they occasionally have dinner or meet at Embassy or governmental functions. What specific measures might give permanent secretaries incentives to consult more widely?

Sixth, by what processes do permanent secretaries decide whom to consult? Do they decide in the privacy of their offices, without consulting anybody? Do they discuss matters with their Ministers (elected officials), or other civil servants? What laws might broaden the process of deciding with whom to consult?

Seventh, what <u>ideology</u> guides the secretaries in making their decisions? Do ministerial norms exist, requiring them to consult particular interests? Does their ideology point them to consult the powerful and privileged, and not the poor? What educational or other measures might create a learning process through which they might change their notions with whom they should consult?

Finally, what <u>agencies</u> exist to implement the formal and informal rules that define the Secretaries' position in regard to consultations? What new implementation processes and agencies might help ensure that permanent secretaries consult widely?

In like manner, Grand Theory may generate the middle level, explanatory propositions to explain the counterproductive social behavior of key role occupants in state institutions affecting all arenas of development. To test these empirically, researchers can structure research programs that systematically investigate the available evidence. Upon those hypotheses that the evidence warrants, lawmakers can structure proposed legislative solutions, each addressed to overcoming the causes of the inadequacies of the particular governmental institutions to facilitate greater mass participation.

VI. Conclusion

To answer the question, What went wrong with the way the newly independent African governments utilized the state and law, global theories like pluralism or Marxism may contribute to identification of the issues and to general hypotheses. They do not, however, easily yield middle-level explanatory propositions that might help to lay a foundation for how, in the future, a government dedicated to transformation and development could do better. Neither do theories damning central government and all its works. Central governments exist. The liberation movements fought for political power because their experience taught them that a central government in the hands of their oppressors became a tool of oppression. The issue then became, how to ensure that, once the liberation movements attained state power, they could exercise it to help the people, and not themselves slip into the oppressors' shoes.

That requires changing the institutions, the repetitive patterns of social behaviors, that caused Africa's poverty and vulnerability. It requires understanding how society's formal normative structures, with its rules, sanctions and implementing processes—the legal order—shape those patterns of social behavior. More than that: It necessitates investigation at a very concrete level in specific country circumstances as to how, once a liberation movement gains state power, it can use that tool to reshape the government and the legal order, not to increase people's vulnerability, but to empower them.

To do that requires research to test middle-level explanations that link global theory directly to how central actors, role occupants, behave in the face of rules of law.   ROCCIPI categories, plus a consideration of how people interact in complex organizations, suggest those kinds of explanations.   Participatory research that tests those explanations may lay the necessary foundation for changing the legal order in ways more likely to create democratic, participatory state institutions capable of realizing a new vision of self-sustainable development in Africa.

Endnotes

1. Coming from very different points of departure and experiences, two of the authors, Seidman and Selassie, both of whom have long taught courses and written about the State and the Legal Order in Africa, had earlier arrived at conclusions similar to those set down in this chapter (Seidman 1978; Selassie's *The Executive in African Governments* (1974) and *Reflections on the Future Political System of Eritrea* (1990). Addis served as coordinator of the Task Force on the State and Law in Phase I of its work.   Selassie has assumed that responsibility for Phase II.

2. By "legal order" we mean the normative system governing the totality of state behavior and its interactions with civil society, including not only the rules of law, but also law-making and law-implementing institutions.

3. The preceding chapters of this volume essentially review the way the state, in its underbearer role, has contributed to Africa's poverty and powerlessness in each of the fields examined by the Task Force.

4. This list includes only official roles. The exclusion of some elements in civil society from the law-making process constitutes a principal point below, in Section IV-B.

5. In fact the social bargains postulated by pluralism never existed, except on "as if" assumptions: One can understand government policies "as if" social bargaining between elites representing various interest groups had taken place.

6. That the system frequently excluded issues from arising created a category of what two critics of pluralist theory called: "non-decisions" (Bachrach and Baratz, 1963: 632).

7. It might be claimed that the pluralist explanation implicitly fostered the 1980s focus on non-government organizations as a catalyst for development.

8. In Chazan and Rothchild, 1988.

9. For a critique of the basis-superstructure metaphor, see Seidman in Marasinghe and Conklin, 1984; also Jessop, 1982: 15-16.

10. The notion of the state as instrumental to class power must be distinguished from the concept of the law as serving as an instrument to change behaviors.

11. Engels, in a letter to Schmidt, argued against this simplistic position (Marx and Engels) In "The Eighteenth Brumaire," Marx explained the state sometimes played a relatively autonomous role (Id.; See also Reuschemeyer and Evans in Evans et al, 1985: 44, 47).

12. See also Nadel, 1953: 265.

13. For critique, see e.g., Michelman, 1983; Magketla and Seidman, 1987; Samuels, 1974.

14. On the appropriate style for adequately communicating the substance of a legal text, see Dickerson; Thornton In lieu of tight prescriptions of role-occupant behavior, modern legislation might well couch itself in terms of either the goals the legislature desires that the implementing agency pursue, or generalized statements to the agency of how to go about allocating its resources in the course of implementation. On the actual communication of the law to its addresses in a way that promotes understanding of it, see Seidman, 1972: 680.

15. The role of the electronic media, especially radio, in facilitating communication in rural Africa, deserves special attention.

16. Where the subject-matter of the proposed bill relates directly to economic affairs—like legislation on restriction on competition, developing new transportation routes or systems, and the supply of energy—sophisticated economic analyses based on the economic interest of the role-occupant may at this point become relevant.

17. Frequently, one or more of the categories will seem obviously satisfied. For example, when analyzing an official as a role-occupant, frequently the situation makes it obvious that the official knows of the rule and its content.

18.   The usual input-output decision-making model purports to explain particular decisions by examination of particular inputs, feedbacks and how the conversion process worked in that instance. See, e.g., Huse. This model underwent withering criticism (Bachrach and Baratz, 1963: 632) on the ground that it did not explain "non-decisions", that is, the failure to address issues which never even entered the system; as a result, it remained static, a device to ensure that change never threatens the structures of power. The model here proposed aims to avoid this problem by examining not particular inputs, but the processes and structures that determine the <u>range</u> of inputs, feedbacks and conversion processes, and therefore the <u>range</u> of outputs (see Seidman, 1978: 194.)

19. Huse, 1975: 37: "A role consists of 'one or more recurrent activities, which in combination, produce the organizational behavior"; See also Katz and Kahn, 1966.

20.   Kalyalya et al, 1988, describe a pilot project research using the ROCCIPI research agenda to involve members of small projects in a participatory evaluation process directed at improving development assistance.

Bibliography

Allison, Graham T. 1971. *Essence of Decision: Explaining the Cuban Missile Crisis.* Little, Brown and Company, Boston.

Allott, A. 1981. "The Effectiveness of Laws", *Valparaiso University Law Review,* Vol. 15, 229.

Amin, Samir. 1990 "Peace, Security and Development." In Robert E. Mazur, Ed. *Breaking the Links.* Trenton, NJ. Africa World Press.

Anton, A.E. 1979. "Legislation and its Limits", *Dalhousie Law Journal,* Vol. 5, 233.

Anyang' Nyong'o, Peter. 1987. "Introduction", in P. Anyang' Nyong'o. Ed. *Popular Struggles for Democracy in Africa*: 14-16. Tokyo: United Nations University; London, Atlantic Highlands, NJ: Zed Books.

Bachrach, P. and Baratz, M.S. 1963."Two Faces of Power", 57 *Am.Pol. Sci. Rev.* 632.

Ball, H.V., Simpson, G.E. and Ikeda, K. 1962. "Law and Social Change: Sumner Reconsidered." 67 *American Journal of Sociology.* 532.

Barth, F. 1966.   "Models of Social Organization", *Royal Anthropological Association Occasional Paper No. 23.* Glasgow: The University Press.

Berg, E. 1982. *Accelerated Development in Sub-Saharan Africa*. World Bank, (1982)

Black, Donald. 1977. *The Behavior of Law*. New York: Academic Press.

Branch, Taylor. 1989. *Parting the Waters: America During the King Years 1954-63*. New York: Simon and Schuster.

Braybrooke, D. 1955, Ed. *Philosophical Problems of the Social Sciences*. New York: MacMillan.

Bretton, H. 1962. *Power and Stability in Nigeria: The Politics of Decolonization*. New York: Praeger.

Burman, S.B. and Harrell-Bond, B.E. Eds. 1978. *The Imposition of Law*. New York: Academic Press.

Carnoy, M. 1984. *The State and Political Theory*. Princeton, NJ: Princeton University Press.

Chambliss, W.J. and Seidman, R.B. 1981. *Law, Order and Power*. Reading, MA: Addison Wesley, 2d ed.

Cardoso. 1979. "On the Characterization of Authoritarian Regimes in Latin America", in Collier (ed.), *The New Authoritarianism in Latin America*. Princeton. Princeton University Press. (51)

Chazan, N and D. Rothchild. Eds. 1988. *The Precarious Balance: State and Society in Africa*. Boulder, CO: Westview Press

Chazan, N., Mortimer, Ravenhill and Rothchild, D. 1988. *Politics and Society in Contemporary Africa*. Boulder, CO: Lynn Rienner Publishers.

Collier. Ed. 1979. *The New Authoritarianism in Latin America*. Princeton: Princeton University Press.

Cranston, R.F. 1987. *Law, Government and Public Policy*. New York: Oxford University Press.

_____. 1978. "Reform through Legislation: The Dimension of Legislative Technique", 73 *Northwestern University Law Review*, 873.

Driedger, E.A. 1976. *Composition of Legislation* (2d ed, rev). Ottawa: Department of Justice.

Ellickson, R. 1986. "Of Coase and Cattle: Dispute Resolution Among Neighbors in Shasta County", *Stanford Law Review*, Vol. 38, 623. 623.

Erlich, E. 1936. *The Fundamental Principles of the Sociology of Law*. (W. Moll: trans.) Cambridge, MA: Harvard University Press.

Evans, Peter, Rueschemeyer, Diedritch, and Skocpol, Theta. Eds. 1985. *Bringing the State Back In: Strategies of Analysis in Current Research*. Cambridge: Cambridge University Press,

Festinger, L. 1957. *A Theory of Cognitive Dissonance*. Stanford, CA: Stanford University Press.

Friedman, Lawrence. 1969. "Legal Culture and Social Development" *Law & Society Review*. Vol. 4, 29.

Ghai, Luckham, Y. R. and Snyder, F. Eds. 1987. *The Political Economy of Law— A Third World Reader*. Delhi: Oxford University Press.

Gouldner, A. and Miller, S.M. Eds. 1965. *Applied Sociology—Opportunities and Problems*. *New York: Free Press*.

Hale, R.L. 1952. *Freedom Through Law: Public Control of Private Government*. New York: Columbia University Press.

Hart, H.L.A. 1961. *The Concept of Law*. Oxford: Clarendon Press.

Hay, D., Linebaugh, P., Rule, J., Thompson, E.P., and Winslow, C. *Albion's Fatal Tree: Crime and Society in Eighteenth Century England*. London: Penguin books, 1975.

Huse, E.F. 1975. *Organization Development and Change*. St. Paul, MN: West Publishing Co.

Huntingdon, S. 1968. *Political Order in Changing Societies*. New Haven: Yale University Press.

Hyden, G. 1980. *Beyond Ujamaa in Tanzania*. Berkeley: University of California Press.

International Monetary Fund (IMF). 1985. "Impact of the External Environment and Domestic Policies on Economic Performance in Developing Countries", *World Economic Outlook*. April.

Jessop, Robert. 1982. *The Capitalist State: Marxist Theories and Methods*. New York: NYU press, 15-16.

Jones, H.W. 1968. *The Efficacy of Law*. Evanston, IL: Northwestern University Press.

Katz, D. and Kahn, R.L. 1966. *The Social Psychology of Organizations*. New York: Wiley.

Kautsky, J.H. Ed. 1962. *Political Change in Underdeveloped Countries: Nationalism and Communism*. New York: Wiley.

Kalyalya, D., Mhlanga, K., Seidman, A. and Semboja, J. Eds. 1987. *Aid and Development: Evaluating a Pilot Learning Process in Southern Africa*. Trenton, NJ: Africa World Press.

Kennedy, Paul. 1988. *African Capitalism—The Struggle for Ascendency.Cambridge*. Cambridge University Press.

Kitch, E.M. 1983. "The Intellectual Foundations of Law and Economics." *Journal of Legal Education*. Vol. 33, 184.

Korten, David. 1989. *Towards the 21st Century*. Hartford: Kumarian Press.

LaPalombara, J. Ed. 1963. *Bureaucracy and Political Development. Princeton*. NJ: Princeton University Press.

Levine, Andrew. 1981. *Liberal Democracy; A Critique of its Theory* New York: Columbia University Press.

Lystad, R.A. Ed. 1965. *The African World: A Survey of Social Research*. New York: Praeger.

MacPherson, C.B. 1977. *The Life and Times of Liberal Democracy* London: Oxford University Press.

Majone, G. 1989. *Evidence, Argument and Persuasion in the Policy Process*. New Haven: Yale University Press.

Makemure, K., Ndlela, D., Seidman A. and Seidman, R.B. 1986. *Transnationals in Southern Africa: Papers from a conference on Maximizing the Benefits of Transnational Corporations*. Harare: Zimbabwe Publishing House.

Makgetla, N. and Seidman, R. 1987. "Legislative Drafting and the Defeat of Development Policy: the Experience of Anglophonic Southern Africa." *Journal of Law and Religion.* Vol. 5.

Marasinghe, M.L.and Conklin, W.E. 1984. *Essays on Third World Perspectives in Jurisprudence.* Singapore: Malayan Law Journal.

Marx, K. and Engels, F. 1969. *Selected Works. Moscow: Progress Books.*

McCelland, David. 1962. *The Achieving Society.* Princeton, NJ: Van Nostrand.

Michelman, F.I. 1983. "Reflections on Professional Education, Legal Scholarship and the Law-and-Economics Movement" *Journal of Legal Education,* Vol. 33, 197.

Miliband, R. 1969. *The State in Capitalist Society.* New York: Basic Books; London: Weidenfeld & Nicolson.

Myrdal, G. 1968. *Asian Drama: An Inquiry into the Poverty of Nations.* New York: Twentieth Century Fund; and Parthenon.

Nadel, S. F. 1953. "Social Control and Self-Regulation." *Social Forces* Vol. 31, 265.

Nkrumah, K. 1977. *Dark Days in Ghana.* New York: International Publishers.

Nzongola-Ntalaja. 1987. *Revolution and Counter-Revolution in Africa.* London: Institute for African Alternatives; Zed Books Ltd.

Packer, H.L. 1969. *The Limits of The Criminal Sanction.* Stanford, CA: Stanford University Press.

Posner, R.A. 1986. *The Economic Analysis of Law.* Boston, MA: Little, Brown and Co.

Robertson, J.A. and Teitlebaum, P. 1973. "Optimizing Legal Impact: A Case Study in Search of a Theory." *Wisconsin Law Review.*

Roche, J.R., and Gordon, M.N. "Can Morality be legislated?" *New York Times Magazine,* May 22, 1955.

Rodney, Walter. 1972. *How Europe Underdeveloped Africa.* Dar es Salaam: Tanzania Publishing House; Washington,DC: Howard University Press, 1974.

Rubin, E.L. 1989. "Law and Legislation in the Administrative State." *Columbia Law Review.* Vol. 89, 369.

Samuels, W.J. 1974. "The Coase Theorem and the Study of Law and Economics" *Natural Resources Journal.* Vol. 14, 1.

Schumpeter, J.A. 1947. *Capitalism, Socialism and Democracy.* New York: Harper.

Seidman, R.B. 1972. "The Communication of Law and the Process of Development", *Wisconsin Law Review.* 686.

_____. 1978. *State, Law and Development.* New York: Croom-Helm.

_____. 1978b. "Why Do People Obey the Law? The Case of Corruption in Developing Countries" 5 *British Journal of Law and Society.* Vol. 5.

_____. 1982. "On Restructuring the Colonial State: How a Bill Became a Law in Zimbabwe", *Africa.*

Selassie, Bereket H. 1974. *The Executive in African Governments.* London: Heineman.

_____. 1990. *Reflections on the Future Political System of Eritrea.* Trenton, NJ: Africa World Press.

Snyder, F.G. 1980. "Law and Development in the Light of Dependency Theory." in *Law & Society Review.* Vol. 14.

Stearns, Lisa. 1983. "The Dilemma of Struggle Through the International Order" in *International Journal of the Sociology of Law.* Vol. 11, 65.

Stokey, E. and Zeckhauser, R. 1978. *A Primer for Policy Analysis.* New York: Norton.

Sumner, W.G. 1906. *Folkways: A Study of the Sociological Importance of Usages, Manners, Customs and Morals.* Boston: Ginn.

Szentes, Tamas. 1990. "Socialism in Theory and Practice," In Robert E. Mazur, Ed. *Breaking the Links.* Trenton, NJ. Africa World Press. pp. 66.

Thorton, G.C. 1987 (2d ed) *Legislative Drafting.* London: Butterworths.

Wallerstein, Immanuel. 1986. *Africa and the Modern World.* Trenton, NJ: Africa World Press.

Weber, M. 1946. *From Max Weber: Essays in Sociology*. (Gerth and Mills. Eds.) New York: Oxford University Press.

Weber, M. 1968. *Economy and Society* 7 (G. Roth and C. Wittich, Eds.) New York: Bedminister.

Weber, M. 1947. *The Theory of Social and Economic Organization*. (A.M. Henderson and T. Parsons (Translation); T. Parsons (Ed.) New York: Free Press.

Weiner, M. Ed. 1966. *Modernization: The Dynamics of Growth*. New York: Basic Books.

Winch, P. 1958. *The Idea of a Social Science and its Relation to Philosophy*. London: Routledge & Kegan Paul; New York: Humanities Press.

World Bank. 1989. *Sub-Saharan Africa—From Crisis to Sustainable Growth. A Long-Term Perspective Study*. Washington, DC: The World Bank.

Wunsch, J.S. and Olowu, D. 1990. *The Failure of the Centralized State: Institutions and Self-Governance in Africa*. Boulder: Westview.

Chapter 9

New Structures for Participatory Problem-Solving research

I. Introduction

At the Washington workshop that concluded Phase I of the Task Force's work, the researchers from Africa and the Task Force coordinators designed a participatory, problem-solving research process to gather the evidence needed to resolve the policy debates outlined in the previous chapters, and build a sound foundation for a people-oriented strategy for self-sustainable development in Africa. This chapter describes that process, the criteria for selecting priority research projects, and the specific research projects proposed[1].

II. A Participatory Problem-Solving Methodology

As a central feature, the proposed further research will involve mobilization of African researchers together with representative segments of African peoples for two reasons: (1) those who experience a development problem know the most, not only about the details of its impact on their own lives, but also the nature of the evidence relating to its possible causes; and (2) in the process of gathering evidence as to the causes of the problem and monitoring the consequences of policies implemented to overcome them, they will learn the skills and confidence to achieve greater self-reliance. Therefore, the research process aims to involve representatives of relevant population segments, together with selected policy makers, in formulating the analysis and gathering the evidence the problem-solving approach requires at each of the following stages[2]:

1. <u>Statement of the problem</u>: Teams of researchers will involve selected policy-makers and representatives of relevant segments of the African community —peasants, workers, unemployed, intellectuals, and small businesspersons—in identifying the nature and scope of the problems they confront.

2. Explanatory hypotheses: The research teams will engage selected policy-makers and the community participants in testing the full range of available alternative hypotheses as to the causes of the problems[3] to determine which seems most consistent with the available evidence.

3. Proposals for solution: Together with community participants and selected policy-makers, the researchers will examine the evidence concerning existing constraints and resources to determine which specific measures seem most likely to overcome the causes of the problem they have identified.

4. On-going evaluation: The researchers will help institutionalize the on-going involvement of community participants in evaluating the consequences of the specific policy measures implemented. Inevitably, these measures will encounter unanticipated difficulties and new problems. In future phases of the project, the researchers, together with the community participants, will seek to explain these, thus laying the basis for new measures to overcome them. Thus, the researchers and community members will engage in a continuing iterative participatory learning process.

A. Criteria for selection of research projects

Recognizing that research, itself, utilizes scarce human and financial resources, the Washington workshop participants identified the following criteria for selecting priority research projects:

1. New areas, not currently being investigated by other kinds of research: Africa has the resources required for development. Multilateral agencies have already gathered extensive data and begun various kinds of modelling exercises that describe their allocation. The proposed research need not waste the funds or humanpower required to duplicate these efforts. In the course of the proposed research, however, an advisory team of African and US statistical experts will work with each task group to help the participants evaluate the existing modes of collecting, storing and analyzing the data in terms of their implications for the proposed new vision of development.

2. The proposed participatory research process will focus, in particular, on explaining the behavior of institutions that historically have allocated resources in ways that perpetuate the poverty and powerlessness of so many Africans. This will help build the pool of information essential to transform those

institutions to re-allocate Africa's rich resources to meet the African peoples' basic needs.

3.   The projects selected will <u>utilize participatory problem-solving research</u> to involve the African people, themselves, in a learning process designed to help them create a new vision of their own role in the attainment of self-sustainable development.

B. The specific proposals for collaborative research

Within the framework of the overall participatory problem-solving methodology and guidelines, the joint Task Forces endorsed the following specific proposals for collaborative research.[4]

1. <u>Economy and regional integration</u>. The close interrelationship between factors hindering economic development and the arbitrary balkanization of Africa justify coordinated research relating to economic development and regional integration.

The problems: On both a national and regional scale, disarticulation constitutes the primary characteristic of Africa's economy. In most countries, relatively capital-intensive 'modern' industrial, mining and agricultural sectors remain externally dependent, linked by management, finance, technology and markets to the metropolitan centers of the North. This aggravates uneven development as subcenters of wealth and power emerge to dominate national and regional economies; in Sub-Saharan Africa, these include the South African military-industrial complex; and the 'modern' sectors of Zimbabwe, Kenya, Ivory Coast and Nigeria. Outside of these regional subcenters, increasing numbers of people among the continent's rural populations, especially women and children, experience growing impoverishment and poverty. In the context of the resulting distorted pattern of resource allocation, growing un- and underemployment appears in the form of expanding informal sectors, most of whose members, especially women, wage a daily struggle for bare survival. The burdens of heavy external and internal indebtedness and inflation, aggravated by subsequent austerity programs, further impoverish the majority of Africans.

Widespread theoretical agreement suggests that coordinated use of regional resources, markets and investable surpluses would facilitate building modern industry and agriculture that benefit from economies of scale. Yet over one hundred existing attempts to achieve regional cooperation have so far achieved relatively limited success.

Explanatory hypotheses: The highly skewed income distribution resulting from this historically-shaped pattern of resource utilization in all sectors of Africa's economies—including informal ones—limits national and regional markets. Investments, shaped by short-run profit-maximizing criteria, cannot foster the kinds of domestically-oriented industry and agriculture required to spread productive employment opportunities and rising living standards. Both state and major domestic and foreign investors have, instead, invested primarily in the production and sale of crude materials and trade geared to external markets. To the extent that any investments take place in manufacturing industries, they depend on capital, technology and material imports; remain capital-intensive; provide relatively few jobs; and produce a limited range of goods for the narrow domestic high income group. They seldom manufacture local materials to make appropriate tools and equipment to increase productive employment, or consumer necessities to improve the quality of life for Africa's impoverished majority. Since third world competition for overcrowded export markets inevitably causes worsened terms of trade, these kinds of investments have accelerated an on-going vicious cycle. To continue investing, African countries have borrowed heavily. Heavy repayments on past external debts forces them to borrow still more to buy the imports on which their economies remain dependent.

Existing institutional structures foster the drain abroad of a major share of African countries' domestically generated investable surpluses. In the past, urged by conventional wisdom as the price of attracting foreign investment, this loss took place primarily in the form of repatriated profits. More recently, as foreign investment has dried up, these outflows have taken the form of fees and transfer pricing to foreign providers of technology, management, and markets; and, especially in recent years, high rates of interest on accumulated foreign debt.[5]

Furthermore, colonially-shaped national boundaries and institutions thwart African nations' efforts to coordinate regional trade and payments. National currencies, tariff and tax policies, ministries and planning institutions—only marginally altered from those imposed by the colonial scramble for Africa—still thwart efforts to expand regional productive activities to enable African industries to take advantage of modern economies of scale.

In the course of the research project, the research teams will disaggregate these general explanatory hypotheses into sets of interrelated, testable, middle-level explanatory propositions relating to industry, agriculture, the informal sector, and regional trade. They will need to identify the special factors that exclude women from the economic development process; and the particular characteristics of the state and the legal order that contribute to perpetuating distorted patterns of investment. These will guide the gathering of evidence required to test and revise them to make them more consistent with the objective conditions prevailing in specific Africa countries. As revised in light of the evidence, these middle-level explanatory propositions will logically suggest the range of specific policies and institutions required to overcome the causal factors identified. For example, at a micro-level, by exposing how existing institutions—legal restrictions, potential providers of credit and inputs, etc.—impede the efforts of informal sector workers, especially women, the research will suggest the kinds of specific measures required to ensure they contribute to increasingly productive informal sector employment directed to meeting the communities' basic needs. At the macro-level, by identifying specific mechanisms by which existing institutions—importing firms, banks, government rules and regulations, etc.—foster the misallocation of nationally-generated investable surpluses, the research will lead to proposals for changes to redirect those surpluses to domestically-oriented productive employment, including that in the informal sector. In short, by detailing and gathering evidence to warrant middle-level explanatory propositions as to the complex interrelated factors that hinder national and regional economic development, the research teams will contribute to the pool of information policy makers require to formulate policies more likely to lead to increasingly productive employment opportunities and an improved quality of life for the peoples of Africa.

To test the explanatory hypotheses as the basis for a new economic development strategy: Working with the economy task group, individual African scholars will coordinate the establishment of the research teams to work out detailed research designs in selected countries in two regions: Southern and Eastern Africa, including Zimbabwe, South Africa, Tanzania, Mozambique, Zambia and Kenya; and West Africa, including Senegal, Benin, Nigeria, Ghana and Zaire.

2. Education. The problem: At the outset of the post-independence era three decades ago, most African regimes and external bilateral and multilateral agencies (and experts) perceived education as the single most important variable in promoting economic development and institutionalizing participatory democratic state structures. Viewing formal educational credentials as the sine qua non for improved life-chances and enhanced living standards for themselves and their progeny, the citizens of the new African nation-states, too, voiced a strong demand for education.

Unfortunately, the phenomenal expansion of educational opportunities in African countries neither met the needs of many

Africans nor paid the predicted social, economic and political dividends. At every level—primary, secondary and tertiary—growing numbers of school leavers, especially women, remain un- or underemployed. Recent United Nations and World Bank data confirm that, in the mid-1980s, for the first time in the post-colonial era in many African countries, the percentage of school-age children attending school declined (in some countries drastically). At all levels, due to the scarcity of resources, the quality and relevance of classroom instruction declined significantly. Confronting endemic economic crises, political instability and repression, and the deterioration of university and research institutions, thousands of educated Africans have left their countries to work abroad.

Moreover, Ministries of Education and African educational policy-makers at all levels have become increasingly dependent on external (bilateral and multilateral) aid to meet recurrent budgetary commitments as well as to finance new educational programs and institutions. As a result, in many African countries, external funding agencies have acquired unprecedented and unparalleled influence in shaping educational policy.

All these problems attest, not only to a failure of educational institutions and policies, but to the high degree to which the educational arena is interconnected with and impacted by changes in the international arena and the structures (and crises) of the African state and economic systems.

Initial explanatory hypotheses: The problems plaguing African educational systems have arisen in part as a result of the colonial development of western-style formal education. The focus of much controversy, educational curricula and structure frequently became reactive and restrictive, reflecting uncertain and ambiguous (if not contradictory) political colonial agenda. Yet after independence, as most Africans still viewed education as the sole mechanism to achieve improved life chances and societal goals, the new governments expanded them with little change.

The inherited educational systems, which served the nascent ruling elite well, often resulted in the further institutionalization of educational structures and policy processes which contradicted the participatory and enabling goals of education for liberation and development.[6] These reflect both the economic employment structure dominated by the non-productive service sector (largely state bureaucracy), and contemporary—though sometimes fleeting—cumulatively and temporally sedimented educational ideologies and practices, often but not exclusively external in origin. They latter inculcate, produce and reproduce skills and ways of knowing, doing and interpreting values.   At best, these do not prepare students for economically productive and personally enriched lives. At worst, they contribute to maturation of young adults with attitudes, values and "ways of interpretation/evaluation" antithetical to personal, community and national development.

The economic crisis exacerbates these structural and systemic problems by reducing government funds for education. Many urban workers (and growing numbers of unemployed) and rural dwellers cannot afford the increased school fees and hidden costs associated with attending school, a major factor causing the decline in school enrollments at all levels.   Lack of government funds has also forced African Ministries of Education to turn increasingly to external donors. Along with their aid, these have been even more generous in policy suggestions—making African educational policy-makers more susceptible to external policy directives than at any time since the end of colonialism.

The research process will involve researchers and selected representatives of relevant population groups and educational policy-makers in disaggregating these initial hypotheses into sets of middle level explanatory propositions for testing. In so doing, they will fill in a gap in existing research by making cross-national comparisons that rigorously and systematically examine the historical and contemporary relationship between educational structures and policy, on the one hand, and, on the other hand, the political, economic, and social gestalt in which schools function and educational policy-makers formulate and implement policy. In this context, they will explore the implications of the differentiated "interest groups" in civil societies, including elites, social classes, ethnic and religious groupings.

To test the explanatory hypotheses as the basis for a new educational strategy: The research team will undertake a comparative case study in the Southern African Development Coordination Conference (SADCC) region[7] involving Botswana, Kenya, Zambia, Zimbabwe, Mozambique, Namibia, and potentially South Africa.[8] In each country, they will involve the participation of selected representatives of actors intimately involved in policy-articulation and implementation or who are directly affected by schooling and educational policy.   These include state officials, educational policy formulators, mid-level bureaucrats assigned to implementing and enforcing policy, school administrators, teachers, parents and students. The research will examine, not only issues of structural relationships, but also the factors influencing these actors' decisions. By involving students, parents and teachers in explaining causes of their educational difficulties, and articulating new initiatives and strategies, the research will contribute to creating the necessary conditions for their implementation.[9]

3. Health. The problem: Since at least the late 1970s, the poor in Africa have enjoyed less and less control over the spaces they inhabit and the resources they require to satisfy their basic health needs. Growing numbers of urban squatters, as well as rural people, have seen their real income and the provision of health care shrink. They find it increasingly difficult to maintain the nutrition and health of their children. They receive less help when they or their children fall ill. One in ten Africans suffers some disability of one form or the other. Maternal mortality is shamefully high. Of the 30 countries with the highest death rates for children under five years of age, 21 are in Africa. These children die of diseases preventable by immunization, basic sanitation and simple community-based primary health care. On top of all this, Africa's rapid post-independence urbanization has fostered serious new health risks. These include HIV infection, food poisoning, exposure to toxic waste, residential fire, rape and other forms of abuse.

The insights into urban health hazards by those at risk are an underutilized body of knowledge. A participatory research process that identifies the specific ways in which "development" institutions and projects undermine individual and environmental health will lay the foundation for a range of policy measures to ensure that future decision-making processes take these human needs and capacities into account. In addition, a participatory process will reveal the creative responses of children, youth and low income women to health risks in their daily environments. Such coping activities could well be incorporated into the programs of municipal governments and ministries, non-government organizations and donor agencies.

Initial explanatory hypotheses: Africa's seriously deteriorating health conditions interact with the causes and aggravate the consequences of many of the problems analyzed by other teams in the Task Force. First, deepening economic hardship in the rural areas is forcing greater numbers of people to migrate to the cities and even to abandon their children. The survival strategies of these children and youth can include such high risk activities as prostitution in areas of AIDS endemicity, heavy porterage of goods and recycling of dangerous materials like glass. Sick or injured children, youth and women place added burdens on the system of health care already under stress.

Second, in most African countries reduced government expenditures have decreased the availability of health services. Marginal groups, including the homeless, street children, youth, and low income urban dwellers, never had much access to these, and now have less. Falling real incomes of the working poor and semi-employed people have compounded the impact of deteriorating health facilities. In some cases, attempts to increase economic growth in and around African cities have introduced new risks, including dumping of toxic wastes that pollute the water and air, and unsafe working conditions.

Third, the "business-as-usual" activities of local and national institutions, whether public or private, simply do not take into consideration the environmental and health requirements of most people, especially the poor and such impoverished groups as the homeless, street children, and low income urban women. Exclusion of these groups from decision-making processes at all levels has meant that even measures supposedly directed at improvement of the situation through "development" have often had the opposite effect.

Fourth, the causes of deteriorated health conditions lie deeply intertwined with the causes of those studied by the gender and education task force teams. Explicating these should help to formulate new policy and action proposals, including improved use of the tools of non-formal education, job training, mobilization and self-organization to empower these impoverished groups to cope with the challenges of their rapidly changing urban environments. Finally, whereas many health problems, especially those in Africa's rapidly growing cities, only emerged as especially serious in the 1980s, legal safeguards and entitlement have failed to keep pace. Thus, urban environmentally-linked health problems of marginalized children, youth and women constitute a major challenge for the state and its legal apparatus.

To test the explanatory hypotheses as the basis for a new urban health strategy: Regional and national researchers will engage the participants in a learning process to identify and test more detailed, middle-level hypotheses. At the national level, they will train student researchers to involve women, urban children and youth at risk in defining their own health problems and gathering evidence as to the access they have to health services and resources for satisfying their other basic needs; and how they cope with the health challenges in their environments. On this basis, they will work with women, youth and concerned policy-makers to design more appropriate health strategies and the institutions required to implement them. The action phase of this participatory research will begin almost immediately as the participants (children, youth, women, and agency representatives) share their varying perceptions. In the final stages, the research teams will draw together their findings from all participating countries in a form useful to African agencies like WHO's regional office, the UN Economic Commission for Africa, the African Development Bank, national government ministries, regional donor agencies and non-governmental organizations.

The proposed country studies will be undertaken in West Africa (Nigeria, Ghana, Sierra Leone, Senegal, Cameroon, and Cote d'Ivoire); and East and Southern Africa (Kenya, Tanzania, Zimbabwe, and Mozambique).

4. Environment. The problem: Donor assistance to Africa increased from levels of approximately two billion US dollars per year in the early 1970s (when awareness of the disastrous impact of the drought was just beginning to become known) to something like nine billion per year in the latter years of the 1980s. Hundreds and perhaps even thousands of donor-driven projects took place in areas of agricultural research, food crop development, integrated rural development, population and family planning, water development, reforestation, commodity imports, technology transfer, food imports, and health—to name but a few. Yet these projects seem not to be working. A recent evaluation classified one third of the World Bank's major agricultural projects in West Africa and half of those in East Africa as failures.

Persistent and dramatic project failures have led to a gradual shift away from project development to interventions at planning and policy levels, and broader structural adjustment programs. Preliminary research, however, indicates that the new "conventional wisdom" actually accelerates African's environmental crisis. Impoverished people constitute high percentages of the populations of countries—like Sudan, Chad, Mali, Mozambique, Angola, and Mauritania—where per capita GNP is below $330. Attention to market prices seems to bypass the rural and urban poor who participate only marginally in market-oriented production. Privatization of production traditionally brings rewards to those who already have access to productive resources and weakens those who do not. Finally, market-driven pricing does little to bring resources or attention to marginal ecological systems or the marginalized people forced to live in these environments. In short, privatization and growth-centered development may actually exacerbate declines in soil, water, and tree cover, causing further decreases in productivity of the marginal ecosystems that spread over more than half of the African continent.

That these marginalized groups comprise the vast majority of Africa's people and resource users underscores the importance of a search for alternative strategies that start with rural communities rather than with macro scale institutions; that places the burden for analysis, planning, and implementation on local institutions rather than external or national agents; and that identifies local leadership and rural organizations as the most effective agents for undertaking rehabilitation of Africa's degrading ecosystem and launch truly sustainable environmental development.

Explanatory hypotheses: The causes of Africa's environmental crisis are deeply-rooted and multi-faceted, and there is no single or simple solution.   Explanations center on three clusters of factors: 1) External factors, including those that go back many generations, like the impact of the slave trade and the colonial experience; the current terms of trade which some argue are continuations of colonial dependency; the debt crisis and negative capital transfers which afflict many African nations; the externally-planned development investments and management processes; and inappropriate technologies; 2) causes internal to individual African states, including weak or ineffective government institutions; internal civil and military unrest; skewed access to land; corruption; officials' personal political ambitions; and weak infrastructure in areas such as financial management, communications, and transport; 3) a range of pressures which run parallel with and aggravate the overall environmental crisis, including drought and climate change; the population explosion of the last three decades; diet change; changes in attitude about urban life as preferable to rural; and growing income and class differentials in the society's changing economic life.

To test the explanatory hypotheses as the basis for a new sustainable environmental strategy: The Environment task group will engage representatives of local level environmental groups, selected government officials and donor agencies in a participatory research process to evaluate the extent to which existing local level models designed to attain sustainable environmental development have succeeded in dealing with these causal factors in four interrelated areas:

1. Local communities, self-contained: To obtain better knowledge of the elements in local systems and community institutions that, through traditional institutions, land and resource management practices, have sustained existing patterns of resource use over the years;

2. Local communities, developed via external intervention: To understand the nature, extent, and consequences of specific institutions (NGOs, government extension, private agencies,

commercial organizations, church groups, etc.) for enabling local community participants to achieve increased sustainable production by incorporating new ideas, institutions, technologies, or systems into their community management system;

3. Regional resources management, based on local participation: To examine the extent and consequences of community participation in the formulation and implementation of the regional plans through which most African governments attempt to deliver transport, health, education, extension, and other services to assist individual communities to maintain sustainable production over extended periods.

4. Policies for government and donor agencies: To explore the existing linkages, methods of participation, and donor relationships in the formulation of national policies and programs required to support local community and regional efforts as a basis for making the changes necessary to implement an alternative strategy for sustainable environmental development.

On the basis of their findings, the research participants will recommend measures for improving local, regional and national efforts to attain sustainable environmental development. The research will take place in three of the following five countries: Kenya, Somalia, Senegal, Mali, and Ghana.

5. Gender relations. Problems: Gender-related problems have two dimensions: (1) in general, at all levels the development process excludes women, who typically fail to receive whatever benefits it may generate; (2) particular difficulties disadvantage women in every field of development-related endeavor. All the task groups recognized that, in every field of development-related activity, women experience special problems. As young girls, they typically receive less education. As mothers, they carry a double burden of taking care of their families and finding adequate sources of income. Together with their children, women especially suffer from environmental degradation and worsening health conditions. In all their endeavors, they encounter discriminatory exclusion from essential resources and job opportunities, and, when they do find them, receive less remuneration. Hence, in general, they experience more than average marginalization. All these problems, merged, aggravate the tragic impact of AIDS on the lives of increasing numbers of African women and their families.

Explanatory hypothesis: The marginalization of women in the development process typically occurs because of the interaction of authoritarian state and non-governmental organizations and structures with traditional institutions and attitudes shaped by an historically-biased sexual division of labor. In every aspect of their lives, these typically exclude women from participating in the decision-making process and deny them access to essential resources

The participatory research process, involving women, themselves, drawing on their own life experiences, will disaggregate this generalized hypothesis to formulate interrelated, testable middle-level propositions to explain the specific ways in which, in specific contexts, family, community and state institutions marginalize women. Representative women, themselves, will participate in revising and warranting these initial middle-level propositions in light of the available evidence. As a kind of learning process, this will empower them to contribute directly to the formulation of specific proposals for improved institutions and educational programs that will enable them to make their full potential contribution to realization of self-sustainable development.

Two proposals to test the explanatory hypothesis as a basis for formulating new gender-related strategies: The gender relations task group proposes to undertake two kinds of research to explore the full implications of the institutionalized process that excludes women from decision-making and access to the resources they require for development:

1. The gender relations task group will hold an initial continent-wide workshop involving researchers, representatives of grassroots women's organizations, and relevant policy-makers. There, to analyze the causes of the marginalization of women, the participants will detail middle-level explanatory propositions for incorporation into the research designs of all the other groups. Individual participants from this continent-wide workshop will then undertake assignments with the other task groups to ensure the latter provide adequate opportunities to gather evidence to test those propositions. After the other task groups complete and assess the implications of their findings, the gender relations group will reconvene to reexamine, revise and deepen the middle-level propositions that comprise their own initial hypotheses. On this basis, they will propose generalizable measures to

empower African women to participate more fully in all aspects of efforts to attain self-sustainable development.

2. To illuminate the tragic consequences, as well as the institutionalized causes of the marginalization of women, the gender relations task group will convene a regional workshop to design a participatory research process to investigate the complex interrelated causes of the impact of AIDS on women and their families. The research process will involve the researchers together with women, both young and old, in formulating and testing detailed middle level propositions as to the way, in the context of the current crisis, the present structure of gender roles shapes family and community responses to AIDS. The process will focus on empowering women to take a more proactive role in identifying specific measures to change the family and community institutions that have left them helpless victims of the disease. The research will take place in three communities in Southern Africa: Siavonga in Zambia; Arusha in Tanzania; and Harare in Zimbabwe.

6. The state and the legal order. Two kinds of problems: Two kinds of problems characterize the state and the legal order: (l) state structures tend to be hierarchical and militaristic, and neglect peoples' inputs and basic needs; and (2) as illustrated in all the problem areas mentioned above—economy and regional integration, education, health, environment and gender relations—undemocratic state policies and procedures foster counterproductive decisions that affect all aspects of African development.

Tentative explanatory hypotheses: Largely inherited from a century of colonial rule, several interacting characteristics of typical African state structures foster emergence of a new internal class—some call it a "bureaucratic bourgeoisie"—that contributes to both kinds of problems in the following ways: i) its members seek to employ authoritarian, hierarchical and often militaristic institutions to enhance their personal power and privilege; ii) in their competitive efforts to gain or retain state power, members of this class not infrequently stimulate ethnic conflict; iii) institutionalized external pressures—including transnational corporations, bilateral and multilateral agencies, and various kinds of donor groups—exercise undue influence on the new rulers through existing state structures, strengthening undemocratic decision-making procedures; and iv) confronted by mounting popular protest, the new rulers utilize increasingly repressive measures. Nevertheless, the state does not constitute a single "rational" (or "irrational") actor. Rather it comprises the contradictory, conflicting social behavior patterns of central actors in complex institutions.

Differing explanatory hypotheses focus on the relative importance of the internal as compared to external factors that fostered these negative developments. Some assert primarily external transnational corporations and multilateral agencies' policies pressure African governments to adopt counterproductive state strategies. Others argue that African domestic interests and state structures pursue those policies in their own efforts to achieve power and privilege. Logically, of course, these differing explanations lead to quite different strategies for development. The proposed research will include examination of evidence to resolve that debate.

To test the general hypotheses, research teams will formulate middle-level propositions that take into consideration all the factors the various hypotheses suggest may shape the behavior of key state institutional actors. This will ensure that the research teams obtain the evidence required to lay the basis for formulating and implementing measures to improve the state's role in the development process.

To test the explanatory hypothesis as a foundation for formulating a new strategy for creating democratic state structures: Given the importance of the state in all aspects of the development process, the proposed research designs in the other six areas should incorporate features specifically devoted to investigating the institutionalized factors that constitute governmental behavior. To facilitate this, the task group dealing with the state and the legal order will hold an initial continent-wide planning workshop to detail the middle level testable propositions that underlie the more general explanatory hypotheses concerning the state. Individual participants from this workshop will then join each of the other task groups' research teams to ensure their research design includes gathering evidence to test those propositions. This will assist each research team to identify measures likely to facilitate creation in its field of democratic participatory state institutions to support self-sustainable development.

Once the other task groups have completed their work, the state and legal order researchers who have worked with them will meet in a final evaluation workshop to assess the implications of their findings for a generalizable explanation of the states' past negative role in the development process. This will enable them to propose generalized measures aimed at achieving more democratic, participatory institutions to ensure the state and the legal order as a whole contribute more positively to the attainment of self-sustainable development.

7. <u>Data Evaluation Team</u>.   Self-evidently, all the researchers must gather and analyze relevant evidence with which to test explanatory hypotheses. African governments and multilateral agencies, including various departments of the United Nations, the World Bank and the International Monetary Fund collect and aggregate vast amounts of statistical data.   Together, these agencies enjoy far greater resources than the joint Forces which will make no pretense at duplicating that task.   The researchers will, however, explore the complex issues that surround data access, collection, consistency, measurement and interpretation.   They will assess the presence of the minimal conditions required for a state or region to collect adequate data.   These include: (1) the availability of sufficient financial resources to hire qualified persons, with adequate knowledge of techniques of data collection and storage; and provide them with the necessary equipment (computers, vehicles, etc.); (2) qualified managers to effectively supervise the data gathering activity, identify weak performances, conduct necessary training, and evaluate and improve the data collecting apparatus;   (3) competent people, with a long term perspective, to assume responsibility for strategic planning about the collection and use of data; (4) general societal agreement that accurate data serves the general interest, avoiding incentives to "misreport" data for personal benefit; and (5) the recognition that, since data analysis serves the public interest and contributes to improving the quality of government, government officials must accept the risk and uncertainty that may result from its objective collection, assessment and publication.

Beyond that, all the Task Force researchers will have to assess the kinds of data available, and how it is collected, aggregated and analyzed.[10] During Phase I, the UNDP-World Bank team preparing an aggregated country-by-country statistical data base for Africa invited the Task Force members to review and make suggestions for a draft computerized version.

In Phase II, the Joint Task Force will establish a Data Evaluation Team to serve in an advisory capacity to the seven task groups. Consisting of six members, three African and three US-based researchers, this team will seek to answer critical questions such as: For a given country or sub-region, are reliable relevant current data available to researchers and policy makers? How is data actually collected, stored, aggregated and tested for validity?   What institutions, procedures, and pitfalls lie behind the numbers?

C. The proposed participatory process

The Washington workshop participants proposed a generalized framework[11] to facilitate operationalization of their proposed five step iterative participatory research process (see Figure 9-1). Over the next three year period, in each of the seven task group areas, this framework will enable researchers to work together with relevant segments of the population and policy makers to design and implement research programs.   In the course of implementing the five step iterative process, they will institutionalize on-going mechanisms for participatory research to evaluate   and suggest improvements in whatever strategies the policy makers eventually adopt.

Figure 9-1

Diagram of the proposed framework
for participatory policy-oriented research

Step 1:		Initial regional planning workshop	
Step 2:	Planning workshop in country A	Planning workshop in country B	Planning workshop in country C
Step 3:	Implementation of research in country A	Implementation of research in country B	Implementation of research in country C
Step 4:	Evaluation workshop in country A	Evaluation workshop in country B	Evaluation workshop in country C
Step 5:		Final regional evaluation workshop	

At each step, the Joint Task Force coordinators will work with the research teams in each research area to undertake the following tasks:

Step 1:   In each research area, researchers from the African universities and research institutions in the selected African countries will meet together with representatives of relevant population segments and selected policy-makers in a regional planning workshop to formulate a detailed research design. Depending on the nature of the problem the researchers seek to explain and solve, population representatives and policy makers will be chosen in consultation with researchers and non-government organizations in the relevant community.   Where appropriate, specified US Africanists will be invited to bring background information and experience expected to facilitate the process; and to arrange possible exchanges of researchers and students to help build African research capacity for the future. Qualified observers may also be invited from other regions.

Step 2: The researchers and population representatives will then return to their own countries where they will meet in planning workshops to work out the country-specific details of the research design with university students selected to conduct the field research, additional representatives of relevant population groups, and national policy-makers. Involvement of senior or university graduate students in the research teams is not only cost effective, but will also help to build up the national capacity for undertaking future participatory problem-solving research.   Wherever possible, the students' participation will be incorporated into university curricula, and receive university credit. Qualified US Africanists and observers from other regions may also be invited to participate in those workshops.

Step 3: Over a period of six weeks to two months, each national research team will conduct the research according to their design. They will involve relevant population segments and policy-makers in examining the nature of the problem and testing alternative candidate explanatory hypotheses against the evidence to determine which seems most useful for identifying specific institutional changes required to overcome the obstacles to self-sustainable development. In light of the findings, the national research team will discuss with the relevant participants how to revise and deepen their explanatory hypotheses and, on that basis, the formulation of possible new development strategies. In the process, they will identify necessary changes in relevant theories and models or propose new ones to provide better guides for more effective future research.

Step 4: The national researchers, population representatives, and policy-makers will meet again in an evaluation workshop in their own countries to draw tentative conclusions as to the implications of their country-findings both for the theory and the practice of development.

Step 5: Finally, the researchers and selected representatives of population segments and policy-makers from the separate countries will bring their country-findings and proposals for new development strategies to a second regional workshop. Again, qualified US Africanists and other observers may be invited to participate. The regional workshop will re-assess the implications of the whole process, further revising and deepening explanatory hypotheses as the foundation for a range of strategies more likely to contribute to the attainment of sustainable development.

D. Overall summary and conclusion

Attainment of self-sustainable development in Africa requires bold new initiatives that, building on the lessons drawn from the failed development projects of the past, enable the peoples of Africa to realize their vast rich continent's full development potential. As a whole, this book constitutes a summary of the findings and the research framework formulated in a year long process designed by what became a joint Africa-US Africanist Task Force effort to mobilize researchers to contribute to that goal. The chapters survey the evidence currently available to assess which of the alternative theories purporting to explain the factors plaguing Africa's past development policies seems most likely to guide more effective future strategies. Adapting and developing a critical participatory, problem-solving research framework, this final chapter outlines several case studies designed to involve those affected by specific aspects of Africa's crisis in probing more deeply into the evidence. In the resulting learning process, they will discover how best to utilize their own human, physical and financial resources, as well as help to formulate more effective national and regional development strategies.

Self-evidently, the tasks the joint Task Force proposes to tackle far exceed the scope of any individual or even any group of researchers' efforts. It necessitates strengthening the existing networks and building new ones to facilitate collaborative efforts involving all concerned researchers. Hopefully, the materials in this book will also encourage and facilitate the efforts of university faculty members, students and community members to re-examine the theoretical premises underlying alternative policy prescriptions in light of the evidence in their own fields of work; and undertake additional participatory research projects designed to improve theory as a guide to assist policy-makers in devising more effective development strategies.

Over time, working together, and extending their efforts to comparative studies of other regions, researchers will improve their theoretical analyses and their methodologies for gathering, assessing and comparing evidence to facilitate improved policy-making in all parts of today's increasingly interrelated world. They will disseminate the findings as widely as possible, both in Africa and the United States, to the academy, the public and policy makers. This seems the surest way that researchers can contribute to deepening relevant theories as guides to rational formulation of self-sustainable strategies for increasingly productive employment opportunities and an improved quality of life for all Africans.

Endnotes

1. For the structure, membership and relationships of the joint Task Force mechanisms they established for coordinating their work, see Appendix I.

2. For the theoretical background and an illustration of this methodology, see Kalyalya et al, 1988: especially Chapter 2.

3. The chapters prepared by the Task Force coordinators suggest the range of alternative explanatory hypotheses proposed by conflicting theories. Logically, each set of theories led to fundamentally different—even conflicting—strategies.

4. The evidence cited for each problem area discussed below is drawn from the review chapters that comprise the bulk of this volume; interested readers should refer to those chapters for the sources.

5. As Dr. Adedeji observed in his keynote speech to the ASA Annual Meeting in Baltimore, in the late 1980s Africa experienced an annual net loss of almost six billion dollars—a sum equal to roughly three quarters of the total official development assistance received by the low income countries of sub-Saharan Africa (excluding Nigeria). See also World Bank, *Sub-Saharan Africa—From Crisis to Sustainable Growth*, Washington, DC 1989.

6. This not withstanding that all African states have attempted to Africanize/nationalize their curricula, especially in the social sciences (including history) and humanities. In these disciplines, curricula are no longer "Euro-centric."

7. SADCC involves the 10 independent countries of Southern Africa and will undoubtedly include a liberated South Africa.

8. The Education task group has been in close contact with representatives of the African National Congress's education office who have expressed interest in including South Africa in the research process, contingent on the existence of a political environment that permits the type of participatory research envisioned.

9. For example, declining school enrollments may not result solely from lack of government or even parents' lack of financial resources. Other economic, social or cultural factors may also influence a student's decision to leave school. Only an accurate interpretation of these factors can ensure proposed initiatives adequately deal with them.

10. The Economic Commission for Africa's critique of the World Bank's data used for assessing the impact of structural adjustment programs illustrates the debatable issues involved.

11. This generalized framework adapts the approach used in Southern Africa, as described in Denny Kalyalya et al, 1988: Chapter 2.

Appendix

Joint Task Force Members

A. TASK FORCE MEMBERS

   1. Advisory Committee members:

Goran Hyden

Political Science Department
University of Florida,
Gainesville, Florida

PhD, University of Lund; taught and conducted research for 13 years in universities of Dar es Salaam, Nairobi, and Makerere; served two years as Nairobi Ford Foundation representative for Eastern and Southern Africa; consultant to several African governments and international agencies; external examiner for universities of Ibadan and Makerere; member, Board of Directors, African Studies Association; author of several books, including *No Shortcuts to Progress: African Development Management in Perspective* and *Beyond Ujamaa in Tanzania: Underdevelopment and an Uncaptured Peasantry*, and other books as well many published articles.

Georges Ntalaja-Nzongola

African Studies and Research Center
Howard University
Washington, DC

PhD, Political Science, University of Wisconsin-Madison; Taught and conducted research for 5 years in National University of Zaire, Lubumbashi, one year in University of Maiduguri, Nigeria, and one year in El Colegio de Mexico; served as Board member, Vice-President and President of African Studies Association; author of several books, including *The Crisis in Zaire: Myths and Realities* and *Revolution and Counter-Revolution in Africa* as well as many articles and chapters in edited books.

Beverly Carolease Grier

Department of Government and International Relations
Clark University
Worcester, Massachusetts

PhD, Yale University; Ford Foundation and National Research Council Postdoctoral Fellowship for Minorities; Fulbright Scholar and Lecturer, University of Niamey, Niger; member, Board of Directors, African Studies Association; author of several articles; currently a Bunting Fellow, writing a book on peasants in Ghana.

Allen Isaacman

International Studies Institute
University of Minnesota
Minneapolis, Minnesota

PhD, African History, University of Wisconsin-Madison; Director, MacArthur Program on Peace and International Security, Professor, History Department, Adjunct Professor, Afro-American and African Studies, University of Minnesota; served as Chaired Professor, Mozambiquan History, University of Eduardo Mondelane; Co-editor, Heineman African Social Science History Series and African Economic History; On editorial boards of Sage Series on African Modernization, University of Minnesota Press; author of four books, including *Mozambique: The Africanization of a European Institution, The Zambesi Prazos*, and many articles.

Ann Seidman, Chair of Task Force

International Development Program
Clark University
Worcester, Massachusetts

PhD, Economics, University of Wisconsin-Madison; Taught and conducted research for ll years in universities of Ghana, Tanzania, Zambia and Zimbabwe, chaired Economics Departments in latter two universities; one year in Peking University; external examiner for universities of Botswana and Swaziland; served as member of Board of Directors, Vice President and President of African Studies Association; consultant to African governments and international agencies; author of a number of books, including *Planning for Development in Sub-Saharan Africa* and *Money, Banking and Public Finance in Africa*, and author of many articles.

2. Coordinators:

Economy:

John Ohiorhenuan (Nigerian)

United Nations Development Programme
New York, NY

PhD in Economics, Sussex; Senior Lecturer, University of Ibadan; on leave as consultant to the United Nations Development Programme in New York; author of book on Nigerian industrialization and many articles.

Ann Seidman (see above: Chair, Task Force)

Regional integration:

Guy Martin (Malian)

The School of International Service
The American University
Washington, D.C.

PhD, Political Science, University of Indiana, Bloomington; has taught in Universities of Nairobi, Kenya, Botswana and De Pauw, Indiana, and the International Relations Institute of Cameroon; served in EC/UNESCO as a member of Study Team on Costs & Benefits, Preferential Trade Area for Eastern and Southern Africa (Zambia); author of *The European Community and the Third World After 1992* (forthcoming) and many articles and chapters of books.

State and legal order:

Bereket H. Selassie (Eritrean)

African Studies Center
Howard University
Washington, D.C.

PhD in Law; Professor, African Studies Program, Howard University; former official in Ethiopian government; consultant and advisor to government and international agencies; author of several books including *The Executive in African Governments*, and *Conflict and Intervention in the Horn* as well as many articles.

Ernest N. Maganya (Tanzanian)

Law School
University of Dar es Salaam
Dar es Salaam, Tanzania

Associate Director, Law School, University of Dar es Salaam; President, Southern African Universities Social Science Conference; Alternative member, Executive Committee of World University Service; author of report re informal sector in Tanzania and several articles.

Environment:

Richard Ford

International Development
Clark University
Worcester, MA

PhD, University of Denver; Professor of History and International Development, Co-Director of International Development Program; author, co-author and editor of many books and articles on environmental and resource use, including *Evaluation of the National Environment Secretariat, Ministry of Environment and Natural Resources* and *Readings in Participatory Rural Appraisal*; and consultant to African governments and local projects on resource management.

Calestous Juma (Kenyan)

African Centre for Technology Studies
Nairobi, Kenya

D.Phil, University of Sussex; Executive Director, Nairobi African Center for Technology Studies (ACTS); author and/or editor of books including: *Biotechnology for Sustainable Development; Gaining Ground; The Gene Hunters;* and *A Change in the Weather*.

Education:

John Metzler

African Studies Center
Michigan State University
East Lansing, MI

PhD, University of Wisconsin-Madison; Coordinator of Outreach Programs, African Studies Center, Michigan State University; taught in Zambia secondary school for six years.

Suleman Sumra

Faculty of Education
University of Dar es Salaam
Tanzania

PhD, Stanford University; Associate professor, University of Dar es Salaam; editor of 3 books; author of many papers.

Health:

Ben Wisner

Hampshire College
Amherst, Massachusetts

PhD, Geography, Clark University; Henry R. Luce Professor of Food, Resources and International Policy, Hampshire College; worked 12 years teaching and conducting research on issues relating to resource use and health in Tanzania, Kenya, Mozambique and Lesotho; consultant to African governments and universities and international agencies; author and editor of several books, including *Power and Need in Africa: Basic human Needs and Development Policies*, as well as many articles in journals, including *Social Science and Medicine* and *Disasters*.

Mere Kisseka (Nigerian)

Department of Sociology
Ahmadu Bello University
Zaria, Nigeria

PhD in Sociology, Missouri University; taught at Linderwood College, Missouri, College of the Virgin Islands for several years, and for 17 years at Ahmadu Bello University where she is now Professor of Sociology and conducts research at the Center for Social and Economic Research; has conducted many research projects, and written many articles and chapters of books, especially related to women, children and health issues.

Gender Relations:

Alice Nkhoma (Tanzanian)

University of North Carolina-Chapel Hill
Carrboro, North Carolina

MA in Library and Information Sciences, London University; founding member and for 3 years Convener of Tanzanian Women's Research and Documentation Project (WRDP); member of the Association of African Women for Research and Development (AAWORD), and on board of African Voluntary Development Organization; currently a PhD candidate at University of North Carolina-Chapel Hill.

Brooke Schoepf

Woods Hole, Massachusetts

PhD in Economic and Medical Anthropology, Columbia University; taught and conducted research in Africa for 11 years, many of them as member of Rockefeller Foundation's field staff at University Nationale du Zaire; led collaborative CONNAISSIDA participatory action-research project on AIDS prevention in Kinshasa; edited *Role of US Universities in Rural and Agricultural Development* and has published over 50 articles in journals and collections.

B. AFRICA TASK FORCE STEERING COMMITTEE

1. Co-directors:

Ernest Wamba dia Wamba

History Department
University of Dar es Salaam
Dar es Salaam, Tanzania

Associate Professor, History, University of Tanzania; served as Chef de Cabinet of Minister of State in-charge of labor, Zaire; taught in Brandeis, Harvard, and Claremont universities in US; helped organize and served as officer of participatory research network in Africa; author of many articles in English and French.

Alice Owano (Kenyan)

Kenyatta University
Nairobi, Kenya

PhD in Education, Kenyatta University: lecturer at Kenyatta University; served as Director of Research and Evaluation, Kenya Institute of Education, and conducted extensive grassroots research with women's groups, out-of-school youths, and on pre-school education.

2. Members:

Donald Chimanikure (Zimbabwean)

Zimbabwe Institute of Development Studies
Harare, Zimbabwe
PhD

Thoahlane Thoahlane (South African)

National University of Lesotho
Lesotho

PhD, Sociology, Columbia University; headed Sociology Department and served as manager of District level Planning and Rural Development Project in Institute of Southern African Studies at University of Lesotho; edited *Black Renaissance*; author of several reports on rural development and institutions in Lesotho.

Moussa Okanla (Beninois)

University of Benin
Cotonou, Benin

Law degree, University of Benin and PhD in Political Science, University of Michigan; Assistant Professor of International Relations, University of Benin; served as Visiting Fellow on African Regional Security at UN Institute for Disarmament Research, Geneva, and is national representative of African American Institute in Benin.

Index

Union douaniere et economique de l'Afrique centrale (UDEAC) 8, 69, 74, 79-80, 88, 93
Union douaniere et economique de l'Afrique occidentale (UDEAO) 76
Union monetaire ouest-africaine (UMOA) 82; see also Franc Zone System
Union of the Arab Maghreb (UAM) 9, 10, 71, 73-76, 90, 91, 95, 96
United States' influence in Africa 3- 4, 77, 169, 252
United States AID 27, 257
Unit of Account of PTA (UAPTA) 84, 86; see convertibility, Federal Reserve Bank of New York
Universities 167, 218; use of university students in participatory research, Ch. 9; see also education
Urban bias 26, 159, 186, 244; see also urbanization
Urban health problems 12-14, Ch. 5
Urbanization 12, 30, 150, 155, 156, 162, 167, 168, 105, 217-219, 222-224, 292
Urban squatters 12, 162, 292
User fees 27, 134, 158, 221, 291

V

Values and attitudes 107, 126-127, 203-214, 221, 251, 252, 261, 263- 264, 266, 290-291, 295; see also culture
Village environmental programs 191
Village health committees 165
Vocational education 106-107, 123, 124, 140

Vulnerable groups 1, 167, 249, 259, 275; see also women, children, handicapped, poor, elderly

W

Wages 25, 26, 31, 38, 151, 208, 213, 217, 225, 296
Washington workshop 3, 4, 17, 205, 285, 301
War 150, 151, 160, 163, 165, 167, 209; see also militarization
Water supplies 149, 151, 153, 155-156, 165, 166, 168, 186, 188, 260, 293, 294
West Africa 14, 16, 69, 71, 73, 82, 90, 92, 289, 294
Wildlife conservation 186
Working rules 47; see also Law
Women 1, 12, 13, 14, 15-17, 25, 28, 30, 37, Ch. 7, 287, 288, 289, 293, 296- 298; and education 102, 103, 106-107, 127-130; and health 149, 150, 157, 158, 160-162, 164, 165, 166, 168; and environment 166, 185; and state 266; see also gender
World Bank 1, 3, 7, 23, 24, 26, 27, 28- 29, 31, 32, 33, 34, 38, 40, 50, 69, 77, 294, 300; and education 103, 108ff, 131-133, 289; and health 150, 151, 158, 159; and ecology 187, 188, 189; and gender 214; and the state and law 257, 264
World Conference on Education for All, Jomtien, Thailand, 1990 103-105
World Health Organisation (WHO) 14, 150, 294
World Resources Institute 190
World Summit for Children 149
World systems theorists 256